And That's How It All Started

by

STONEY MCGURRIN

PAGE PUBLISHING, INC.
New York, NY

First originally published by Page Publishing, Inc. 2019

This book is a production of Stoney Leitrim Inc.

ISBN 978-1-64462-451-7 (Paperback)
ISBN 978-1-64462-452-4 (Digital)

Printed in the United States of America

Acknowledgements

I would like to thank the following that helped make this book possible.

John Healy, for encouraging me and taking this book from pencil to print, and Jim Gerding for also motivating me.

They have been listening to me for many, many years, and they said you've got write these stories.

Henri and Madeline Taylor for proofreading and suggestions along the way.

Vin McCarthy for copyediting and some suggestions.

After all I never wrote anything before, except a few checks.

To all the characters in the stories both living and dead without them I would not have all the stories.

Last but not least to James Dennison in Co Sligo, who made me look great on camera for my DVD 18 tracks of other stories.

I hope you, the reader, enjoy this book, "That's How It All Started".

Stoney.

WHERE IT ALL STARTED

It was on April 2nd, 1941, that I was born on a farm three miles from a small town called Dowra in County Leitrim, Ireland. It is the first town on the River Shannon, the longest river in Ireland.

The River Shannon is two hundred and twenty-four miles long and has three large lakes on it: Lough Allen, Lough Ree, and Lough Derg, all about four miles wide. It flows into the Atlantic Ocean from the estuary at Limerick City. Tourists come from all over the world for the fishing and leisure cruising.

The Shannon River starts five miles from Dowra, in County Cavan at a place called the Shannon Pot. It's a hole eight foot round that's so deep that when the local government dropped a chain two miles long down the hole, it still did not reach the bottom. The water bubbles up at such a speed that it becomes a river four hundred foot wide when it reaches Dowra. There's a big bridge that leaves half the town in County Leitrim and half the town in County Cavan.

Like all the places in the world, people who live in one area always seem to think that people from other areas are a little different than they are and they make jokes about them. Cavan people are supposed to be very thrifty and cheap.

Here's one joke making fun of them: The Pope needed a special blood type and said he would pay fifty thousand euros for it. A Cavan man who was the correct type had a doctor draw the blood and it was sent to the Pope. A year later, the Pope needed more blood and the Cavan man was very eager to send it again. This time the Pope mailed him two hundred euros. So the Cavan man asked, "Why fifty thousand euros the first time but only two hundred euros the second time?" The Pope answered him, "But I've got Cavan blood in me now."

* * *

My first memory of life was when I was three and a half years old. It was morning and my mother was baking a cake and my older sisters, Vera and Bernadette, were going out the door to school by the way, I had eight sisters and one brother. I asked my mother when I can go to school and she said everybody starts school at four years old.

I remember my first day at school. My older sisters, Bernadette and Vera, took me to Mrs. Clancy. Mrs. Clancy took me by the hand and sat me in the front row and started to teach.

A few minutes went by and she started beating a girl. The girl was crying and she still kept beating her and I don't know for what. I thought then, I don't think I like school.

Two days later, Father Lynch comes to the school. He lines up the six-, seven-, and eight-year-olds along the wall and starts asking them questions. One boy and one girl each didn't know the answer. He slaps her around the head, her hair flying from side to side. Now, I'm scared, now I really don't like school. We walked three miles to school; some kids walked six miles, all at four years old.

* * *

School in Ireland was much worse in my parents' day. I recall going up into the mountains at Tullaghan, where my mother's farm was. We rode the horse and cart. Sometimes, we would sit and let our feet hang down; sometimes we would stand. We would pass by four or five farmhouses on the way. One house was owned by Yankee Fallon, an odd man, odd because he was very hard of hearing. He would sit at the window and look out at the countryside. He had a big apple tree that grew out over the road, with apples hanging out of it.

One day, my father Pat and I were standing on the cart. The horse was walking slowly and as we went under the apples, I reached up and pulled one. My father said, "You shouldn't have done that."

"Why?" I asked.

"Because if he's looking out the window, he will be out to talk to us on the way back."

I asked my father how long was Yankee Fallon in America. He said he never was in America.

"Why, then, is he called Yankee Fallon?"

My father says he's a little older than him but they all went to the Rock School. The school was above on a rock. Back then the schoolmasters were really brutal. The master's name was Flynn. If you came home and told your parents the teacher beat you, they would say you must have deserved it and then maybe hit you again. My father said that when Fallon was twelve years old, he was a tough kid—he would stand up to anybody.

One Thursday, going home from school, he got into a fight and he outboxed the other kid. He figured if he didn't go to school on Friday, by Monday it would all have been forgotten. Monday came and he went to school late. Master Flynn had his back to the door, writing on the blackboard. He heard the door, creak, creak, creak. He turned around and it was Fallon.

"Well, well, well. You were not here on Friday and you're late today. Where were you?"

"I was in America," said Fallon.

"Oh," says Flynn, "we've got ourselves a Yankee."

And he proceeded to beat Fallon until blood came out of his ear. He's been deaf in that ear ever since.

I heard a man once say that kids on a farm were born to work, and their fathers started them very early. When the father came in at night, he put his shoes at the end of the stairs that went up to the loft or, if the family was well off, went up to the bedroom on the second floor. In the morning, he would sit by the fire and put his socks on and when the kid was able to crawl, the father would say, "Go get the shoes! Go, go, go!" He would point, "Go! Go get the shoes!" And the kid would crawl down and then look back and the father would say, "Ya—ya bring it!" The kid would put one little hand in a shoe and, with a big smile, crawl back. The father would rub his head and say, "Good boy, good boy! Now go! Go get the other one!" This was his introduction to work.

Killing Rats

We would pick the new potatoes in September, bring a couple of cartloads home for food for the winter, and then put the rest of the potatoes in a pile called a heap. We covered them with ten to twelve inches of clay so that the frost wouldn't get at them. In the spring, we would bring them in from the field.

I recall one time, James E. Dannel, who was a full-time worker for my father, was on his knees, sorting the good potatoes from the bad ones. We all knew there were rats inside, from the holes they had made. Well, this one big rat jumped out by James's knee. James grabbed the rat with both hands and wrung its neck and threw it to the side. We kids all screamed and ran away.

Now that I'm remembering stories about rats, all farm-houses kept cats and terrier dogs to control the rats and mice. One day, we were bringing the oats in when we got to the bottom of the stack and saw there were holes in the ground.

This guy Tim Dolan put his hand all the way down into the burrow. He pulled a big rat out, holding it tightly around its neck. He walked around tapping the rat on its head and with a finger on his other hand, saying, "You're going to die, you're going to die!" and he killed it.

Shop and Gossip

Our house and shop were two hundred yards from the post office. People would come every Friday to get their old-age pension one-pound notes. If they could not come themselves, their neighbor, son, daughter, wife—whoever was going that way—could pick it up for them. They would then come to our shop and pick up a few things they might need. The bus stopped at the shop three days a week at 10:00 a.m.

There was a road between the shop and the post office that ended in a T-junction at the main road. One mile up, there lived a man named James Cournan. James had a brother named Tom who was a traffic cop in Dublin from the time he was nineteen until he was sixty-five. He retired and came home to live with his brother. After a few years at home, he went senile.

Back then, when a man in Ireland became a cop, he had to buy his own uniform and he was allowed to take it home when he retired. When Tom went senile, he would put on his uniform and go down to the T-Junction and direct traffic but there was no traffic, only the mail van at 8:00 a.m. and the bus at 10:00 a.m. Both drivers knew Tom and he would put his hand up and they would stop and wait and wait until he finally waved them on. We kids loved it.

The people who owned the post office were Lizzy and John. As a kid, I was there every chance I got. Lizzy baked her soda bread and walked across the street and put it on a hedge, which grew over into the field, to let it cool for an hour.

When I was four years old, I would go into the field and go under the hedge and pull the raisins out and eat them. Being a kid, I thought nobody would know, until, one day, I ran into Lizzy's kitchen like I did every chance I got, and she was making a cake. She told me a story. She said that when she put her loaf of bread out on the hedge that a little bird would come and eat the raisins from the bottom. She looked at me and said, "You know what I'm going to do? I'm going to make a small loaf. Then the little bird will eat the raisins from the small loaf but leave the big loaf alone." From then on, I took raisins from only the small loaf and I was convinced that Lizzy really thought it was a bird that took the raisins.

Lizzy, her husband John and their son Robert were Protestants. There was a parson named Sides, but most of the Protestant population was old, except for one or two young people. As a Catholic, one must learn the Catechism at the age of seven, in order to receive First Communion. It tells you that at the age of seven, you are able to reason. (I can think for myself.) It tells me I must love my neighbor. (Son of a gun.) You must do good to those who hate you. All this is running through my mind and one day–I'm still seven—I ran to the post office and Lizzy is standing in the door enjoying the good weather. I stood alongside of her and she talked to me like I was a little grown-up man. Her husband was out, as he often was, wandering around, picking up old branches and other pieces of wood for the fire.

As we were standing in the door, we saw her husband, John, coming. She said to me, "There's your man. Here he comes." As John reaches the door, as he's going in, he falls back on her. Lizzy grabs John by his shoulders and said, "Grab his legs! Grab his legs!" I was small but I got in between his legs, like I was holding a wheelbarrow. I'm backing into the kitchen and then she turns and she backs, into the bedroom and we get him onto bed—he's dead!

My father and mother knew how much I loved Lizzy and John and so I was allowed to stay up late at the wake. The second night of the wake, I went outside at about 8:00 p.m. and I saw four people standing about a hundred yards up the road.

It was Paddy Kelly, John McParland, John Clinton and Mick Lavin. In today's world, they would be called Yuppies. Even as a kid, I knew they were the hotshot cool dudes. They didn't know what to do when they got inside the wake house; they wanted to know if you stand or kneel by the bed. I told them, "Everybody kneels and says a prayer." I felt like a big little man telling the cool dudes what to do at a Protestant wake.

The next day, being a Sunday, most of the Catholics went to church. Father Lynch gave a sermon on the death of John Paterson the Protestant. Knowing there were not enough young Protestants to carry the coffin, he shouted from the pulpit that it would be a mortal sin for any Catholic to go inside a Protestant church and you would go to hell. I'm all confused.

Catechism is teaching me to love my neighbor, to love even those who hate me and now this man of God is telling me that I can't go into Lizzy's church. What is Lizzy going to think of me? But I was in luck. My father had some clout, mostly because he had the shop. He went to talk to his very good friend, Jim Connors. I went with him. He said to Jim that John Patterson and his family had been around a lot longer than Father Lynch and it would be a bigger sin if we didn't show the family respect and bury him. Then they went to the other neighbors and John got a good send-off. I was so happy, but now I'm thinking about Lynch and God, but I still have to do what I'm told.

My father was a character. He would be locked up today for some of his devilment. When you are ten years old you go for Confirmation and you take the pledge that you won't drink until you're twenty-one. It's a big day for all the families as this is the only day you see the bishop. It's happening in the big church in the town called Drumkeeran. We go very early, my mother, father and sisters. We all got in the horse and trap. My father drops my mother and sisters off at the church. Then he and I go up a back road to a big back yard called Dolan's.

Dolan's is the distributor for all the country stores plus has a bar and restaurant. Back in the 1950s, all bars in Ireland had little room called a snug, where two or three people can go for privacy. You go in and order a drink through a small door that you would slide open, and the bartender doesn't know who's in there.

My father meets a friend, George Bolls. We go into the snug. They start discussing me going for Confirmation. George, being Protestant, says to my father, "In your religion, does the kid have to take the pledge until he's twenty-one?"

"That's right," says my father.

"Well," says George, "if it's okay by you, I'd like to buy him a shot of whiskey before he takes the pledge."

My father looked at me and said, "Is that okay with you?"

I looked at him and nodded and nodded again, okay.

"Yes," said my father.

George slid the board over and ordered three shots of Paddy's whiskey. We all tipped glasses and I threw it right back. I can't remember if I drank something with it, but I'm sure I did. I must have done such a good job that my father said to George, "Well, by God, he's my son! And if you can buy him one, so can I!" He slid the board over and said, "Three more Paddy's." We tipped glasses again and I threw it back again. I found it very interesting but I didn't feel a thing. It had no effect on me and I wondered why people drank.

About my father, in 1958 he left for America to live with my sister in Long Island. He got a job at a race track, which was good as he loved horses.

After the Confirmation, I'm still questioning Father Lynch, God and the Catechism. Already I'm having my doubts. I had never met such good people as Lizzy and John. So, when Sunday came, Mother and Father and my sisters went to the local church in the horse and trap for 10:00 a.m. Mass. I would jump on the bike and say I'm going with Mick Corrigan to Drumkeeran for the 11:00 a.m. Mass. Mick was a bachelor who lived half a mile away with his uncle, Pat Guicken. Pat's brother John willed the farm to Mick; the deal was he would take care of Pat until he died. Mick and his friends, all aged twenty-five to forty, would stand at the back door of the church for fifteen minutes and then go to the pub, me with them, drinking a soft drink called Stone Beer.

The Mission

Every seven years, the Catholic Church brought in fire-and-brimstone preachers for two weeks, one week for men and one week for women.

I never did understand why they separated the men from the women.

There was one man named Staffy Nelly. Staffy said he traveled the world. He once told us he was walking for days and came to within three miles of hell. We asked him, how did you know? He said that he had six eggs and that he had put them on a rock and they fried in ten seconds. He knew it was then time to turn back. As kids we loved his stories. Staffy never went to church. When the missionaries came, all the women that were heavy into religion wanted to save Staffy's soul. They kept nagging him when they all met in the shop. He finally gave in and went one night to the missions.

Those missionaries, not only would they put the fear of God into you, they would scare the hell out of you. The night that Staffy went to church, this mad preacher was walking up and down the aisle saying that bad people went to hell and that his own father was a bad person and he was in hell.

That was it for Staffy. He got up to leave, but the preacher yelled, "You come back here and sit down!" But Staffy just kept on walking. And so, the preacher yelled "If you go out that door, then you're going to hell.

Staffy stopped, turned around and said to the preacher, "Do you have a message for your old man?"

This was talked about for years.

"If she ain't working out, shut her down"

There were lots of families in the area named McPartland. We used to hear people talk about a man, Seamus McPartland, who went to Chicago and became a millionaire and owned supermarkets.

We did not know what supermarkets were back then.

After twenty years he came back on vacation and he really looked the part. He wore a white suit and a big hat, and he shipped home a big American car for himself. Drumkeeran was where the Catholic Canon Renn lived and he put out word that he would like to meet the returned Yank, Seamus McPartland, but Seamus did not want to meet him.

One day they met in the middle of the town. The Canon started telling Seamus that it was the education he got in Drumkeeran that gave him a start in life to become a millionaire in America, and now the local church needs a new roof and a sidewalk, etc.,

Seamus never opened his mouth until Canon Renn was finished. Then he said, "As they say in America, 'If she ain't working out, shut her down.'"

Those guys who returned from the States, they're not giving the clergy the fear and respect that they were used to getting. I'm very happy.

There were a lot of characters around. A family, the McFaddens, Teresa, Jack, Willie, Hughie and Peter, had the nickname "Oaties". Back in the Easter Rising in 1916, Jack was an officer in the IRA, the Irish Republican Army. He was in a battle with the English and got wounded and goes into hiding, or "on the run" as it was called.

The English put a price on his head, a reward for his capture. Every cop and English soldier had his picture in his pocket. For two years, neighbors kept hiding him and feeding him. Eamon De Valera got him a passport so he could get to America.

He had to travel to Belfast, get a train from Bellcoo, County Fermanagh, at 7:00 a.m.—very dangerous. As Jack told it in a letter, he is standing on the platform, a cop strolls by, stops, keeping his hand close to his chest, takes out the photo, and says "Is that you Jack? Hope you make it," and strolls on by.

Jack made it to New York, got an apartment on Ninth Avenue and got a job. His sister Teresa came to New York with two friends that she went to school with. They all got work with the same family on the East Side of New York as housemaids. They always had Saturday nights off.

One Saturday night at 9:00 p.m., as they are getting ready to go out, Teresa said she needs face cream and lipstick from the store across the street. She said, "I will be right back."

She was never seen again.

Years later, in America, I was telling this to a police lieutenant, Flaherty, who I got to know very well. He told me that back in 1920s and 1930s, the mob used to kidnap young girls off the street, drug them, and put them into prostitution.

The following year Jack was coming into his hallway and two guys mugged him and killed him. The father died shortly after. Neighbors used to say that the mother was able to come to terms with Jack's death but not with the loss of Teresa. Since she was never found, the mother never got over it.

When Father Lynch was new in the parish, he wanted to get all the people to attend Mass and he heard that Mrs. Oatie was not attending Mass. He drives in his big car to her house and up the lane, walks to the house hoping to get her back to the church and she meets him with a pitchfork. He ran for his life. She yells after him, "When God tells me where my Teresa is, I might go back to the church." They were the most words she had spoken in twenty years.

Two Faiths and None

There was Parson Sides for the Protestants and Father Lynch for the Catholics. Parson Sides was a lovely man; Lynch was more of a bully than a priest. When a Catholic and a Protestant married, the Catholic would never convert. The Protestant would give in and become Catholic. But we had a rare experience. Tommy Coyle married Rita Patterson and converted to the Protestant faith. He was considered wild.

There was a hill with turns going down from the shop. Tommy would buy the paper, get on the bike, open the paper wide and read it while he went down the hill. Sometime after his marriage he was going down the hill. There was a large truck coming and he lost his balance and went over the ditch and broke his leg.

The following Sunday, Father Lynch made it his sermon. He said we have a member who strayed from the true religion and what happened to him was a warning to him, to come back to the true religion before something really bad happened to him.

In the Protestant church, Parson Sides was giving his sermon. He said, "We have a new member in our congregation. He has had a little accident. He's very lucky he came over to our side or he might have broken his neck."

My Grandfather Dies

Half a mile down the road there lived a man named Francy Sean Travers with his wife. They had no kids. His uncle Bobby lived with them. Uncle Bobby had his own farm two miles past our shop. Every day, he would go to his farm, check his house and cattle and come back by the shop. My grandfather, Peter, about the same age as Bobby, was his friend. They would sit on the stoop going up to the house and talk and argue. Bobby always felt he was right. Then Peter got sick. He went to bed and never got out of it.

He died in about two months. Every day, Bobby would go check on his house and cattle, come back and sit on the stoop for an hour, then go home to his nephew's house. On the morning Grandfather died, Mother looked out and saw Bobby sitting on the stoop. She said to my brother Jim, "Go tell Bobby that Peter passed away at 3:00 a.m. this morning."

My brother went out and sat where Peter used to sit and said, "Bobby, Peter passed away at 3:00 a.m. last night."

Without hesitation, Bobby asked, "How old was he?" My brother told him he was ninety-three. "He's a liar!" said Bobby. Bobby always had to disagree, even with a dead man!

Bobby showed no emotion in any situation, but he was a likable rogue. He left Ireland when he was twenty years old and went to Scotland, married a girl and lived with her for two years. Then he left, went to Australia, married again, stayed a few years and then left the second wife and went to New York. He got married there also, left her, too, and went home to live with his nephew.

A neighbor, Mick Flynn, told us that when he was in New York, he saw Bobby and ran up to him and said hello. Bobby said to Mick, "I don't know you. You've got the wrong person. That's not my name." Mick figured that Bobby was living in New York under an assumed name and walked away. Now it was the 1930s and the depression had hit all over the world. A lot of people felt that they could survive better back home rather than where they were.

Bobby went back home to Francy, his nephew. Bobby was odd. He would never give you the answer you were looking for. We had a nosy neighbor, Kevin Flynn. He had heard Bobby was in Chicago and Kevin had an uncle there. He asked Bobby what he did there and Bobby told him that he had a wheelbarrow and his job was to wheel daylight into dark corners.

Back in Edinburgh, Scotland, Bobby's first wife, Alana, was living with her sister and her husband. Her sister gave her a month to get out. Alana started going through her boxes with letters and, lo and behold, she found Bobby's name and where he lived in Ireland, in Corry, County Leitrim. With nothing to lose and two pounds in her pocket, off she went. She took the boat to Belfast, took the train to Belcoo and asked the conductor for Corry, County Leitrim. He told her, "You're in the North. Walk across the bridge and you will then be in Blacklion, County Cavan. Anybody there can steer you right for Leitrim." She walked twelve miles to reach Dowra and when she got there, she hit some luck and asked a man, Tom McKeown. He told her it's three miles out the road and that he was going that way. He walked her right to the house. It was 10:00 p.m. She looked in the window and said to McKeown, in her Scottish accent, "That's me boyo." He was sitting in a chair by the fire and smoking his pipe. My father and a few other neighbors were in the house. She knocked on the door and Francy's wife opened the door, and this strange woman said, "I'm here to see Bobby."

"Come in."

She walked right up to Bobby and looked down at him. He took his pipe out of his mouth, looked up at her as if he had seen her the day before and said hello.

Stoney on the Farm Horse

Stoney with His Best Friend the Dog

Kathryn and Patrick McGurrin 1922

Peter Mcfadden His Granddad on Mothers Side

Francy's wife must have seen an opportunity. She told Alana how Bobby had his own house, land and cattle. Alana said, "I'll stay here tonight, the floor is fine and tomorrow, you and I, Bobby, will go home."

The next day, bright and early, off the two of them went to her new home. He never complained. For weeks she was painting, scrubbing blankets outside, hanging them on clotheslines. She was using a six-foot stick to beat the dust out of the clothes.

She worked hard. Bobby liked to sit down and watch her work. The neighbors loved her. She lived there for twenty-two years, died there and was buried there. She never talked about Scotland. I guess there was nothing in Scotland for her. When she died, Bobby moved back to Francy and the wife and died there.

Unwanted Babies

Back in the 1900s through the 1950s, there were orphanages for babies from unwed mothers, which the government paid the church to run. These children were considered by the nuns and the priests to be the Devil's children and they were treated badly. Here we go again! I kept asking myself, "Where is this invisible character called God?" In the spring of 2017 in Tuan, County Galway, the skulls of seven hundred and eighty babies were found in a graveyard at a convent.

Let's continue.

Since the orphanages were getting overcrowded with older kids, the Church came up with a plan for all those kids to be adopted. Here's the way it worked: if you were a man who had a trade, you did not have to be married to adopt a boy, and there were a lot of men who had never been with a woman and a lot of women who had never been with a man. Back in those days, a woman could not go and talk to a man and a man could not talk to a woman. You had to have a go-between called a matchmaker.

Now back to the adoption.

This man Tom Dorsey was a shoemaker who lived up in the mountains. Single and heading towards fifty years old, the neighbors said, "Tom, you're getting on in years. Use this as an opportunity to get a young boy to help you. You can teach him the trade and you'll be looked after when you get older." He filled out the paperwork to adopt a boy and was approved. He got himself a young boy named Peter Murphy, twelve years old. As Peter told the story years later, the house had three rooms. When you walked into the house, there was the kitchen, which was used for making the shoes and for cooking. There was a bed in the corner that was where Peter slept. (He didn't mind, as it was the warmest room in the house.) There was a room that had a bed but was never used. Tom slept in the upper bedroom.

Three years went by and Tom was at the fair. He saw this woman and enquired who she was. He found out her name was Mary Coyle and that she lived alone on a small farm that her father had left her. The matchmaker tells Mary that Tom would like to marry her and it would be nice for her to have a man and a boy. The boy could look after her land and cattle and she could go every day and see her own house and then go to Tom's house and cook and have company to talk to.

She was very nervous. She had never been with a man but she liked the idea of a man looking after her, her land and the cattle. She said, "I'll do it." The match was made and the church date was set.

Everybody was in the church. When the priest finished with the 'I Dos', he asked for ten pounds. Tom said, "Ten pounds! Jesus Christ! Ten pounds! If I knew it was going to be ten pounds, I wouldn't have got married at all!"

They got married at 8:00 a.m. and they took the 10:00 a.m. bus to Sligo for the day. They had to be back by nighttime to milk the cows.

Now comes their first night together. I must explain that back in that era, men wore long white nightshirts that came down in a V-shape to your knees.

As Peter told it, he was sleeping by the fire. Tom and Mary went up to their room. After ten minutes, Mary started screaming, came running down out of the room, still screaming, "No! No! No!" with Tom right behind her with an erection so hard that his shirt was sticking way out. Into the other room they went and she was still screaming, "You're not going to stick that thing into me!"

Tom was saying, "But—but we're married now, Mary." He didn't get his way that night.

Peter stayed with Tom and Mary. They had no kids. (I often wondered why.) Years went by and Mary died. When Tom died, he willed the house and the small piece of land to Peter.

Peter married a lady called Bee Daniels. They had two daughters, Mary and Sue, and a son, Frank. Bee and the daughters went to America. Mary went to night school and became a registered nurse. She met a doctor and lived in Connecticut. Bee worked for a family on Park Avenue in New York City. They loved her. Sue met a Wall Street businessman, married and lived in Westchester.

Frank stayed home in Ireland with the father. This I must explain. There was a small plot of land in front of the house where there was a large bank of clay. One tree grew on it. The tree was ten foot tall with a few branches from six foot up to the top. At night, when you opened the door, this lonely tree looked scary. Frank got up late at 10:00 a.m. one morning and when he opened the door to look out, there was his father, Peter, hanging from the tree. This tree was already scary enough to look at and now your father is hanging from it. I guess Peter never got over it. Back then in Ireland, if you were born out of wedlock, even the priests liked to remind you of it.

Love your neighbor. Good on ya, Father Lynch.

On The Farm

With the turf stacked by the road at the bog, it's time to cart all the cow manure to the fields, one to two acres, and plow or dig ridges and set potatoes.

Then we set oats grain with a harrow tied behind a horse in the field where we grew the potatoes last year.

Now, we have to cut the hay and dry it and put it in big piles called rucks and bring it into the haggard in August or September and still we kids had to do our homework for school. I don't know how we learned anything.

Now I'm going to tell you about taking home the turf. Every farmer stacked his turf by the side of the road at the bog. It took two or three days to bring the turf home from the bog and neighbors would lend each other their donkeys until the turf was brought home. Each night we would take the big baskets, called creels, and saddles off the donkeys and ride them to the gate going out on the hill. Our neighbor Tommy Tryer had the crazy one. When we pulled the donkey's hair, he would jump and kick and we kids would fight each other to ride him. The second night when we removed the creels, I was the first on the donkey's back. I was only four years old. My sister Bernadette jumped up behind me and tried to get up front by holding my shoulders and putting her right leg in front of me onto the donkey's neck and trying to jump in front. The donkey was standing on the cement walkway that went from the house to the road. We both fell off, her on top of me. I screamed in pain. They took me into the house and they figured my arm was broken, so they wrapped it in a blanket, gave me hot milk and told me they would take me to Manor Hamilton Hospital the next day. I have no memory of the pain or of being in the hospital. I do remember coming home with a plaster of Paris cast on my arm from my fingers to my shoulder.

One month went by. They took me back to the hospital where they removed the plaster of Paris cast and, much to their surprise, they had missed an elbow break. There was a lot of talk for a few days and then they dropped the bomb. (Back then, hospitals were not held responsible for their mistakes.) They told my father that my arm would have to be amputated. My father said, "No. There has to be another way." Then they told him about Jervis Street Hospital in Dublin. My mother took me by train to Jervis Street and left me there. I remember crying. A week went by. A neighbor, Casey Flynn, came to see me. I remember making it very hard for her to leave. Every time she would get up to leave, I'd cry. I wanted to go home.

The doctors at Jervis Street could do nothing, but they found a doctor who could, a specialist in Paris, France. Father had to pay to bring him to Dublin. I never heard my mother or my father mention what it cost. People never mentioned money ever, but I do think I'm the reason we all had to come to America, my mother at fifty-nine and my father at seventy-two, and they both got jobs, my mother in a restaurant called Schrafft's, my father in the stables with horses, which was right up his alley. What a big change, from being your own boss all your life to this, and at such an advanced age.

Anyway, I was at the Jervis Street Hospital for three months. The French doctor's name was Dr. Chance. He told my father he would take a vein from my right arm, six inches up from my wrist and put it in my left elbow. My arm couldn't straighten out but someone who didn't know me would have to be told in order to notice it. Dr. Chance told my father he must never stop reminding his kid that he must never talk about his arm, because at school kids can be mean if they knew about my arm not being able to straighten out. When I got into a fight, my arm would be what they would jump on and if it got broken again, that's it. It would have to be amputated.

I had a lot of pain in it until I was fourteen but I never talked about it, only to my parents and then only once in a while. They would tell me, "Be a man; it's only growing pains." I'd believe them but when I was about eleven, the pain had become very bad and they found a doctor with his own practice twelve miles away. "Off you go," they said to me, "get on your bike and go see him."

I rode my bike to Manor Hamilton. The doctor brought me to his office. He sat across the table from me and asked me what was wrong. I was scared to mention the pain so I told him that my elbow creaked a lot—it did. I moved my elbow and he could hear it creak, creak, creak. He stood up—he must have been six foot four inches tall—and lifted his hand up and twisted it around and his shoulder blade went creak, creak, creak. Man, it was loud! He looked at me and said, "All great men have creaks. Get out of here.

No charge." I had creaks in my elbow until I was twenty-five but I never complained about them again.

My father was so proud that my arm did not have to be amputated. When I was at a bar with him and his friends, he would brag to his friends how he managed to find Dr. Chance, who was able to save my arm. He would say to his friends, "You see, I took a chance on Dr. Chance."

Church and Land

Priests and the Catholic Church in Ireland. When God's power corrupts, the result is absolute corruption.

Back in the 1800s, when England owned Ireland and controlled the country, the best land was owned and run by English landlords. The people worked and lived on the land for no pay, just like slaves. In 1880, the people decided not to work. That was the beginning of what was called the Land Wars. The people got evicted from all the landlords' land; these evictions by the English go back to the 13th century. They started living along the sides of the roads traveling from county to county. They learned a trade making tin cups, saucepans, and buckets and, down through the generations, they became known as tinkers and tinsmiths. They loved their lifestyles.

Today, they're called Travellers. They will deal in anything. They would rob anything and everything and they loved horses and they fought among themselves at the drop of a hat. Bar owners hated to see them come into their bars.

The Land Wars worked. They were very successful. In County Mayo, there was a landowner named Captain Boycott. The Land Wars were so successful that Boycott went broke and left Ireland and went back to live in England for good. In the dictionary, you will find the word boycott. The word meant when people are told not to help their neighbors, and even to let them die.

When the English had to give the land back to the Irish people, they divided the land into small farms, in such a way that all farmers had access to the road but often the road was closer by going through a neighbor's land. They called it the "shortcut." This worked fine until there was a fight and then the farmer could no longer use the shortcut. The one who lost the shortcut would run to the English establishment.

The English had spies and the English thinking was genius.

Then came 1920 and Ireland got its freedom, had its own government and ran itself, but the Catholic Church had more power than the government and used the same technique, boy-cotting, on their own people. All the Protestants saw it coming and all who could get out did so and went north.

There was this man, Frank McFadden, who lived next to John Sully. Sully owned a half-acre field close to Frank's home and the field was Frank's shortcut to the road. Frank always stayed friends with Sully and he always asked Sully to sell him his half-acre field. Finally, Sully gave in and Frank got his half-acre and the shortcut to the road was his.

Two years later, Sully died. Sully's wife, Bridie, never liked Frank. At Sully's grave, she told Frank that she wanted the half-acre back. Frank said, "Not now." She went to his house the next day and demanded the half-acre back.

Frank said, "I've been trying to buy that half-acre for twenty years. It's of no benefit to you, it never was, and now you want it back so you can make me go the long way around. It's a big asset to me. It's mine now and I'm not giving it back."

Bridie was very friendly with Father McGuinness. Bridie went to Father McGuinness and asked him to help her get the half-acre back. McGuinness agreed to help her and went to Frank and demanded that he give it back, but Frank said no.

McGuinness said, "I'll have you boycotted." The follow-ing Sunday, McGuinness gave a sermon saying that Frank McFadden was the Devil and as of next Sunday, he would be boycotted. "I want the pipe and drum band here and nobody to leave after the Mass is over." Man, did priests have power.

The next Sunday, after Mass, McGuinness lined up the band and lined up all the people behind the band. He got in front like Moses and with the band blaring, marched through the countryside for six miles to Frank's house and then marched around it, still banging drums, three times for the Father, the Son and the Holy Ghost. He shook holy water and then he said, "This devil is done for! Nobody talks or does anything for him."

And these are the people who told me when I was a kid to do good to those that hated me.

Back then everybody needed flour to make bread. My father went to Frank late at night. They hatched a plan. My father would go to the top of the hill and hide a half bag of flour under a tree. Frank would come at one or two in the morning and pick it up. If anybody saw them and ratted them out, my mother and father would be boycotted and that would be the end of the shop.

My Father's Family

My father's grandfather was a blacksmith. He had four sons and he taught them all the trade. Each one of them had their own blacksmith shop, one each in Doballey, Dowra, Creavelay, and Drumkeeran. The father of the four sons had the home place in Corry. When he died my father's father, whose name was Simion, got the home place. His three brothers decided to quit the blacksmith trade and travel to America. We heard they settled in Boston and upstate New York.

My father had one brother, James, and one sister, Mary. The father, Simion, had a bad accident and died at the age of thirty-three, the same age as Jesus Christ. The mother sent them all to America. His brother James put himself through school and went on to become Commissioner of Jurors, County Clerk of Manhattan, head of the Irish Historical Society and speaker for the New York Democratic Party. When FDR came to New York, he would give the introduction speech.

Mary married Joe Carney who had a brother, Tom. They both worked for the Brooklyn Gas Company, Tom days and Joe nights. They both drove their cars to work. One day Joe was running late going to work. He was speeding, ran a red light and went head on and crashed into his brother Tom. What aco-incidence. Tom was seriously hurt. He was in the hospital for months and couldn't work for a year.

Back then people did not have any insurance. Joe paid all his bills and mortgage for two years.

My father got a job as a conductor on the Ninth Avenue trolley and fell between two cars and was dragged four blocks. He was in the hospital for ten months. He got what was a huge settlement for that time, three thousand dollars. His brother, James, and sister, Mary, suggested that he return to Ireland with all that money and take care of his mother, and so he did go back and built a new home.

Our land was all around the main road. The house was about two hundred feet from the road. He knocked it down but kept one thatched room, I guess for sentimental reasons. He built a two-story slate roof house with the thatched room attached to it. Then he built a two-story shop at the road, a cow barn, a dairy house, a hen house, a horse shed, a shed for oats, a turf shed, and a shed for all the farm machinery. It looked like a small village. He was in his thirties when he met my mother; she was eighteen years old and lived up the mountain. She loved him until the day he died, and after he died. I used to joke with her, "Mom, you saw the money and that was your chance to get out of the mountain."

New House Built in 1965

Old House Built in 1923

Been Taught Not to Hate

When I was a kid I slept in the thatched room with my father. He always slept on his back. I would sleep with my legs over his belly and we would talk ourselves to sleep. I must have been eight or ten years old and the schoolmaster was teaching us Irish history, about how the English invaded us, killed the men, kidnapped all the young girls, and burned homes. I was really getting to hate the English. One night in bed, I say to my father, "The English are very bad people. Can you tell me something about them?" I look back and think of my father as a man who knew how to teach his kid not to hate.

He said to me, "Well, I recall one Sunday evening, we knew there was going to be no fighting, the English army, two hundred of them, were leaving Ballinaglera, going along the road marching fifteen miles to Manor Hamilton. We were all out by the shop watching them march by. One young man stepped out of line and asked for a mug of water. I asked your mother to get it." "He drank it and handed the mug back and ran on. We watch him get back in his line up by the post office." My father says that that young man did not want to be marching roads in Ireland on a Sunday evening, he would rather be back in his home with his family having tea.

I still want to see a thirty-two county united Ireland before I die, but that history teacher was not able to get me to hate all English people like he did. Thank you, Father.

Romance in the Town

Jack McDonough and Martin McSharry did business with each other. Jack and his brother, Packie, were butchers in Drumkeeran. Martin and Tom McSharry were jobbers—cattle dealers. The McDonough's bought cattle from the McSharrys for slaughter, which made them all friends of sorts.

The McSharrys were very highly respected. Martin was six foot five inches tall. He never fought, but if a man hit him, they never forgot it. Nobody tried him on because they all knew what the result would be. Martin was brutal when he got mad, but he loved to laugh.

Stoney and His Five Sisters
Back Row: Ann and Josephine
Middle Row: Bernadette and Vera
Front Row: Stoney and Nuala

Jack McDonough would fight with his fingernails and he would "sly rap" you, hit you when you weren't looking. People stayed away from him. Jack owned his own house and a car and he did something nobody had ever heard of in that part of the country, he put in a bathtub in the house. Many people asked how it was done. We were backward in those times.

Jack married a tall, blonde school teacher. She looked like she should have been in Hollywood. It must have been the bathtub that did it since Jack wasn't Hollywood material. They were married for six years and had no kids.

Martin lived on a big farm and was married to a small woman, five foot two inches. They had six kids, four sons and two daughters. Martin and his wife stood out when they walked through the town, him being so tall and she so small. On a market day in Drumkeeran, he sold a lot of cattle to Jack. When the market closed, Martin and Jack went drinking at Kelly's Pub, Jack got sentimental and said to Martin, "I'm going to ask you something personal."

"Okay," Martin said with a smile, "Why not?"

Jack said, "Martin, there must be a secret to it. Now listen, Martin, you're married to a small woman and you've got six kids. I'm married to a tall beautiful blonde. I've been trying but can't have any kids. How do you do it?"

"Well," said Martin, "here's what you've got to do. First of all, everyone is talking about this thing they call the bathtub. You fill it with warm water and have your wife sit in it. Get a nice warm cloth with some soap and rub her up and down. Then, stand her up and dry her off and wrap her up in a big towel but don't let her walk—pick her up and carry her to the bed and lay her down." Then Martin said nothing.

Jack couldn't help himself, he had to ask, "And what do I do then?"

Martin said, "Then you send for me"

Well, if there ever was a time Jack would sly rap a man, this was it. He ground his teeth but he knew that if he hit Martin he would lose.

With neither radio nor television in those days, that story was the entertainment for a long time.

Ghosts and Fairies

I think back and wonder why we were so backward in our thinking. The older people were scared of God, ghosts, priests, lights and fairies. I've always thought to myself, "I'm scared of things that I can see. I ain't gonna live my life being scared of things I can't see, such as ghosts and some invisible bastard who, if he did exist, he'd have to be a sadist."

When the Protestants died off, Parson Sides got a new parish near Dublin. The Parish House, as we called it, was a castle with cobblestone yards and two large gates by the main road. The castle was a short distance from the road and everybody talked about it being haunted. A bunch of us would hang around the large gates at night but nobody would go up to the castle.

One night, we all started talking about the ghosts and this guy, Andy McTierney, said, "I ain't scared of no ghost." And Mick McGuire said, "I'll bet you one pound you won't go up."

"I'll go right now," McTierney said.

"No," said McGuire, "tomorrow night at twelve o'clock." (Everybody thinks ghosts come out after midnight.)

"Okay," said McTierney.

The next night, we all show up. McGuire shows McTierney the one pound note and says, "You've got to go up the stairs to the top of the steeple." It was three stories up.

McGuire says, "We're scared so we ain't goin'. Here's the deal, Andy, so we know that you went up.

Here's a hammer and a six-inch nail. When you get to the top, you hammer this nail into the banister.

Tomorrow, we'll check. If the nail is there, you'll get your one pound." Off went Andy.

When he got to the castle, he started up the stairs. We could hear his footsteps because the windows had all been taken by local people. Also, it was winter and frost was in the air, and sound travels further in the frost. Andy made it to the top. We heard hammering and then the hammering stopped.

Silence and then more silence.

Then a yell, "No! No! No!" And then another yell, "Please! Please! Let me go, please!"

We then heard Andy tumbling down the stairs. I was the youngest in the group but the others took off running and so did I. Nobody wanted to fight the ghost.

The next day, we all went to Andy's house. He was there. He had cuts on his face, elbows and legs but nothing was broken. McGuire said, "Here's your money. You earned it."

We left Andy and we all went to the Castle. Even though it was daytime, those grown men seemed to me to be a little scared. I stayed behind them. We got to the top and lo and behold!

Andy, the man who said he wasn't scared of ghosts, had been wearing a long coat and gotten so scared that when he started to drive the nail into the wood, he caught the nail in the end of his coat and drove the nail through the coat. When he stepped to go down the stairs, the coat held him back and, already being scared, he thought it was the ghost, and he started pleading for mercy. He had pulled so hard, he had torn the bottom of his coat off and there it was with the nail through it.

A Haunted House

The grown-ups used to tell us as kids ghosts cannot cross water. I guess it had something to do with keeping you from having a heart attack; if the ghost is on one side of the river and you're on the other side, he can't get to you.

I'll tell it this way. When I was thirteen, a young man named Tony Gray brought movies (we called them pictures) to Dowra. He used a petrol (gas) generator and it used to break down a lot but we didn't care.

Nobody had seen movies. They were a big hit.

Every Thursday night, the girls would come from Ballinaglera. I knew one, Lisa McPartland, from the Technical School. I rode my bike home with her. After, I had to come back through Dowra and then it was three miles home. It would be one o'clock in the morning by the time I got there.

On the way home, I had to pass a vacant haunted house. I was still young and I'm thinking maybe—just maybe—there are ghosts in there. As I get past the haunted house, I'm pedaling away and, suddenly, I'm finding it hard to pedal. I start to pedal harder. I have a quarter of a mile to McCarter's Bridge. I feel something holding the carrier of the bike. I feel it wants me off the bike. If I can only make it to the bridge and get over the water, the ghost can't follow me. Now I'm up off the saddle, pedaling faster and the sweat is pouring off of me. The bike is really being held back. I'm getting closer and closer. I feel I'm doing only one mile an hour and as I get over the bridge, the bike shoots forward so fast that I fall back on the saddle.

The next day I ride down to the haunted house. I turn around and pedal back to the bridge. I go back to the haunted house, pedal it again, faster this time. I do it again as fast as I can go. Then I have it figured out. I'm like Andy. Subconsciously, I think there's a ghost. So, no matter how hard I pedaled, it wasn't hard enough, and my mind was telling me that when I get over the water, the ghost won't follow me. I'll be safe.

Another story of a haunted house. There was a teacher who we knew as Master Flynn. He was the son of Master Flynn Senior, who taught my father. He had a house about four hundred yards from our house and shop. When he was going to college to study to be a teacher, he failed the Irish language subject. Therefore he was not allowed to teach in the South of Ireland. So he found a teaching job in the North of Ireland. He was not married so he stayed in the North Monday to Friday and his house was vacant for five days. He would return on weekends. He had a caretaker named Pat Guicken to mind his house. This guy told everybody that Flynn's house was haunted. Some nights we would see lights, but not every night, sometimes twice a week and in some weeks, three nights. Those lights seemed to be in a bedroom on the second floor.

Master Flynn told a story of how he ran over a person with his car one night in front of his house and when he got out of the car, there was nobody on the ground.

One night, my father came home late with supplies for the shop. We helped him put away the supplies and he put the horse out to pasture. We looked towards Flynn's house and there was a light in the second floor bedroom. My father says to me, "Let's go up and see the light." I am scared, but I did not want to show my fear.

We walked to the house. My father found a small window he was able to open, "Okay," he said to me, "You hop in and go open the front door for me." I get in and it's dark. I am in the parlor. I walk to the kitchen and fall over a chair. Wow, am I scared! I get to the door and open it to let my father in. My father starts up the stairs with me behind him, both walking slow. We get to the top of the stairs, and we look in the bedroom. In the middle of the floor is a tall candle burning in a metal container. It still had a few inches to burn to the end. Pat the caretaker made his job easy. He did not have to check on the house every night, just had to light the tall candle to keep people away.

And there you have your ghost.

Card Games in Houses

Mike Corrigan's house was half a mile from ours and I used to visit there a lot. His two uncles were John and Pat Guicken. Pat had been the caretaker for Master Flynn's house. When John died he left the house and land to Mike. That house was great for having card games. The house would be packed with locals. The prizes varied for the big games: a pig's head, a goose, a turkey at Christmas, or even a new pair of shoes someone got as a gift from America that didn't fit him, and if they didn't fit the guy who won them, he would raffle them.

Some of the locals were great characters. John McTige was very witty. He had lost a leg in the Second World War and had a wooden one. Jimmy Paw McPartland was a bachelor who was paranoid and thought everyone was talking about him, so he was always early for the game so nobody could talk about him behind his back. He had to stay home one night as he had a cow giving birth. The next night Jimmy arrived late. He wanted everybody there. Then he stood at the door and said in a loud voice, "I guess ye all had a good time last night talking about me."

John McTige was so fast, he said, "Last night we talked about only good people, and your name was never mentioned."

Time went on and Pat Guicken got ill and was bedridden. We used to turn him in the bed four times a day, but he still got bedsores, then they got inner tubes from car tyres and inflated them and lifted him onto them. Finally the day came. I was nine years old. Mike told me to hop on my bike and go to Willie Oatie and ask him to come because Pat was near the end.

Willie was the man who took care of the dying. He arrived at 6:00 p.m. and went into the room, came out and said he only has a few hours. All three of us sat by the fire drinking tea and every fifteen minutes one of us would check on Pat. At about

10:00 p.m., I went to the room and his mouth was open. I came up and told Willie. "Okay", says Willie, "he is leaving us," and all three of us go down.

Willie takes the prayer book and jams it under his chin to close his mouth. He then got two half crown coins, they were heavy coins, and he puts them on his eyes to keep his eyes closed. We wait for an hour and Willie and Mike put his best shirt, tie and jacket on him. They straighten out his body with a pillow under his head. Pat Guicken is ready to party.

The next morning, I tell my mother in the shop and Lizzy in the post office that Pat has died; the wake is tonight. Mike will be over for supplies, food, drinks and Guinness, and get word to a few musicians, so Pat can get a good send-off.

Curfews

Every Thursday, I went to Dowra, met Lisa and came home late. No more ghosts. Boy, was I smart for my age! Then my father and mother found out about me seeing a girl in Ballinaglera. They didn't tell me that they knew. That's the way people did it back then. They would come up with another excuse, "No more late nights. We need you early in the morning. No more Dowra for you."

My excuse was that the movie was a continuation from the prior week and I had to follow the story.

"No, you're still too young."

"But I'll be fourteen next year."

"Then you'll wait until next year."

Back then, we were always told you were a man at fourteen. Grown-ups valued your opinion; you took on responsibilities. I look back and laugh at the nerve of me. I recall that when I was eleven years old, my father hit me a slap for getting out of hand. I stood up to him and shook my finger in his face, and said, "Three more years!"

Anyway, I knew it wasn't working. So early in the week, I started planning for Thursday. There was a big deep drain down past the shop and I hid the bike in it. That night I said I was going to Dowra and started to dress. My mother was baking bread for the next day and my father was sitting by the fire in his socks, reading the paper. My mother tried to stop me from getting dressed.

My father said, "Let him get dressed. He's going nowhere. Bolt the door."

Now I'm dressed and I go to sit on the stairs. Then I go up the stairs. Mother comes up and I meet her. She goes back down and I sit on the stairs again. Then I go up again and she goes to come up, but I was already going down the stairs. She goes back down. She was a little at ease then. There's a window on the second floor over the porch outside. If only I can get it open and then go back down like I'm staying. I'd sit at the top of the stairs while Mother was baking away. I went and opened the window and I knew she heard it. I came flying back and met her on the stairs. She turned and went back down.

When I finally got my chance, I ran and jumped out the window. I had to land on the concrete. "It's now or never!" Down the walkway to the road, then to my bike. I knew my father had to get the bolt off the door but he could run. He prided himself on his running. I got to the bike. I got it out of the ditch and jumped on it. The pedals were spinning and I couldn't get my feet on them. Finally, I got my feet on them. I felt my father's fingers touching the carrier on the back of the bike. I made it to the hill and I looked back.

I got him. I waved my hand and yelled, "So long, Pat!"

That night when I came home, I was watching for my father. There was no sign of him. I got past the house and went to the neighbor's house, Mick Corrigan's. I often stayed with him. The next day I came home. Mother was in the shop with neighbors and she would never say anything with people around.

She told me that my father was in the big meadow. I went down there. From the road, I saw him working by himself. I went into the field. He was bent down, doing something with potatoes. He straightened up and looked at me.

Before he opened his mouth, I said, "If you're going to hit me, that's it. I'm going to England." At that time, men as young as twelve were going to England and getting jobs.

He said, "Okay. Not another word. Go to work."

At twelve years old, I left National School and went to the Technical School in Drumkeeran. Drumkeeran had a big building with a fifty-ton generator that gave light to the town but broke down about five times a week.

The Technical School taught woodworking, chemistry, mechanics, etc. They had three rooms for boys.

They taught sewing, knitting, cooking, etc. They had three rooms for girls.

There were no suspensions or penalties if you didn't go every day. But there were three days a week we boys never failed to go.

Those were the days the boys and girls from Doballey, Ballinaglera and Dowra went to the Technical School and there were a lot of girls. It was too far for them to walk, so the only days they went were the three days that the bus went to Sligo. Because the bus didn't come back to Drumkeeran until 7:00 p.m., the best way to control the boys and girls was to keep the school open until the bus arrived. In the winter, it was dark by 4:30 or 5:00 p.m. When the generator broke down, no lights.

I often think of how naive the teachers were. All the teachers, can you imagine, all of them, they would lock us in the school and go up to the town to check on the generator. Doors locked. No teachers. We boys went flying off to get our favorite girl.

Pitch black dark. We were grabbing every girl. They were running and screaming. It was a game until you found the one you liked and she liked you. Then she'd laugh and say, "It's me! It's me!"

What a time and what fun we had until the lights went back on and then everybody would run back to their rooms and be back where they were supposed to be when the teachers came back.

Electric Power

The government planned to use water from Lough Allen to bring electricity to our part of the country by building a power station on the other side of the lough. There were men from all over the country working on the project. All the locals got jobs and loved to be working. My father was working in our quarry. He was selling stone by the ton to the government for the road. We were finally going to have a tarred road and electricity. The Twentieth Century was coming, even though it was half gone!

I was almost fourteen years old. I used to go to Drumkeeran on my bike. I met Tom Coyle, who I went to school with, at seven o'clock one evening. He was dirty like he had been working hard. I asked him, "Who are you working with?" He told me he had found a job in the power station. I went there the next day and got hired.

There was a guy, Joe McNiff, who worked at the power station. He had a car and he charged so much a week to bring me to work. I walked two miles to his house and he picked up four other guys along the way. It was a good deal. I worked with an old man, Tom McLaughlin, digging holes eight foot deep for the electric poles. We had a foreman, Tom Lynch, from County Cork. For whatever reason, Lynch seemed to dislike Tom, and I guess me too. One day, Tom and I had finished digging out holes by lunchtime. While we were eating lunch, the sky opened up and the rain came lashing down. After lunch, Lynch pointed to Tom and me and said, "You two, dig a trench at the back of the shed to stop the rain from coming in."

"In this rain?" asked Tom.

"Yes," said Lynch.

So off Tom and I went. We dug that drain fifteen feet in the lashing rain.

The next morning, we were lined up waiting to be told what to do. Lynch said, "You two, the weather is good today. We don't need that drain for water. Fill it back up with the clay you dug out yesterday."

Tom said to me, "What did we ever do to this guy?"

There had been large pipes stacked up for about a year, so large that you could crawl through on your honkers. Now they had to be welded to carry water from the lough, but there were no welders in Ireland at that time, so they had to get them from Germany.

The German welders arrived and for the first two months they built offices and workshops with heat. We were fascinated. In the morning, they drove in, in Mercedes Benzes, dressed in suits and ties and then changed into their work overalls. They went slow and calculated every move, and never had to redo anything. They asked people to fill out job applications. I was one of the first and I got a job. I was working with the Germans. I was then able to go to work, put on overalls and leave work clean.

On my first day, a German took me into his workshop and took out a large leather holder, what looked like what the American Indians carried their arrows in with a strap. He hung it over my shoulder and filled it with welding rods. He walked out the door and waved at me to follow him.

We got to the lough. There were large cranes lining up the giant water pipes together. When that was all done, he pointed to me to jump on the pipe and sit on it. He then reached up and pulled a welding rod out and then put it back. He gestured to me. I then pulled one out. He nodded his head and knelt down and started scrubbing the pipe with a wire brush. Then he muttered to me, "Ein anderes," and I answered with a welding rod. That was my job and I was good at it. Man, did I love this!

The next day, Joe McNiff, our driver, was wheeling a wheelbarrow full of muck and my ex-boss Lynch was yelling at him. Lynch would look over at me and I would pull out a rod and put it back, pull it out again and put it back again. I could see the anger in his face. Maybe Old Man Tom was right—Lynch didn't like us.

On Saturdays, we got paid and went to the pub. I broke the pledge at fourteen. Every Saturday evening, I went to the pub with twenty-, and thirty-, and forty-year-olds. I was a man; I was fourteen.

On Sunday nights, I dressed up and went to the local dance.

One Sunday night, I was in the New Bridge Dance Hall. I saw this girl, Sheila. She was dressed up nice, and her face had make up on, powder and lipstick like she was twenty years old. She was with a taxi driver, Gene McGorty, who was twenty-seven years old. He was driving her and her two older sisters who were home from America. They dressed up their younger sister to look like them. When I got to know her, I found out that she was the same age as me.

I thought she was the cat's meow, very pretty.

The sisters went back to America and McGorty went out with her for a month. Then one night in Tess Lee's Dance Hall in Drumkeeran, I saw her with Frank Earley, a cousin of mine. He was twenty-five years old. I felt safe and I asked him if I could dance with her. He yelled, "No!" and I walked away.

A month later, a guy, Mike Keegan, had bought a car. Four of us hired him to go to a dance thirty miles away and what do you know? She was there with her older brother. I made a date for the following Thursday evening for nine o'clock and her friend Monica Gallagher to join me and a buddy of mine, Johnny Flynn. We were to meet on the mountain road near where the girls lived.

The following Thursday it's snowing hard. I meet Johnnie in Drumkeeran, we say to each other, why go four miles up the mountain road? No one in their right mind would wait in the snow for us. We meet Mike Keegan with his car and, for a laugh, we pay him to drive us up the mountain. We're an hour late and to our surprise we see two people walking in the snow. It's them. Sheila says we should go to her house. Her parents are away and her younger brother Myles is at a neighbor's house.

Her parents had put in a generator for electric light. She takes us up a flight of stairs over the cowshed. It was full of hay and very warm from the breath of the cows. Sheila and I go to the end of the hayloft and get under the hay, we giggle, and the four of us are talking back and forth and laughing. Then we hear footsteps coming up the steps. Sheila says, "My father!" and she and I dig deep in the hay to hide.

We hear the light switch click on. Not a word. It seemed like forever. I stick my head up slowly over the hay and there is Myles, her brother, trying to stop himself from laughing. Johnnie had hid Monica under the hay and most of himself, but his arse was sticking out from the hay like an ostrich. We all roared our heads off laughing. Then we went in the house for tea, and later Johnnie and I walked the seven miles home.

More people were getting cars by now. The dance halls were paying for big bands but Lynch the priest used the local bands, for which he didn't pay too much. The other dance halls stayed open until 2:00 a.m. but Lynch stayed open until only midnight.

So he used religion again. He got on the altar and made it a mortal sin for anybody to go to a dance hall that stayed open after midnight, but younger people were changing.

Mad Ass

Most of us farm boys and girls started going to dances at twelve or thirteen years old. Sunday night was the only night people went dancing. There were four dance halls within a four-teen-mile area. We would cycle to Crevealey, Drumkeeran, New Bridge, and Doballey.

Doballey is in County Cavan. There were some young people who were very clannish of their town or area, and were suspicious of people from other areas. There was a mountain area some miles from Doballey dance hall. There were families up there, the McGoverns; they were very protective of their girls.

This story is about Paddy Kelly, one of the cool dudes, who asked me at the Protestant wake some years before, what should he do. One Sunday night in Doballey at the dance, he took one of the McGovern girls home to the mountain. The next Sunday night, the McGovern boys get around him and tell him to stay away from their girls, and stay off the mountain. I must say he had nerve and he took her home again.

The following Sunday, Kelly is there again with the girl. Love is blind. The McGoverns leave the dance early and go back home to the mountain and wait for Kelly. It was a beautiful, clear moonlit night. They have it all planned what they are going to do with Kelly.

They had rounded up the wildest ass (donkey) off the mountain. They had cut a blackthorn bush with a lot of thorns and got a rope. Kelly, because he got the girl, he leaves the dance early. When he reaches her house, they grab him and give her orders to go home.

They take every stitch of clothing off Kelly, tie him on the donkey's back and then tie the blackthorn bush to the donkey's tail, so that every time the donkey moves the bush hits the back of its legs. They hit the donkey on the arse and he takes off down the mountain road towards the dance hall. The mountain road is very steep and the crowds of people coming from the dance have to jump into the ditch on both sides of the road to let this mad ass by, braying with pain from the prodding of the blackthorn bush on the back of its legs with this naked man strapped to him, screaming with fear.

They say love is blind, but I think Kelly got the message.

Dublin Trip

There were ten of us in our family. There were about two years between each of us. I was the second youngest. Mary, the eldest, went to England before I was born. When we were planning for me to go the United States, we had to go to Dublin to get me a passport. I had never met Mary, so my mother wrote a letter to her saying that it would be nice if she could take the boat to Dublin to see me before I went to America.

My mother and I took the train to Dublin. Another sister, Josephine, was living in Dublin. She was the only one of us who never left Ireland. She went to college, became a schoolteacher, married a schoolteacher and lived happily ever after.

We all met Mary in the Green Rooster Restaurant. My mother introduced me to her. She was a quiet, shy woman. I was sixteen and was shy also. We all had lunch. I don't remember much conversation. We finished lunch, shook hands and said good-bye. Mary got the boat back to England and we returned to Leitrim.

Within a few months, I'd be in America and that didn't seem to bother any of us. I guess it was the times.

If you can't do anything about it, then make the best of what there is.

My mother always said that when she was young, people felt there was one thing that they must do when people died and that was to give them a good send-off. They felt that life was so hard for the living, this was a way to make them happy on the last trip to the beyond.

The family would buy pipe tobacco, papers to roll cigarettes and a half-barrel of Guinness and get musicians from all around to come and play, and they would dance and sing until dawn. Then we buried them. They called that a good send-off, "An Irish Wake."

She said they did the same thing for a person going to America. The only difference was that he or she was alive at their own wake. But when they left the next day for America, walking fifteen to twenty miles to the train station, they were never to be seen again.

They called it "The American Wake."

I did see my sister Mary again. My other sisters once brought her to America for two weeks.

The Army and Me

A lot happened when I was twelve to fourteen years old.

The army recruiting officers came and set up shop in New Bridge Hall and recruited anyone who wanted to sign up. They would measure you for shoes and a uniform. They would come to the Hall every Thursday for four hours of training and you had to do two weeks in the Midlands.

I wondered if they would take me—and me not yet thirteen years old. Can you imagine such a thing happening today? I said to Mother and Father that the Army was recruiting and that I'd like to go to the meeting to see if they would take me. "Sure, son. Your brother was in the LDF (Local Defense Force) when he was twelve."

Off we all go, twelve-, thirteen-, fourteen-, fifteen-, sixteen-, seventeen- and eighteen-year-olds signed up and got measured for shoes, uniforms, a visor cap and short leather leggings that go above the shoes so the pants come over them by two or three inches.

It took about a month, but they arrived with a truck and everybody got their new outfits and a bolt-action rifle. We took all of this home. The rules were only to wear the uniform at meetings and outings that had to do with the LDF, but the rifle you could keep. You could use it to shoot rabbits, but you had to keep it spotless and oiled.

I became such a good shot that I won a rifle contest at a bazaar. I beat out guys who were thirty years old. I look back and wonder; by today's standards, what we were asked and expected to do was mind-boggling, but we loved it. It also taught us a lot about respect. Always keep your rifle pointed at the ground. If you got into a bad argument, throw your rifle to the ground, go at it with your fists and take your beating. You might never win, so swallow your pride and get into a line of business where you won't have to fight.

Today, the motto is, "Don't make him work, he's only a child!"

"Oh, look at what you've done? You've upset him. He wants to stay in his room and watch the best violent movies of all time and stay on the computer."

"How are you, Son?"

"I'm bored. I'm going to kill everybody at school."

Simple Times, Simple People

Around the fireside at night, our parents would sometimes tell us stories from when they were young. Our mother told us of tough times when there were a lot of diseases, like tuberculosis, polio, etc., and doctors were scarce. People didn't marry for love. They would think of their own kids and would never marry into a family with sickness in it. Years later I was telling this to a friend born in New York. He said, "Jesus Christ! That sounds like the Hitler Plan."

My mother also told us that when she was very young, nobody had ever seen their own face, except in the water when they looked into the river.

The men used to go to Dublin to work with the English landlord farmers. Once, my mother's neighbor, Patrick Doyle, was walking down a street in Dublin to the train station, going home. A guy on a corner said to him, "You want to buy?" Pulling his hand from inside his coat, he flashed a mirror. He let Patrick look into it. Then, just as quickly, he put the mirror back into his pocket.

Patrick was about fifty years old and thought that he had seen his own father. He said, "Where did you get my father? I have to have him." So the fast talking guy got a little extra money from him. When Patrick came home, he couldn't help himself. There wasn't a day that he didn't go into his pocket and look at his father.

One day he and his wife were working in the field making hay. It was hot and so he took his jacket off and put it down. She had been watching him for a long time going into his pocket and she was curious. She went to his jacket and pulled the mirror from the pocket. She looked into it and said, "So, this is the old hag you met in Dublin!" She had never seen herself either.

My mother told me that when she was a child, nobody had ever heard of, or seen, a car or a bicycle, so people had no clue what they looked like. She told me the story of a woman, Mrs. Keane, who was fifty years old when my mother was five. Once a month, she used to walk fourteen miles over the mountain to the nearest town to do her shopping.

About thirty-five miles away there was a rich family called the Lards. Nobody knew they had bought a car. It had big round headlights and an air horn on the side to blow with your hand. They had two sons in their early twenties who decided to drive the car through the mountain roads and scare people with the lights and the horn.

They were on the mountain road near my mother's house when Mrs. Keane is walking on it and she hears the horn. She looks back and sees the big round lights. She's so scared that she starts to run and runs right through a hedge outside my mother's house, in through the door, and puts her back to it and, hands against the door, yells, "Close the window! I just saw the Devil!"

The Spanish Onion in the Irish Stew

Eamon De Valera was elected President of Ireland in 1959. He was born in Manhattan on October 14th, 1882. His father, who was Spanish, died when he was two years old and his mother, who hailed from County Clare, sent him back there to be raised. In 1938, he was made Minister for External Affairs.

He was acclaimed a statesman for keeping Ireland neutral during World War II. England wanted to use Dublin ports for their ships during the war, but De Valera refused them, saying it took eight hundred years to get you out and we are not letting you back in. This made De Valera very popular.

When the war ended, England stopped buying beef and lamb from Ireland. Because Ireland had been part of England's commonwealth for so long, it was in the constitution that Ireland could only sell beef and agricultural products to England.

The price of land and cattle fell so low that it was hard to sell any at a profit. I recall myself being at a fair with my father where a neighbor had a pregnant cow for sale. He was asking ten shillings for her and he had to pay the fair sixpence to hold her in an area known as the green. He couldn't sell her, so in the evening he left her on the side of the road and walked away.

In 1956, twenty-two families left our part of the country. Eighteen of those were offered nothing for their farms, so they just abandoned them. This hardship was equal to the hardship of the dust bowl of the southern plains of Oklahoma and Kansas in America in 1930s.

People were leaving by the thousands. The joke was that the last one out of Ireland should switch out the light.

Murder on the Bridge

Tim Pat Tady lived in Glan, County Cavan, about two miles from Dowra. He was about five foot six inches tall and he was about six or seven years older than me. I would see him at the pictures in Dowra and at dances in Ballinaglera. He never traveled far from Dowra. He was such a little weasel; he would show you his fist and say, "Look what I can do with this little fist."

I was in America when I heard that he had killed a young man named McGoldrick on the Dowra Bridge. McGoldrick was an only son, whose father had died of a heart attack. His mother had asked the blacksmith if he would shoe their horse on a Sunday so that her son could start work early Monday morning.

As he was riding his horse home across the Dowra Bridge, he came upon Tim with a few of his mates, bragging. Tim, trying to look like a big man, stepped out in front of the horse and took a penknife out of his pocket. He said that he would cut the horse's head off. When McGoldrick stayed on the horse, Tim decided to pull him off and that's when a freak accident happened.

The knife went into McGoldrick's heart and he bled to death right there on the bridge. Tim jumped on his bike and rode off. Tim's mates carried the body to a house in town. They banged and banged on the door until they heard the occupant of the house coming and then they took off.

I had heard Tim got ten years in Mountjoy Jail in Dublin. He came home and committed suicide. I heard wrong.

Many, many years later, in New York, I met a man named Kevin Healy and, in conversation, he told me he had been a policeman in Dowra. I told him I was from Dowra and I said that the biggest thing that ever happened there had happened after I left, the first murder on the bridge ever, by Tim Pat Tady.

"I was there when that happened," Kevin told me.

I asked him to tell me about it. "Well," said Kevin, "people were very hush-hush. The people who found him on their doorstep saw nobody. We as town cops never had anything like that to contend with. The Sligo cops were called, who didn't know much either. We had everything closed off. The cops arrived from Sligo and the first thing they noticed was that there was a footprint in the blood on the bridge. They measured it lengthwise and widthwise and said that if they find the shoe that made this impression, they will find the killer.

The bloody footprint went up the street to the station house and in, and up the stairs into the room of a cop named

Jerry. He was asleep. All the cops lived in the station house back then. Big excitement. Close off the police station. A cop did it.

Jerry the cop was fond of the drink like many cops in the country stations. It was his day off and he was drinking in Gillday's Pub on the other side of the bridge. On his way back to the barracks, one of his shoes stepped into the blood and he was so drunk, he never noticed it. If this had been a big city—there goes another innocent man!

Kevin said that within a week, the truth was known. Tim was arrested and convicted and sent to Mountjoy Jail. Years went by and one day the phone rang in the station house.

It was Mountjoy Jail telling us to inform the family to meet Tim at the train in Carrick-on-Shannon. Tim was coming home. His sister had gone to America, the father was dead and the mother was home alone.

Tim should have been on his way to Sligo to the insane asylum and not going home to live with his mother. She was scared. Tim was home two months when his neighbors called us to tell us to come to the house because Tim was going to kill his mother.

Myself and Jerry went out to the house and found Tim in the kitchen with his mother up against the wall, with a knife to her throat. We tried to talk Tim into giving us the knife, but no dice. I thought Jerry had made a bad move but it worked. He jumped Tim and grabbed his hand and got the knife. Jerry was a religious man and when we were walking him to the door, Jerry turned Tim around and said, "Apologize to your mother," but Tim would not.

Tim got convicted again and was sent back to Mountjoy.

Tough convicts don't like guys who abuse women, kids or their mothers.

Tim never got to go home to his mother again.

Stoney at Cove, Co. Cork, Leaving by Ship for America
Left: Joe Rodden, Middle: Mick Carrigan, Right: Stoney

My Mother Arrives in New York

I was still living with my brother Jim in New York at the time my mother arrived.

She arrived on a Thursday night. As I tell this story, you must keep in mind that my mother worked on the farm, ran the shop, had ten kids, and had never seen electricity. She had only been in the local town a total of three times in her life.

She was fifty-nine when she arrived in New York by ship. At 9:00 p.m., she got to 114th Street in Richmond Hills, Queens where my sisters lived.

My sisters Vera and Bernadette had to get up for work early. So they all went to bed early. The next morning when they got up and got ready for work, they looked in on my mother but she was not there. Mother had been an early riser all her life and it was not unusual for her to be up so early.

My sisters returned at 7:00 p.m. and Mother was not home. They waited until 9:00 p.m. and then called my brother, who lived two miles away. He said to me, "Let's walk over, and by the time we get there, Mother will be there."

He and I walked slowly and got there a little after 10:00 p.m. No sign of her. My sisters said we had better call the cops that something must have happened to her. She wouldn't know where the train was. It was too far away.

Jim said, "Make some tea. We'll wait until 11:00 p.m."

"Okay, Jim, it's 11:00 p.m. We've got to call the cops," Vera said.

"Now," Jim said, "you know what we'll do? We'll wait until midnight."

She said, "No way! I'm calling them right now!"

"Wait, wait!" said Jim.

"Okay. 11:30."

"Okay."

It was 11:25 p.m., and Mother walks in the door.

"My God, Mother! What happened to you?" asked Vera.

"I found a job."

"But where?"

"In town," Mother said.

"You mean Manhattan?"

"Is that what you call it?"

"But how did you get the train?"

"Well," said Mother, "I was dressed and out of the house by 5:30 a.m. I saw this well-dressed young man walking like he was going somewhere. I asked him how I could get to City Center. He said that he really didn't know what I meant. I told him that back home they call the middle of the town the City Center. I'm going to look for a job and I think that that would be a good place to start. 'Well,' he said, 'I'm going to 34th Street and Sixth Avenue and that's pretty central.'

"We chatted away and when we came up on the street, he wished me luck. He was smart too. He told me I should look for a job in a restaurant. He said they have women waitresses, women in the kitchen and women at the cash registers. Lots of jobs for women.

"So off I go. After going in and out of places for hours and just hearing no all the time, I figured I was asking the wrong people. I decided that when I went into the next place, I'd ask for the manager. I went to four places. This was not working either. I went into the fifth place and it was so busy.

I asked the girl at the register if I could see the manager and she pointed to the back. I pushed my way back and found him. He looked confused. I asked him if he had any work for me. He hardly looked at me and asked me to follow him to a stairway. He pointed to the bottom of the stairs and there must have been more than a hundred cups, saucers and plates, and knives and forks, and food. He pointed to the big trash cans and asked me if I could clean it all up. I said, 'Absolutely!'

"I took my coat off and went down the stairs and had it all cleaned up and swept clean in about fifteen minutes. I went back up to him and before I could say anything, he said was it too much for me, but I told him that it was all cleaned up. He went back and looked down the stairs. 'I can't believe it!' he said. I asked him if he had anything else.

He told me there was a young man picking up all the dirty plates, etc., from all the tables with a big wheeled cart and that we were running out of clean plates. I told the young man to stop doing what he was doing and bring up the clean plates, cups and saucers. He got upset, went crazy and threw the cart and everything down the stairs and walked out. I was stuck at rush hour. 'If I show you what to do, do you think you can do it?' the manager asked. I said, 'Sure.'

"He came by after a few hours and was surprised to see that I had finished everything and was mopping the floor. He told me he had never seen anyone work like that and that I didn't have to mop the floor, that they had someone for that.

I told him that I have to keep working, that I can't sit down. He asked me if I thought I could do a double shift. I asked, 'You mean work late?' 'Sure,' he said. I told him yes and so that is why I am late coming home."

The name of the restaurant was Schrafft's. Mother worked there until it was bought by Marriott Hotels. Marriott got the franchise or concession to supply all the airplanes at JFK Airport. They liked Mother so well that they got her a job at the airport. Then she only needed to take the Lefferts Boulevard bus to work.

Her job was to prepare all the salads but she would have that done in half the time. Then she would wash the dishes. Her boss was a large lady named Mrs. Johnston. She used to tell Mother to slow down, but Mother never did. Mother weighed only ninety-eight pounds. She told me that one day when she had done all of her work and she was helping wash the dishes, Mrs. Johnston walked in and said, "Kate, I told you to slow down." Mother told her that she couldn't slow down and that that was the only way she knew how to work. She said that then Mrs. Johnston picked her up and danced her around the kitchen and said, "If you don't slow down, I'll knock you down."

Mother got the bus every morning at 5:00 a.m. on Lefferts Boulevard at Atlantic Avenue. There were the same bus driver and the same six passengers every day, and everybody said good morning to everybody and everybody sat in the same seat.

One morning, as usual, she gets on the bus says good morning and sits in her usual seat. Her feet kicked something and when she looked down, she saw it was a briefcase. She picked it up and put it on her lap. She tried to open it and the top flew open.

It was packed tightly with hundred dollar bills. She slammed it shut, jumped up and ran to the bus driver. She told him it was full of money. He took the case with his left hand, put it alongside his left foot and said he'd turn it in when he got to the bus depot. She never saw him again.

I said to her, "But Mother, wouldn't you think to take the money home?"

"Oh no, son! Money like that is bad luck. You've got to work for your money."

Back then in the 1960s, Mike Wallace and Harry Reasoner, of the 60 Minutes TV show, did a story on drug money. They said that a briefcase full of hundred dollar bills could hold over a million dollars.

Maybe Mother was right; if it was drug money we'd all be dead.

My Brother Jim Returns to Ireland.

My sister in Ireland, Josephine, plans to get married. Jim says, "I must go back and walk her down the aisle," and he did. He came back with a different frame of mind; Ireland is the only place to live, he says, and to raise kids.

Here's a guy who spends twelve years trying not to be Irish in America, comes back from Ireland, and sells everything. He sells his station wagon to me, his kid brother. When I went to pick up the station wagon, he had the back seat down. I went to bring the back seat up, but he stopped me, telling me it looked better down. I was easy to handle, so I said okay.

Two weeks later my buddy Desmond Fallon and I were at Rockaway Beach and we picked up two girls. Desmond picked up the back seat and when they jumped in, their feet went right through the floor to the street! My brother had sold me a car with no floor in the back. The Fucker.

Jim lived in Ireland for fifteen years. His warped mind followed him. I always said he should've been a politician. He could look you straight in the eye and say, "How can you say that about me?"

In Ireland, Josephine and her husband, Noel Hogan, were both schoolteachers. She asked Mother to come back to Ireland and babysit her five kids. Can you imagine this? So she retired from the Airport. To her surprise, the big bosses at Marriot knew about her work ethic and threw her a big retirement party at the Marriott Hotel. We were all invited. It was a great party.

My Father returned to Ireland to the farm he had a stroke Josephine got him in to a nursing home in Dublin. He lost his speech. The home place had not been sold. It was in my father's name but we all agreed that whatever money it sold for must go to our mother. Jim said he knew a lawyer, so he would get the paperwork done for the sale of the family home. He was in a big rush to sell it. He went to a cousin, Johnnie, and sold it within weeks.

Mother asked him for the money but he said that he had invested it for her. She never saw the money. I said, "Mother, I'm doing okay now and I'll see to it that you'll be fine." The nice thing about this was that within a year, the property went up and up in value. I was so happy for my cousin. Jim tried to buy the property back from him, but Johnnie had always wanted to live on the main road. "I'm here until I die," he said. And he was.

Mother was living with Josephine and Noel, and she didn't like living there on the weekends when they were home from school. I went back for vacation, went to Dublin and stayed in a hotel Jim found me. I told him I'm going to Navan to see Mother and he said he'd go with me. We go there and while we are talking, Mother said that cattle had come through a hole in the bushes.

Jim said, "Let me check it for you."

While he was gone, Mother said, "I hoped that that would get him to go outside for a while. Look Stoney, I'll talk fast. I have enough money for a down payment on a house, maybe you could get somebody to look for a house for me in Dublin."

We could see Jim, the thief with no conscience, coming, and I said, "Mother enough said. Leave it to me." Jim walked in.

I said, "Okay, Mother, we're leaving." Jim said, "Stoney, you're always in a hurry."

Come in, say hello, and then go out, that's me!

I was leaving for New York the next morning, so I called Sean Flynn. Sean was a close family friend from home. He said, "I'll get Peter McHugh, also from home. He's in real estate and he will write to you in New York." Peter wrote to me and said he had a house that was perfect for my mother but he needed all the money transferred to his bank in Dublin and he gave me the address. I asked myself, "Should I do this?" Then I said to myself, "There can't be two Jims." So I emptied out my bank account. The bank manager told me I was doing a very foolish thing, but I didn't listen.

Two months went by and no word from Peter. I wrote and asked him what was going on and I got no reply. "Well," I said, "Mother has no house and I should have listened to the bank manager."

Two more weeks go by. The mailman comes with a large envelope for me from Ireland. It was from Peter:

"Sorry Stoney, it took longer than I thought but here it is. Sign all these papers at the Xs and the house is yours. I will give the keys to your mother. She can move in right away."

I went back the following year and saw Mother, and she was so happy. When Josephine and Noel walk in the door Friday evening, she walks out and is on the bus for Dublin.

Mothers-in-law should not stay in their children's house when there is no work to be done.

She tells me, "Jim was over in your house." She always called it my house. "He says to me, 'Mother, I just can't believe it that Stoney would go to a stranger and buy his house and having his own brother here in Dublin.'"

She said to me, "Where did he come from?"

I didn't see Peter McHugh when I was home, so I called him on the phone to thank him again. He tells me, "I met your brother Jim in Dublin recently and I had to keep my hands in my pockets."

I fell for it. I said "Why?"

He said, "So Jim couldn't get his hands in."

I thanked him for getting the house and he thanked me for the business.

I told Mother that I was going down to Leitrim. She said, "Stoney, you can't, Jim has destroyed our good name." I went down anyway and met my good friend Katie Flynn, Sean's mother, and she confided in me that Jim found out that they were going to visit their daughter in England for two weeks.

He asked to use the house with his kids. Katie and her husband Francy told him that they would love to have someone they know living in the house while they are away. They tell Jim he has the run of the whole house but for one room, which is locked because they have some gold coins, silver and antiques in there. Talk about the fox minding the hen house.

They come back from England; he had broken the lock to the room. Coins were missing, etc. He said, "Oh, the kids must have broken the lock."

Mother said, "I thought I was going to die here, so I bought a grave plot here in Dublin, but now I can't bear to meet people I know. When Josephine's kids don't need a babysitter, I think I'll go back to New York."

A few years later, I bought a house in Flushing, Queens. I wrote my mother and told her I got a two-family house with a backyard. When your babysitting job is over, you'll be able to grow your own vegetables in the backyard. She came back to New York and the first thing she did was buy one grave plot deep enough for two bodies. She thought I'd be buried with her, but I'm going to be cremated.

When some of Jim's children came to America, he quit his job and came also. One day the phone rang and Mother picked it up. "It's Jim. I'm coming over to see you," he said and he hung up.

Mother asked, "What does he want to see me for? He's got everything I had."

My sister Nuala was visiting when he arrived. Jim liked to talk politics. He starts to talk about the Kennedys and he told Mom that they were a very tragic family.

She said, "What do you mean, Jim?"

Jim said, "Oh, come on, Mother. The oldest son Joe was killed in the War. John F. was assassinated. Bobby was assassinated, and there was a sister in a mental institution." He says, "That is tragic."

Mother said, "Jim, that's no tragedy. These are hard things that happen to families as they go through life, but that devil Teddy went over that bridge and killed that girl and destroyed the family name. Now, Jim, that is a tragedy."

A little while later Nuala asked me to drive her home. We're in the car and Nuala says to me, "Did you get that answer Jim got?"

Well, I said I heard what she said so Nuala explained to me: "She was letting him know what he did to our family."

I said, "You know he didn't get it because he justifies everything and I didn't get it until you said it."

Many years later, I felt I got even with my loving brother Jim. When my business started to make money, he had the nerve to call me on the phone. I answered it, and said "Hello."

He said, "I am so glad I got you, this is Jim. I hear you are doing very well. I need to borrow twenty from you."

I said, "Jim, twenty what?"

"Twenty thousand dollars," he says.

Can you imagine the nerve? I told him no more lending for me, "I lent a guy ten thousand dollars for plastic surgery and now I don't know what he looks like."

Mother lived with me until she died at ninety-two. Jim came to the funeral and when he found out that I could be buried over my mother, he suggested that he be buried with her. We all laughed. He must think he can get his hands in her pockets now that he's on top.

Well, what do you know? He died in California broke. His children took up a collection in the bar that he owned. They did not seem embarrassed about that. My sisters asked me about him being buried with our mother.

Did I mind? I did mind, but Mother always said you don't know the difference when you're dead.

Hard Times, But Good Times

It's good to be born in the 1940s. When you're young, you're working like a grown-up but you have so much energy that at the end of the day you still have the spirit to jump on your bike and go. If you're hurt, you're taught not to show it, and if the other person isn't pulling his weight, make a joke if you have to. Do his work if you have to but keep going. It's a matter of teaching your mind to not complain.

You have used up extra energy and you'll sleep better. All of this makes you a happy person as you get older.

We all left Ireland at different times. Mary went to England and became a nurse, Una to Edinburgh, Scotland. Kathleen, Ann and Jim came to Aunt Kathryn in Queens, New York. She was married to our mother's brother, Uncle Mike. He was a motorman on the railroad. They had three kids of their own, a son, Hughie, and two daughters, Geraldine and Beebe. Aunt Kathryn got jobs for Kathleen, Ann and Jim, washed their clothes, and fed them for twelve dollars a week.

Ann and Kathleen got married. Jim went into the US Army and was stationed in Germany. He didn't have to go to the Korean War. Aunt Kathryn's one son, Hughie, was in World War II. The ship he was on was blown up.

Six months later the government came to the house and gave their condolences and gave her a medal. One year after that, Hughie walked in the door. When the ship blew up, a few survived. He had made it to a friendly island, but he had amnesia for months. Later, he got married and worked for the telephone company. He progressed to the top of his job, retired, and moved to New Hampshire.

My sisters Bernadette and Vera came to Aunt Kathryn a few years after Jim and my other sisters, and she did the same thing for them. Bernadette got a job with the phone company. Vera got a job with American Airlines, with free travel for her family, until she got married.

Then I came. My brother Jim said that his only kid brother would stay with him. By then he was married with three children and he was going to look after his only brother. He always talked like that. It took years to get to know him.

I was one hour in the country when he said to me, "The first thing you do is you must get rid of that accent."

What a thing to say to a farm kid in a new country! I'm wondering that he must be right. He's in New York nine years and has lost his accent. He married an American. I start off in this new country and I'm never opening my mouth. I was a man back home. Now I'm a fish out of water and I don't even know the money!

It's hard to believe today but back then, coming to a new country, you didn't even know the names of the foods. Jim got me my first job, running an elevator in Stern's Department Store on 42nd Street and Sixth Avenue, Times Square.

At lunch hour the first day I worked there, I saw a lot of people go outside. I followed them to a corner place across the street. It had no stools and open windows. There were five guys behind the counter yelling, "You're next!" and I couldn't figure out what they were saying or what they were eating.

When I went home, I told Jim I had gone to a place that day and people ordered food through a window and inside also, but I couldn't understand, so I didn't eat that day.

He said, "All you need is a hot dog."

"A what? Hot dog?"

"Yeah, until you get home."

At his apartment all they had was spaghetti. I hated that also.

The next day at lunch hour, I go out to the corner place, I squeeze inside, and I wait until I get right up to the counter.

The guy says, "You," with his finger pointed to me.

I say, "Hot dog," and it was there in a flash.

He snapped the dollar out of my hand and slapped the change on the counter. I looked around. Nobody seemed to notice my accent. I felt good. Next day I did the same thing. For a whole week.

Then I said to Jim, "Are there any other foods? I'm getting tired of eating hot dogs."

"My, my!" he said. "Order a hamburger."

I said, "What?"

He said, "Hamburger."

I thought to myself, well, I know I'm going to like ham, and I hope the people won't hear my accent. I'll say it fast and get out of there. The next day I squeeze into the counter and wait. The guy points his finger at me and says, "You."

I say, "Hamburger."

He says, "What?" and I say, "Hot dog."

Making Ends Meet

My first week's pay was seventy-five dollars. I think Jim was surprised. He explained to me that I'd have to pay him forty dollars a week rent. All I knew was that I still had money in my pocket.

Two weeks went by and I met a guy from home in Ireland named Jimmy Cullen. He took me to a dance hall at 85th Street and Lexington Avenue called the Jaeger House. Ninety percent Irish. I was in my element. I met a girl named Rita Farrel. She took me home to 97th Street and Lexington Avenue. I stayed overnight, got into work late the next day and fell asleep on lunch hour, and got fired.

Jim, my brother, was not happy. He took me to King Kullen supermarket on Kissena Boulevard in Flushing. The manager was Tommy Farrell, from Longford, Ireland. He said he did not like hiring guys from Ireland, "You guys are always drinking on Sunday night and you're always late on Monday and a lot of the time you don't come in at all, but I'll take a chance on you. Get working papers."

I said, "What does he mean?"

Jim said, "You're not eighteen and you can't work without working papers."

I said, "What about Stern's?"

Jim said, "I knew the manager and he did me a favor."

Okay. I got the papers and got the job in King Kullen supermarket.

What a shock! My first paycheck and the take home pay was forty-six dollars for a week.

Jim said, "You still owe me forty dollars for the rent."

"But Jim, I'll have nothing left."

He said, "This is a good lesson for you. All you need is bus fare and you can eat at home."

I had heard he had paid Aunt Kathryn twelve dollars a week, and she did his laundry and fed him the best. "But Jim," I said, "you only paid Aunt Kathryn twelve dollars."

He said that it wasn't a good house to live in because she never fed you well. When I told this to my sisters, they went wild because Aunt Kathryn was so good to all of them. The sad thing was that he had a wife who was so lazy that she would not clean and would only occasionally cook spaghetti. Her response was to say, "If I had my own house, I'd take care of it."

Bernadette and Vera were still living with Aunt Kathryn, but because Mother was coming over the next month, they got a house with seven rooms on two floors, electricity included, for eighty-five dollars a month. It had to be fixed up. Every night and on their days off, they were in it, painting, cleaning floors, etc.

I have no excuse for what I'm going to tell except that I was nervous that I'd do it wrong if I helped but I remember sitting on the floor watching them work so hard and, to this day, I feel guilty. That's the way we Irish were back then. We would think it but we wouldn't say it. Anyway, they were nicer to me than my loving only brother.

They said to me you've got to get out of that place. With a conniving brother, and his wife and kids, it is no place for a kid brother. Boy, did he stick his heels in. He said he signed the papers to get me into the country. He is responsible for me for five years. If I cost the state money, he would be responsible, and there wasn't a McGurrin ever had cost this country money. We have our pride (except him).

My sisters said, "Stoney is going to be living with his mother and us," But Jim gave it one last shot.

He said, "I could have him deported."

"Jim, what are you saying? And our mother and father here."

He hated losing forty dollars a week, but I was finally out of there.

I got a job at Hession and Connelly delicatessen on Madison Avenue at 35th Street. My pay was back up to seventy-five dollars a week. To pay our rent and run the house cost sixty dollars a week, twenty dollars each. I met a guy I went to school with in Ireland named Desmond Fallon. He also got a job in Hession and Connolly. We worked six days a week, off on Sundays.

Sunday was our only night out back home and we carried that tradition with us wherever we went. We got paid on Saturday. I gave my sisters my twenty dollars for the week. Bought enough subway tokens for me and another person. We knew that we would meet girls and spend the rest of the money. We would make it into work on Monday, often with no sleep.

Desmond lived in Brooklyn with an uncle. It was an hour and a half to work. One morning, he woke up late, jumped out of bed put on his overcoat and took off for work. When he walked in, he went straight into the back and took off his coat.

When he looked down, he saw that all he had on under his coat was his pajamas. He said that he had wondered why people were looking at him on the train.

We were burning the candles at both ends. I slept over with a girl, came in late and unshaven, and got fired again.

I got a new job on Avenue D and 8th Street at a place called Flag Foods. Ten hours a day, ten dollars a day, seven days a week. That will keep me from going out at night!

The manager, Mike Fox, was from County Leitrim. I was there only three weeks when the night manager was locked up for stealing. Mike came to me and asked me to be the new night manager.

I asked, "How much more money?"

Not knowing my parents were in the country, he said, "Oh, no extra money. But think of it when you write home and tell your parents you're managing a supermarket."

I said, "Mike, my mother would be much more pleased to get ten dollars from me and have me mopping the floor in Stern's."

I was told I had to work nights until they found somebody else. Him being from Leitrim didn't mean much. Two weeks later, Desmond my buddy got fired from Hession and Connelly's and he asked me if there's anything going. I told Mike I knew somebody and he said, "Bring him in." Desmond got hired to work nights with me. We closed the store every night at 1:00 a.m.

The neighborhood was mostly Puerto Rican and dangerous. One night, two girls hung around until we closed. They asked us to walk them to the Third Street projects. We got to the elevator and four guys appeared out of nowhere and yelled, "What are you guys doing with our women?" They pulled knives and we started running to Avenue D.

We saw the bus pulling into the bus stop to pick up one person. We screamed and he waited that half-minute and we made the bus. The bus driver closed the door, with the four guys banging on the side of the bus. The driver was white. He said, "What are you boys doing down here?" We told him that we worked down here but we had learned our lesson.

Two, three more weeks went by and Desmond said to me, "It's time we did something else." He said, "I'm going to check out automotive mechanics and where they teach it. Would you be interested?" I said, "Absolutely."

A few days went by. He told me his uncle told him about the Delehanty School in Long Island City. He said his uncle knew my father and mother and he would like to meet me. "Come out with me and stay over one night."

I went to Brooklyn the following Saturday night, we were in the living room talking with his uncle about becoming auto mechanics and he said, "It's a good profession, but I suggest you young men never buy a car. They're very dangerous and remember, trains and buses run all night long."

I asked him if he ever owned a car. He said yes, he had one car. He went on to tell us that he worked for the Fire Department. His job was steering the back end of the fire truck. When the fire truck made a left turn, the guy on the back had to turn his wheels right to get the eighty-foot fire truck around the turn. He had done that for four years and then he bought a car. On his first day out, he drove down the street and made a left turn. Still thinking that he was on the back end of a fire truck, he turned the steering wheel to the right and went into a woman's front yard. He said he called a tow truck and never drove a car again.

I said to Desmond later, "Your uncle's got his mind a little twisted, but when I make money, I'm still buying a car." And

I knew it wouldn't be long, back then you could buy a car for twenty-five to a hundred dollars. My first car, a 1949 Pontiac, cost twenty-five dollars.

Our plan then was to go to Delehanty School but we had to get off working nights. We explained our goal to Mike Fox and we got lucky when two guys on the day shift, Katz and Freddy, were caught stealing. Mike said it might take a week or two, let me talk to Mr. Lawn, the owner. It worked out that two weeks went by and Mike tells us that Mr. Lawn wants to keep you two boys. We explained that we would come in at 7:00 a.m. but we must be out of there by 5:00 p.m., Monday to Friday. Saturdays and Sundays we would work days or nights.

Our first night at school we had a German teacher. He said, "Gentlemen, when you leave here you will know everything about cars. The first thing you're going to learn here is brakes. You must know how to stop a car." He mostly talked about how if you're driving down the highway at sixty miles an hour and you put your foot on a rubber pedal, you expect two tons of steel to stop on a dime.

It took six weeks to get qualified on brakes. I didn't like it. I told Desmond, "That's it for me; I'm finished."

"Why?" he said.

I was only having a laugh so I said, "Back home I knew how to start them. Now I know how to stop them."

I quit and he quit.

So then we were back working for Flag Foods, any hours that they wanted us to work. Mr. Lawn had three Flag Foods: one on Avenue D; one on 56th Street and Eighth Avenue; and one on 65th Street and First Avenue. I was asked to go to Eighth Avenue for two weeks. The first Saturday, I'm working at 10:00 a.m. and a beautiful tall blonde in her twenties filled her shopping cart, brought it up front and walked into the back. I'm working the register.

A long time went by. I said to the guy on the floor, "Alex, I think the blonde left. We should put the meat, fish and groceries back on the shelf."

"Give it a little longer, she'll be back."

Some time goes by and here she comes, and Bill the manager too. Bill tells me this is an account. Ring nothing. Just bag everything and you and Alex make the delivery.

Later, I asked Alex what that was all about. He said some things are hard to believe. He said, "There's a popular show on TV called The Ed Sullivan Show and that blonde is a regular on it. She lives in a doorman building, and yet she comes in here, goes down into a dingy half-lit basement and screws the manager to make ends meet." I made sure to watch the Ed Sullivan Show Sunday night and there she was. I heard years later that Ed Sullivan would not pay unless you were a big star.

They moved me back to Avenue D. Desmond and I were working together again. Desmond was smart; I was always dumb but if somebody had a bad idea I knew enough to stay away and Desmond always had good ones. He told me he was looking into another trade, electric, at the same school. Okay, I said. First week they start us on bells. One door ringer; one bell inside. By six weeks, we were doing intercom systems. I didn't know why. I said that I think I'd like some trade that I can combine with electric. He said he was staying with this.

I said, okay, I'm quitting. He kept going to school but we still saw each other every day.

Hijack Dolan

One night Desmond and I went to Center City Ballroom on 55th Street. It was July and we went by subway. We took two girls home to Brooklyn and said good night, then got back on the train and took it to Rockaway Beach. We decided to sleep under the boardwalk for a few hours, and then get some sun.

We get off the train. As we are walking to the beach, we see a guy wearing only his undershorts. Desmond says, "Ha! That's Jack Dolan." Jack lived near Desmond back home in Ireland. I knew the family also, but I didn't know Jack.

When I was in the country a few months, I was in the car with my brother, who knew Jack well. They were about the same age. It was 2:00 a.m. and we were going over the Kosiuszko Bridge and a bulletin came over the radio with some breaking news.

A man had gotten on a plane at JFK Airport wearing only a dirty t-shirt and pants and carrying a bag. After the plane took off, when the man got refused a drink, he said he had a bomb in his bag and if he didn't get a drink he would blow the plane up. The stewardess ran to the captain. The plane made a U-turn and landed. The cops took him off the plane, checked his bag and there were a few pieces of dirty clothes. That was Jack Dolan. Years later, I would tell people that I knew the first plane hijacker in America.

I visited a cousin of mine in Brooklyn, Eamon Earley, who grew up with Jack and came to America with him. Eamon told me Jack was the hardest worker. But ninety-nine percent of the Irish only knew hard work at that time. He said Jack lived with an aunt here in Brooklyn. Her husband had died. They had no kids but he left her very well off, with a large brick house in Brooklyn and an eighty-acre farm in New Jersey. She loved Jack as a son because he was such a hard worker.

Eamon told me that in 1948, when very few people had money, Jack worked in the meat market, carrying sides of beef— half a cow—in cold boxes. He was also a musician and played in Irish bars and dance halls every Thursday, Friday, Saturday and Sunday nights and he never drank anything but tea or coffee.

He had bought a new car right out of the show room and had twelve thousand dollars in the bank.

His aunt died and left him everything: the brick house, the farm in New Jersey and seventy thousand dollars in the bank. Eamon told me that Jack brought a few guys, including him, to the lawyers' offices, I guess as witnesses. They all left the lawyers' office and a few of the guys said, "You've got to have a drink to celebrate."

So he did. He never knew it, but he was a stoner alcoholic. He never stopped drinking. He lost the job. He lost the car. He sold the farm. Two years later he sold the house. It took six years and everything was gone.

Eamon said "He would come to me when he would be filthy dirty and ask me to let him clean up. I used to put him in the tub and scrub him with a long handled brush. I always had a box of cigars around. I was the same size that he was, so when he came out of the tub and shaved, I'd give him a suit, a white shirt and a tie. What he would say used to bother me. He would light the cigar, stand in front of the mirror and say, 'Eamon the only reason you're giving me this suit and tie is because you were going to throw them out anyway.'"

Sometime later, one of his brothers, Frank, came from England to find Jack and give him a decent burial if needed. Frank found my brother Jim's phone number and then I met him.

Even though Frank was older than me, I kept in touch with him. He told me, "I found my brother Jack in a vacant building in Brooklyn. It took two of us to push the door in there were so many beer cans and bottles behind it.

"When we got in, we could see nobody. We made our way over the piles of cans and bottles and at the far end of the room there were three of them half dead, Jack and two blokes from Mayo. We pulled all three out on the street and called an ambulance for the Mayo men, and I took Jack to the Bronx where I had got an apartment."

I called Frank a few weeks later at the apartment. I asked him how Jack was doing and he told me he was going great. He had gone to the pawnshop and Jack's fiddle was still there. "Listen," he said, holding the phone away from his ear. I could hear Jack giving hell to that fiddle.

Frank told me he was taking Jack back to Leitrim. "My father is building a new house, closer to the road and Jack is a great tradesman so he'll be back in his element."

Years later, I heard Jack worked every day. He kept a fire on all day with coffee brewing. Locals thought it quite funny. Jack built the house, built a car garage, a horse stable and a hay shed. He kept busy for seven years.

Then, one day, he got all dressed up, took the bus to Sligo then the train to Dublin and met a guy, Shane Corrigan, who he had gone to school with. Shane was drinking heavy. Two years later both of them died in a doorway in Dublin's fair city, 'where the girls are so pretty.'

A guy tells me the up-and-coming trade to go into is refrigeration and air conditioning. We have to change schools since they are teaching refrigeration and air conditioning in a YMCA in Bedford-Stuyvesant, Brooklyn, a very bad neighborhood. "We could get killed there, baby," I kid with Desmond because of that incident with the two Puerto Rican girls.

We had a phone booth at the wall beside the register, the kind you could sit in and close the door. There was this girl about two years younger than me. Her name was Ola. She said she was Polish. Every evening she would sit in the phone booth and ask me to walk her home. She was a toughie. I guess she had me figured out and she could be bossy.

One Sunday evening, after I finished work, I'm walking out. She's waiting at the door and she says, "You're walking me home."

She lived on 12th Street, the opposite direction of the Puerto Rican girls. We get up to the Projects and she brings me over the grass, up to the wall, puts me with my back to the wall and starts kissing me. Then she bit my lip.

I say, "What are you doing?"

She spins me around and now her back is against the wall. She grabs my hand and hits her face with it and in a loud voice says, "Hit me! Hit me!"

I say, "Why? No. I can't do this."

She yelled again for me to hit her.

Luck was on my side that she had taken me to where she lived. A window opens on the second floor and a woman yells, "Ola, you come up here right now!"

Ola yells back, "I'll be up when I want to and you shut up!" I ask her if that was her mother. She says yes and I say that I need to go.

She says, "You're not going!"

"I'm going!" and I ran, man!

The next day I was telling Mike Fox. He said there's a name for that. It's called masochism; it's a sex urge. They reach a climax when they're slapped around. That's it for me. I'm going to stay away from the girls on the Lower East Side and go back to school.

Desmond was good with his working hours because he never stopped school. I had to explain to Mike that I needed the same hours. We would come in at 7:00 a.m. but we must be out by 4:45 to get to the school by 6:00 p.m. It was all set up. Get up 5:30 a.m. Get into work at 7:00 a.m. Get out of work at 4:45 p.m. Get to school at 6:00 p.m. Get out of school at 10:00 p.m. Study on the train. Get home at midnight. Sleep four to five hours and start all over. School was Monday through Thursday. Flag Foods was seven days, sometimes doubles on Saturday and Sunday. We did good and two years later we graduated.

In the two years of night school, we had three teachers. The first guy told us he was Jewish. The second guy told us he was Italian. They looked American to me. The third guy didn't have to tell anybody what he was. He was born and raised in Limerick, Ireland. His name was Lynch and I was very impressed.

Here is a man who, when there was no gas or electric in Ireland, came to America, went to school and now he's teaching Americans refrigeration and air conditioning. Maybe, just maybe, Jim was wrong about me losing the accent. If Lynch has one and look at what he can accomplish, maybe I should focus on talking clearly (which I do). If I lose it, fine; if I don't, well and good.

After getting our diplomas, we all have to go back to school. The following night we are all feeling good. Lynch waits until we are all sitting down. Then he stands and says, "You gentlemen must feel real smart with your diplomas, but I want you all to understand, now you know nothing."

A guy in the group, Ralph, he was always a talker, he shook his diploma in the air and said, "Are you dumb or what?"

Lynch said, "All you know is the theory. It will take another two years in the field doing the practical before you can call yourself a mechanical engineer."

Ralph said, "If I served my time for two years and didn't go to school, I'd know more than if I had gone to school."

Lynch said, "I don't know about more, but you would know as much."

There are a lot of jobs where you served your time and know the job. Today they want college degrees and no practical experience.

Before I tell you this: back in Ireland only a few people owned cars. A bunch of us would pay for the gas and we would go forty, fifty, sixty miles to a dance. When we came out here to America, we went everywhere by subway. We would meet girls at a dance and they might live in Brooklyn, the Bronx or Queens. We got to know the boroughs.

Desmond got a job with an air conditioning company on Church Avenue in Brooklyn. He said that in the summer, his company hired high school and college kids. Once, they were doing a job on Wall Street and they were driving over the Brooklyn Bridge into Manhattan and this young guy, eighteen years old, same age as us, he looks at the buildings and he says, "My God they're big."

Desmond says, "You never been in Manhattan before?"

"No," he says.

Desmond says, "Where do you live?"

"Bensonhurst."

"Isn't that in Brooklyn?"

"Yes," he says.

"But wouldn't you want to see Manhattan?"

"I'm from a close Italian family. We stay in our own neighborhood. No need to go to Canarsie, wherever Canarsie is."

We thought it so strange. We didn't want to live with our parents. We couldn't wait to get our own apartment and go everywhere.

Desmond bought a 1953 Chrysler. The first Saturday night, we have two girls to pick up in the Bronx. He asks me to drive his new car to his job and we'll leave from there. (It was hard to be on time for dates because bosses wouldn't let you off early and driving the car, we'd get lost.) It's raining and we're on Church Avenue. Desmond is driving his new car. He says, "I know where I am. We'll make a left here," but there's a car ahead of us.

While we are sitting there, waiting for the light to change he says, "This is good. No more subways on Saturday nights." And then it happened: we got hit from the back so hard that we were pushed into the car in front of us and his trunk flew open.

There goes our dates.

I didn't even get out of the car. Desmond gets out, talks to the guy in front, then talks to the guy in the back, gets back in the car and says to me, "You won't believe this. The guy in front, his trunk is all pushed in bad. The guy in the back, his radiator is busted. But with these big chrome bumpers, I have no damage at all."

He told the front guy to make the left and that he'll make the left behind him and he told the guy in the back that he was going to park across the street and that he should make the left. We wait for the light to go yellow and then we go straight, leaving the two guys to figure it out.

"Man," I said, "that's fast thinking."

As they say back home when they look down at their feet, "Down there for dancing."

Village People—Not Like Home

At work, Desmond met an American-born guy named Murphy and every weekend Murphy took him to all the places he knew. Desmond lost the Irish accent. On occasion all three of us went together to different places on the weekend. One time we went to the West Village. Murphy got talking to an older guy, well-dressed, well-spoken. He told a story about President Wilson in the 1920s.

When a president visits a city, there's a spokesman for the party and he told us that Wilson once came to Madison Square Garden, which at that time was at 24th Street on Madison

Avenue. The spokesman for the party was Chauncey Depew. He introduced Wilson by saying, "And now, I give you a man who is pregnant with the milk of human kindness."

Wilson thanked him for his kind introduction and said, "If it's a boy, I'll call it George Washington; if it's a girl, I'll call it Martha Washington; but if it's wind, like I think it is, I'll call it Chauncey Depew."

The older guy bought us beer for hours. I needed to use the bathroom and he said to me, "Don't use the bathrooms in here, they're very dirty. I'll buy three six-packs and all of you come up to my apartment. I live across the street."

Desmond and I are a little afraid to go, but Murphy is the New Yorker. He has no problem. He winks at us, slapped the man on the back and said, "Let's go," Murphy and him carrying the beer. We get up to his apartment and I'm busting to go to the bathroom but I'm too nervous to say anything. He says the place is a mess. Give him a minute. Murphy is drinking a beer with a smile on his face as if he knows what's happening.

The guy goes into the bathroom and comes out with a pile of old newspapers, which he lays out, on a section of the living room floor. He goes into the bathroom again and comes out completely in the nude, goes down on all fours and says, "Please, please boys! Piss on me!"

I think Desmond was like me. We were shocked. Murphy with a big smile says, "The man bought us the beer. So let's piss."

Murphy had no problem. I was so nervous that it took me a while to get started but then I couldn't stop.

The guy rolled around until we were finished.

Murphy shouts, "The show is over!" and grabs all the beer and we leave. Down on the street, Murphy says, "How do you guys like New York?"

Cars and Boys—1961 Dodge

We had a party at our apartment at 94-32 114th Street, off Atlantic Avenue. Aunt Kathryn, who lived five blocks away on 112th Street and Liberty Avenue, was at the party. She said that she was so used to a full house that it was strange now having it so quiet. The McGurrins and her two daughters, Geraldine and BeBe, her son Hughie, and her late husband Michael—all gone.

Desmond asked her if she would be interested in renting a room. She said, "I'd love to. I'll charge you fifteen dollars a week. Is that okay?"

"Yes, ma'am."

She said, "I have a seventeen-year-old godchild, Brian, there now. It will be nice to have extra company." Deal done.

I bought a 1959 Chevy Impala convertible that was bright red, with a white top and red upholstery. The guy I bought it from was a mechanic and he needed the money. He told me that he had had it souped up and that he had put a big engine in it. He had taken out the automatic transmission and put in a 4-speed transmission with the gear stick on the floor.

He said all it needed was a big rear end axle, what he called a "411" rear end, to match the power of the car. We asked Aunt Kathryn if we could use her garage because we could do this ourselves and she said yes. We went to the junkyard and found a big 411 and we put it in the car. The car was so fast it could do sixty miles per hour in first gear. Forever after that, if Desmond saw a girl with a big ass, he would say, "Now there goes a 411 rear end!!!"

A few weeks went by and Desmond got a call from his first cousin in White Plains, who was a car dealer, telling him that he had a 1961 Dodge, like new.

"Don't let it go," his cousin said. "Give me your address and I will have the paperwork ready and you can drive it home."

The following Saturday, we took a train at Grand Central Terminal to White Plains. The car was ready. We stayed for dinner with Desmond's aunt. We left her house late and decided to stop in the Bronx to meet Jimmy Cullen, also from home. Jimmy decided to come to Queens and visit my mother since he hadn't seen her in years.

We were on the Van Wyck Expressway, the three of us in front back then cars had a long seat in the front called a bench seat, and we get off at Atlantic Avenue and made a right turn. This car with three guys in it comes up on the right side of us. The guy in the back seat has his window down and so does the driver, and they're screaming at us. They go forward and wait for us to go forward, again and again for ten blocks. I'm in the middle.

I say to Jimmy, "Turn the window down." Jimmy turns it down. I yell out to the guys do you want us to pull over?

"Yes, you faggots."

We found out later some people thought that if three guys sat in the front of the car together, they must be gay. So we were going to get a bad beating just because they thought we were gay.

I yell, "If you want us over, ram us."

Desmond yells. "My car, my car! No! No!"

By now we have reached 114th Street and we make a left. The next turn is 111th Street and I see their turn signal going on. I say, "They're turning around, they're going to get us."

We park the car in front of my house and we all jump out of the car, but they're already there. Desmond makes it to the trunk and pulls out the jack. I ask myself why to this day. He throws it to me. I swing it at a guy and he runs back to his car. Desmond yells my name. I turn and I see lots of blood. Desmond has a guy in a headlock, but Desmond is the one who's covered in blood. He tells me to hit him, so I hit him on the head and Desmond lets him go.

The driver in the car starts spinning rubber. I yank his door open and hit him in the ribs with the jack. Someone called the cops and we could hear sirens, so we took off running. I ran across Atlantic Avenue into somebody's backyard. I was so exhausted that I lay there for twenty minutes. I came out to Atlantic Avenue and called my house from a public phone. Mother answered and said that there are a lot of sirens and police cars, and it sounded like somebody got killed outside. I said that I thought I did it. The phone went dead.

I was told later that my sisters called our brother-in-law, Larry Griffin, a detective in the 75th Precinct. He drove in from Mineola to 114th Street. We told him Desmond's car was outside. He said they had traced the license plate to Aunt Kathryn's address. Let's go, he said to me.

We went there and there were two detectives there and they were very pissed off. They wouldn't even talk to Griffin, but I noticed that Griffin kept talking. We knocked on the door and Kathryn's godchild, Brian, answered. He let us in, but the pissed off detective said to Brian, "Desmond Fallon was here and you wouldn't let me in."

Brian had a lot of nerve. He had told them that they needed a search warrant to come in. He said that Desmond wasn't there but they still needed a search warrant. Griffin saved us from getting arrested.

The next day we found out that nobody had died but one guy had a fractured rib. Desmond went to Jamaica Hospital and they gave him seven stitches.

Mother said to me, "I don't wish bad to any family, but I will gladly go to your funeral before I'd have you harm someone else, right or wrong. Let the other family worry about what their son did, but don't you harm anybody."

That straightened me out. Now I knew where I stood.

A month later, Desmond and I got letters. The guy was suing us. The driver of the car was named Simon and he was twenty-four and married. We couldn't believe it, married men out at night, looking for and making trouble. They should be under their father's care themselves.

We showed the letters to Larry. He read them and said, "There's something they missed. Let it go a few weeks and I'll stop by their house."

A few weeks later, Larry stopped by. He said he didn't think I'd be hearing from Simon or his pals. He said he went to Simon's house and he asked him in. Larry told him it was a routine call, that he needed to hear the circumstances of how it started.

Simon said they were on their way home when a car started to bump them. They tried to get away by going down a street. Larry says, "You say they followed you but how did you all finish up outside of 94-32 114th Street, Stoney McGurrin's home? Simon, your story is false. No case."

Luck was on our side.

On another night, Fallon and I drove to the Bronx to the Red Mill Dance Hall on 168th Street at Jerome Avenue. We met no girls but we did meet two brothers, Mike and Johnny Carty, and their roommate, Pete McGrath from Scotland. McGrath was a boxer and he must have been pretty good. He was doing ten rounds in Madison Square Garden. He fought under the name Scot McGrath. He was a little guy who fought bantamweight and drove a white Cadillac. He thought that he was hot stuff.

Mike Carty was the guy who should feel like hot stuff. He was six foot one and slim as a branding iron. All the guys would ask a girl to dance and one after the other, they would get turned down. Mike Carty would fix his tie and walk over and the girl or girls would jump up every time.

One Thursday night Mike Carty, McGrath and I went to the Lorelei Dance Hall on 86th Street, in an area known as German town. Thursday night was the night. All the girls from Germany, England, Ireland, Scotland, etc., were off work. I had heard guys joking about it. They called it "Kitchen Mechanics Night Out."

The three of us were at the bar. The band started playing. McGrath saw this tall blonde and he asked her to dance. She nodded yes. The music was so loud you couldn't talk. When the dance was over, McGrath pointed to the bar, "Will you have a drink?"

She nodded. He was so happy to be with this tall blonde. He ordered a drink and introduced her to Mike and me, asking her name with a Scottish accent.

She asked him, "Are you from Scotland?"

"Yes," he said.

"Good-bye," she said.

He said, "What's wrong?"

She said, "I didn't come three thousand miles to meet you. I could have met the likes of you back home."

We should have had Desmond with us. He didn't want to meet Irish girls and she didn't want to meet Scottish guys.

We all got called up for the Army within a year of one another and we all failed except Desmond. I was so surprised. I knew why I failed, because of my arm. Desmond was called for the Army but he had other options. When you got called for the armed forces, you could choose to join whichever service you liked. Desmond said the Army was a bunch of pussies and that he was joining the Marines. He did the eleven weeks in Parris Island, South Carolina. He told us the top guys from the sergeant on up were all southerners. There was one black guy in his outfit.

The first day the sergeant told the black man to stand up front where he could keep an eye on him. Every day, the black man was leading the pack, for nine weeks. I forgot to mention that for eleven weeks they had no radio, no TV, no contact with the outside world.

One afternoon the sergeant called a halt. He marched all the way up front, turned, and faced the black guy, clicked his heels, pointed his finger into the black man's face and yelled, "You, back of the line. Your friend just got shot."

For the next two weeks the black guy was at the back. When the eleven weeks were over, they got off base to find out that the sergeant had a radio, so he knew that President Kennedy had been shot.

Desmond never wore the uniform when he was out on leave and he didn't like anyone who did. One night we were all at the bar in the Red Mill Ballroom and Joe Ford walked in, in uniform. He was in the Army. Joe was a nice guy. He had no airs and graces to him, but Desmond had to start. He said, "Look at the pussy in an Army uniform."

Then he saw the medal on Joe's lapel. He reached over and flipped it and asked Joe what it was for. Joe, in a nice tone of voice, said that it was for sharpshooting. Desmond asked what is the distance for sharp shooting in the Army?

Joe said, "A hundred and fifty yards."

"We in the Marines call that the John Wayne course," says Fallon.

Mick Carty said that Desmond was so insulting that he was funny.

Desmond didn't like the Marines that much so he went into the Reserves. He had to go away two or three weeks at a time, twice a year. He and I got a two-bedroom apartment on Union Street in Flushing. He got a refrigeration air condition-ing job on Bleecker Street in the West Village. Union Street was not a good neighborhood. There were two bars, Shannon's Bar, mostly black, and the Chestnut, which was mostly white. There were a lot of bad white kids hanging around and watching everything.

We lived over a not too fancy supermarket. There were four apartments. You went up one side of the supermarket for two apartments, front and back, and you went up the other side for the other two apartments, front and back.

We got to know a guy named Neil Mahon who had just joined the NYPD. He lived in the back apartment on the left side. We lived in the front apartment on the right side. They were all two bedrooms with kitchens that had a fridge just inside the front door.

A woman with two kids lived in the back apartment on our side. She let us know when she was leaving and she would leave it open so we could use it as a shortcut to go and see each other. We had very little but we had a TV. Neil had a hi-fi but no TV. We asked Neil if we could run speaker wire from his hi-fi to a speaker in our apartment and we would hide the speaker in the ceiling. When we would put on his long-playing records, our visitors wouldn't know where the music was coming from.

The Police Department rules were that, for the first six months after you join, you have to stay home, but when they called you, you had better answer. Neil, having no TV, would come through the empty apartment to see us and ask to watch TV. We also ran a fifty foot wire from his phone jack to our apartment so that he could answer his phone when he was watching TV.

One Saturday night we asked him if he would take a chance on leaving and come out with us. He said it was not worth it and could he stay there and watch TV. We said sure and left. We didn't get back until 4:00 a.m. In the hallway, there were two doors with glass. First door, glass and lock broken, second door, glass and lock broken.

I said, "Desmond, we are screwed."

Plus our TV is probably gone. We get to the top of the stairs and see our apartment door is open and the lock is broken. The lights are on. Neil is asleep on the couch with his gun in his hand.

Desmond was great for telling somebody else what to do. He said to me, "You wake him."

I said, "What happens if he wakes up shooting?"

Anyway, I thought it was safe. So I got the broom and stood off to the side, and started shouting his name and pushing him with the broom until he woke up.

He tells us, "You guys were gone for no more than ten minutes. I heard the door bang downstairs. I think it's you guys coming back. You forgot something. Then I heard the second door. Then I get up with the gun. They then started on the apartment door. Now I know it's not you, so I put my elbow on top of the fridge with the gun pointed straight at the door two feet away. The door gives and there they are. Their faces went a lot whiter than they were. I grabbed the one closest to the top of the stairs, so the other guy can't get down. I was really going to put a scare into them. I could tell on their faces that they couldn't figure out how I was in there. I have the one guy by the throat and I pushed him up against the wall. The other guy is pleading and the gun went off. I looked down and the bullet went through the toe of his shoe. I got scared but I didn't show it. I lifted him with a push, I didn't mean to but he went tumbling down the stairs. I said to the other guy, 'You too,' and didn't the other guy fall down the stairs also."

He told us for the first six months and always for that matter, you've got to account for your bullets. You can always say that you lost one, but he's a little worried that the bullet hit a water line. He asks me to go down to Esser, the owner of the supermarket, in the morning and see if there's a water leak.

Nine thirty the next morning, I walk in, get milk, bacon and eggs. I go up and down every aisle. No water. But I can't go in the back. I come up to the register and Esser starts ringing. I tell him that we came home this morning and the bathtub was full but I don't think any water came down to you.

Esser stops ringing up the money, which is hard for a Jewish man. "Oh my god! Oh my god! Where? Where? Come with me." He took me everywhere.

I said, "I told you, Esser, that we caught it in time."

I come up stairs and tell Neil, "Okay, no leak. And we're okay."

Drop Dead

We started going to the Chestnut Bar. The bartender, Tommy, was in his sixties. He was six foot three, with a big head of gray hair and he was like a big teddy bear. He never said an angry word. We had heard that some woman owned the bar, and occasionally a woman came in and was very abusive to him. Later we found out that we hadn't yet met the owner and that the abusive lady was Tommy's wife. They lived around the corner.

On Sundays, bars did not open until 1:00 p.m., but Tommy would come to work at 9:00 a.m. to get away from his wife. We were there one Sunday at 10:00 a.m., plus another fifteen people.

She stormed in and ranted and raved for fifteen to twenty minutes. Even the customers were getting tired. When she left she had to pass a window. As the door closed, Tommy said, not too loud, "Drop dead."

As she passed the window her head went down. We all knew something happened. We went out and there was no movement: she was dead as a doornail.

There you go Tommy, you got your wish.

We went to the wake. We felt very funny saying sorry for your trouble.

Gay in the Sixties. What?

Desmond started working for an air conditioning company on Bleecker Street in the West Village. He was there only a short time when he was given a job on the air conditioner system in a doctor's office.

Everything the doctor wants, he does. The doctor is friendly, and asks Desmond why he's not in the Armed Forces. Desmond tells him that he was in the Marines and is now in the Reserves.

The doctor says, "Bet you would like to get out of the Reserves."

"You bet," says Desmond.

"Well," the doctor says, "I'm a doctor for the Marines and I can help you with that. Get me all your paperwork for your time in the Marines, and I'll arrange it from there."

The job was finished and a month went by when Desmond got a call from the doctor's office. He met the doctor, "Sign here and you are out."

How lucky can a guy be? That was the best air conditioner job ever.

Back in the sixties, a lot of people knew very little about gays and nothing about transvestites. Desmond was getting an education driving around the Village, fixing air conditioners, beer boxes and ice machines in all those gay and transvestite clubs. Some weekends, he was on emergency call duty. You had to leave a number where you could be reached. You could get a call at one or two in the morning and off you went.

He talked about one club on Jones Street off Seventh Avenue. It was one of the weirdest. On his first Saturday night, he got a call at 3:00 a.m. He had never seen so many tall girls, and when he walked in, they crowded around him, saying, "You look so hot baby, make our beer cold." He had to go behind the bar to fix the beer system. That's when the bartender who looked normal but was probably gay told him that the girls here are all men. It was an eye-opener.

Desmond's mother in Ireland wasn't feeling well. He decided to go visit and stay a few days in Leitrim and a few days in Dublin where his brother, Shammie, was in the insurance business. When he came back, he told me that Shammie's girlfriend was a schoolteacher and her friend, Lisa, was an airline stewardess. Lisa flew the Dublin-to-Paris route, but she was going to be transferred to Dublin-to-New York.

He told me he gave her his phone number. A month later she called and told him what hotel she was staying at. It was Saturday night. He said to me that he didn't know where to take her. I told him that I had no date so we'll both take her. We'll give her an experience on her first weekend in New York. We'll go to a few half-normal places first and then to Jones Street.

We got to Jones Street about 1:00 a.m. and the joint was jumpin'. Desmond didn't dance, so I asked her out on the floor. She was staring at all those beautiful women and she said to me that she had never seen so many beautiful girls. "Yes," I said, "they are beauties."

When the music stopped, we went back to the bar and she asked to go to the bathroom. I said to the bartender, "Where is the bathroom?"

He pointed to the dance floor and around to the right. Off she went. After about five minutes, she came running back.

She said, "There's only one toilet bowl and I'm waiting. Then a voice says, 'I'll be right out honey.' and the door opens. She had her dress over her shoulders. She had a big belt around her stomach and she was tying up the biggest wing-wang between her legs."

I said, kidding, "You can go back now. She's gone."

She said, "I'm too scared to pee."

Desmond spoke to the bartender and he took her inside the bar and downstairs to the house toilet.

I never met her again but I'd have loved to, to hear her tell the story of a twenty-year-old girl's first night in New York City.

Desmond and I loved to watch the Saturday night fights on TV. He had a cousin bartending on Second Avenue and 90th Street. One night we drove in Desmond's car and found a parking spot on 91st Street at First Avenue. We went to see the fight. As we're going back to the car, we make the turn off Second Avenue on 91st Street and see a large crowd of black people going towards First Avenue. We have suits on. A little kid comes running up the block. He says, "Are you guys cops?"

I said, "What's wrong?"

He says that crowd of blacks searched him and took his only fifty cents.

I gave him a dollar and said, "You're okay now, kid. We'll take care of it."

The kid ran off. We kept going towards the car. The crowd turned and started towards us.

Desmond said, "Let's go back." I said, "Never trouble trouble until trouble troubles you. Why should they bother us?"

Desmond said, "You and your damn rhymes. They bothered the kid. I'm going back." When we got back to Second Avenue, we looked back. The crowd had turned and was going back the way they had come. Our car was at the end of the block and we decided to go back down.

We got halfway. We saw a white couple on some steps, in a doorway. The crowd had turned again. Now I got scared. I said we should go back, but Desmond wanted to run to where the white couple was, but when we get there, there's no couple. I think they lived there and they had run to their apartment.

Now we're in the hallway. It was a long hallway with the stairs in the back. We ran back to the stairs and turned when we got there. Desmond put his hand in his back pocket like he had a gun, but the first guy said, "If you had a gun, you'd have used it."

They kept coming at us on the stairs. Only five of the crowd had come in. Desmond and I grab hands; we're kicking at them but they push us up half a flight. There's a window where we are and we're still kicking, but they push us to the landing and now they're at the window. One of them has gloves on and he smashes the window and pulls out some broken glass and sends it flying into Desmond.

We are still holding hands and kicking. I look over and see six empty Coca-Cola bottles. I break loose from Desmond and run for the bottles. He doesn't know what's on my mind and he's screaming, "Don't leave me!"

I grab two bottles and throw them to him. I couldn't believe that he caught them. I grabbed two more. We broke them on the floor and went after them. The crowd took off. We went up to the roof and went over three buildings and then came down to the street.

When we got down, the cops were there. There was an Irish woman on the steps and a black cop. She said to us, "What are you doing around here? It's a very bad neighborhood. Are you okay?"

Desmond Fallon on the left and Stoney on the right

Stoney and Mike Carty

Drivers Licence

We were lucky it was winter. Desmond takes off his coat and his jacket, pulls up his shirt and the glass had gone through them all into his stomach. The black cop, quite nice man, looks at the cut says you need to go to the hospital.

But leave it to Desmond for an insult. He points to the cut, looks at the cop and says, "Niggers did this."

We decided that I would drive to Bellevue Hospital on 26th Street and First Avenue. We get there and the doctors say they must operate right away. There's glass in the blood and it will move through to the heart if it isn't stopped. I said I'm going to the dance. I don't know what I did but when I came back at 7:00 a.m. Sunday morning, Desmond was sharing a room with an old man who had no chin, and spit and blood coming from his mouth.

A young Irish nurse comes in and Desmond asks her to pull the curtain. She says no. He says, "I'm not going to be here and look at that. I'm sick enough."

She says that if you weren't out there getting in trouble, you wouldn't have to be in here.

He grabs the cord you pull when you need assistance, yanks and yanks on it. Two nurses come in and he says, "I want the doctor." He had such a forceful way that you had to admire him.

He gets the doctor. He explains his case, that the nurse was more concerned with getting her way than with the patient. "I want those curtains pulled and I don't want to see her again while I'm here."

The doctor says, "Yes Mr. Fallon."

Fallon used to say some Irish nurses could be the worst when they came to work with a hangover.

If you were to listen to Desmond, he didn't like Irish girls or Ireland, but it's amazing what can happen. He met an Irish girl who was an only child. Her father owned a dairy farm and wanted a man to marry the daughter and manage the farm.

Desmond and she got married and went back to her village in Kerry, called Knocknagoshel. They ran the farm, had a bunch of kids, and never left. I visited him there in 2016. It was fifty years since we met. He didn't recognize me but he hadn't changed. I'd pick him out of a crowd in Times Square; it must be the country air.

Keeping Cool In The Big City

After refrigeration and air conditioning school, my first job was with Figaria Air Conditioning Company in Manhattan. All they did were window units. They hired extra people for the summer and fired them all in the winter.

I always considered myself not too bright so I never liked being in charge, but I was a little nervous of the guy that I was working with. Our bosses didn't seem to care. One day, on Park Avenue and 50th Street, eighteen stories up, we are putting an air conditioning unit in a window. After we lifted it into the window, he told me to move aside, so I did.

He went to straighten the unit and off it went. We watched as it hit the sidewalk. It missed everybody, one guy by five feet. I couldn't believe it! A few people looked up and then kept going. A few weeks later, he dropped a screwdriver on Madison Avenue, and lucked out again.

The company put a phony ad in the paper to get customers through the door. I was off that detail within a month. It was a twelve-dollar special, and ninety percent of the time the people didn't need anything done.

They had me working very late one Saturday. At 9 p.m., I was told to go to an apartment on 88th Street and West End

Avenue. A Jewish family was having a party for friends and I was going to work on the air conditioner in the bedroom. The brother and sister, both in their twenties, came in and closed the door and started arguing, ignoring me as if I wasn't there.

The sister said the brother invited one guest more than she did and she had bought extra food so he owed fifty cents for one thing, fifty cents for another and seventy-five cents for another. Up to that point in my life I could never imagine family members being like that, but a Jewish friend told me later, "This is good teaching for the business world."

I worked for three more air conditioning companies but they all wanted experienced people. Then I went for an interview at H.O. Refrigeration. H.O. stands for Harry Odelon. I told him, I just came out of school and I have no experience. Harry said, "Well, I like young guys that I can train my way."

I worked for Harry for two years. He worked only on big commercial stuff and he was also a licensed electrician. I was always with Harry, piping-in new jobs and troubleshooting old ones. One day, Harry said, "My top mechanic can't find the trouble on a fifty-ton air conditioner. Let's see what you and I can do."

There was this very large compressor in a basement. The basement was wet except for one spot. Harry was working on the compressor for an hour when he came up with this idea. The compressor had a high side and a low side. The high side was discharge and the low side was suction. Harry turned the electric switch off, took the plug out of the suction side and got a bucket.

He told me to hold the bucket under the hole in the suction side in case there was a drip. Then he went over and threw the switch. The hot oil hit me with such force that it lifted me and threw me six feet across the basement. When I got the oil out of my eyes, there was Harry on the dry part of the basement, laying down with his feet in the air laughing.

Two weeks later all my hair started falling out.

A few guys told me I should sue. I talked to Mother and she said, "Oh, my God! Why would you even think of such a thing? Harry is so good to you, teaching you a trade and giving you work summer and winter. Don't ever talk like that again." My hair did grow back but not like it was before. Mother said that you can live without hair, and I did.

Harry had a deal with the City Housing Department. The Inspector would meet Harry and give him addresses for apartments they thought might have fire hazards. I never did find out how the City knew. Harry and I would knock on the door and tell the people we were there to disconnect their electricity. They would be upset but Harry would disconnect. One morning as usual we met the inspector. He gave us three addresses.

It was 10:00 a.m. and Harry knocked on a door, and the door was open. Harry talked loud. He shouted, "We're from the City. We have to shut off your electricity."

It was a railroad flat. A voice shouted, "In here in the back."

The first thing we saw was an electrical cord going from the front room into the next room. Two more cords plugged into that one, and on it went into the back room, and there was this tall black man sitting on a stool, with a box of chicken on the floor, watching TV. No furniture that I could see.

Harry says it again. "We're here from the City to disconnect your electricity."

The man looks straight at Harry and says, "Every man's home is his castle. Now, this may look like a shithole to you, but it's my castle and you and nobody else is going to turn off my TV show."

He leans down and picks up a big kitchen knife and goes to stand up. That's when I took off, but Harry had taken off also. We got so scared that we didn't see each other and it looked like a Laurel and Hardy scene when we both got stuck in the door. That afternoon, we meet the inspector. Harry hands him the card back and says, "Here's one for you to disconnect."

I said to Harry, "You've got to admire that man. The poor man has nothing but his TV and we were going to take that away. He scared us enough. Now he has his TV. Good for him."

Harry came to like me so much that he brought me to his home in Flatlands, Brooklyn, several times. I didn't know it at the time, but he wanted me to meet his daughter who was beautiful and smart. She was one year older than me, but I couldn't see me with her and I'm sure that she felt the same way.

As work went on with Harry, I also learned electrical and plumbing. One day he gave me an address in Astoria, Queens. He said he'd meet me there. I got lost and could not find it. When I got there, he went crazy and fired me.

I said to him, "All my tools are in the truck."

He said, "You leave everything here."

I said, "No. You can pick your truck up in front of my house," and I jumped into the truck and took off, with him following me, but I got lost.

He got lucky when a police car came towards me. He got the police to stop me and had me put all my tools out on the sidewalk. He locked up his truck and left me there. I hailed a cab, put all my tools in the trunk and went home. I never saw Harry again.

A Working Man

I went to all the Irish bars and got a lot of work repairing air conditioners, beer boxes and ice machines and I signed up about twelve yearly contracts. But come winter it wasn't enough.

I met a guy, Tom Kelly, who worked for his brother, who owned a fleet of yellow cabs. He told me that I should get a cab license and drive a cab whenever I want and also stay with the air conditioning. I went for the test, which I thought was of no use. I remember two of the questions, "How do you go from the Port of Authority to Small Paradise?" and "What street goes river to river but doesn't go through?"

I drove from 4:00 p.m. until 6:00 a.m. My first day, I picked up a skinny little man at 87th Street and Third Avenue. He got into the cab and said, "Aqueduct Racetrack."

I instantly said, "Do you know the way?"

He yelled, "Stop the cab! Stop the cab! My day is fucked! My luck, my luck is gone! A cab driver who doesn't know where he's going!"

He jumped out and ran up Third Avenue. I made the same mistake a few more times and then I came up with a line that worked.

I came to realize that ninety percent of passengers knew where they were going. All I needed was to rephrase my words when they would tell me where.

I would say, "Is it okay for you to call the turns? And I'll make them."

"Absolutely, driver."

A lot of the time, they would say that they liked the driver to go their way anyway.

Tom Kelly and I became good friends. He told me he used to drive a tractor trailer. He said his wife made him give it up, but he still missed it.

I told him, "I don't know what it is, but come every spring, I get this urge to see America and I don't think I'll have peace of mind if I don't do it and get it over with."

"Well," said Tom, "you get yourself into furniture moving and you will find yourself in all of the states."

I stayed in refrigeration. One night, I was at a dance at the Jaeger House. I asked this girl to dance. We got on the floor and the conversation was good. I asked her to have a drink. She asked to look at my hand.

She said, "Why are your nails so dirty?"

I said, "I'm a refrigeration mechanic and it's hard to get all the dirt out from under the nails."

She said, "What makes you think that I would take you home and let you use them on my pussy? No thank you!" and she walked away.

The following Monday I went to see Tom Kelly.

"Tom, how do I get into the trucking business?"

He said, "You'll never run out of work. So I recommend you buy."

Trucking

He seemed to know everything. He made a phone call and the next day he and I were in Commack, Long Island. I put three thousand dollars down on a Ford cab with a Caterpillar engine. I drove it off the lot into his backyard, but I had moved too fast. I discovered that in New York State you need a Number One License to drive a tractor trailer and I didn't have one.

Tom said, "You know Black Willie, the mechanic in the cab garage? Talk to him."

I explained my predicament to Willie and he told me that he knew a guy in Jersey and that one license covers all vehicles there, but you need a Jersey address. I said I knew a family, the Gallaghers, and that I would call them. I knew them well in the past. They were thrilled to hear from me. They all said, "Of course, use our address."

I told Willie I got a Jersey address and he told me, when I came in with the cab the next morning, to wait around for him to get off at 7:00 a.m. and that he and I would drive to Newark together.

On the way out, Willie told me, "It's been so long, I hope I know what he looks like."

I was a little worried but I said nothing. We drive into the parking lot of the motor vehicle department and park. Cars are coming and going. Finally, a white car comes in and a man gets out. Willie says, "I think that's him," and gets out of our car.

He walks over and they talk for a while, then they shake hands. Willie waves to me to come over and I go over and say hello. The instructor hands me a piece of paper with twenty questions and answers and tells me that he has to take a girl for a test.

"I'll be a half hour. You memorize all of these."

I sit in the car and say them over and over until he got back.

He says to me, "You got them all?"

I say, "I hope."

He says, "Don't worry. You've got thirty-five dollars?" I hand him thirty-five dollars.

By now, there's a line outdoors going inside. He stands with me all the way to the door and he gets the attention of a guy, tapping me on the top of the head.

"Now," he says, "the guy inside the door will give you a form with all the questions. You answer the ones you're sure of and sign the paper. Just make sure you go to that guy."

I fill out the paper and go to the guy. He was an Irishman. He takes the paper and tells me to go for the eye test and then leave.

Four days later, Mary Gallagher called me, "Stoney, there's a letter here for you from Motor Vehicles." I registered the truck at their address also.

Kelly brought me to All State Van Lines in Corona, Queens. I was hired immediately. It took us two weeks of driving to the Bronx, Brooklyn and Manhattan to load five families for Los Angeles.

The owner of All State Van Line, Moe Goldstein, told me, "You're young and have no experience. You must hire an experienced man to go with you and I've got the man for you. He's one of the black men who have been working with you all week, Jimmy Reese. You, Jimmy and I go into the office. Jimmy gets to know what he gets paid. You get to know what you get. You pay for all the diesel, the tires, road tax, insurance. I have my own insurance company and I'll give you a deal." He says, "We don't have the rights to go all the way to California. You've got to go to Atlanta, Georgia and pick up papers at Rocky Ford Van Lines and those papers will allow you to travel to California legally."

Jimmy and I headed out. Our first stop was a truck stop in Maryland. When we got out of the truck, Jimmy says, "You diesel up and have coffee. I'm going to call my cousins and tell them I'm coming." I did all that and waited in the truck. Twenty minutes later, here comes Jimmy. The next morning, we were in South Carolina and Jimmy does the same thing. He says, "Diesel up and eat. I've got to tell my cousins where I am."

The next stop is a rundown truck stop outside of Atlanta. He does the same thing. He has to call his cousins. I say okay and I walk to the back of the trailer and I watch him go around a corner at the back of the building. Then I take off running but he's not there, just a wall. Why would he go over the wall? I stand there and think for a while and then give up.

I'm walking back to the truck and there's a screen door into the kitchen. Right inside the door is Jimmy, sitting at a small table. I could not believe I was so dumb. It dawns on me; he can't eat up front.

I open the screen door and go in and sit down. I say to him, "Up in New York you take no crap from nobody. I just realized you can't eat up front."

"That's right and when you're in Rome, do what the Romans do. And you can't be in here either. You get out before we get our tires slashed on the truck."

We left there. It was Friday. We felt that we had plenty of time. We started to panic at 3:30 p.m. We did not want to be stuck in Atlanta until Monday. That's what's called a layover. Twenty minutes later, we find the place. They give us a very hard time, telling us that we should have been there earlier. It's too much paperwork. I say the New York office told us the papers would be all ready. They give us all the papers and two-foot by two-foot cardboard signs that say Rocky Ford. They become very nice to me and they explain that the signs must be taped to each door before we get to Texas. We were so excited to be getting out of Atlanta, I put the signs behind my seat.

Three days later, I pulled on to the scales in New Mexico at 3:45 p.m. I handed the guy the papers and he studied them.

He said, "You're not Rocky Ford."

I said, "Oh man! I've got the signs behind my seat."

"No good," he says. "Pull your rig over there, park it, lock it and come with me."

When I get scared, I start talking. We go inside and there's four other border guards writing up other truckers. I'm still try-ing to talk myself out of the charges.

One of the Mexican guards, who was writing up another trucker hears my voice and stops writing. He looks straight at me and asks me where I'm from.

"Ireland," I say.

He says to the guy who brought me into the back, "Do you mind switching with me?"

His friend says, "No problem."

This little Mexican says to me, "Where in Ireland?"

I say, "Leitrim," And he says, "My mother is from Killybegs in Donegal, Ireland. Do you know it?"

"Yes," I say. "As a kid, we used to go on bus tours to Killybegs."

He says that I had forgotten to display my signs. "Let me get the proper tape. We'll make you legal and send you on your way. My mother will be happy that I met an Irishman who was in her town. You were very lucky," he says, "another ten to fifteen minutes and I would have been off duty and your fine would've been five hundred dollars."

We got to Los Angeles. It took five days to unload, a day for each family. Then you call New York. They tell you where to pick up and where it's going. You find yourself going from state to state. The whole idea is not to travel empty. It's September, and we're in Fargo, North Dakota. The warehouse guy said, we have eight thousands pounds going to Baton Rouge, Louisiana. Jimmy said, "We'll take that." We picked up another five thousand pounds in St. Louis for Fort Bragg, North Carolina. Jimmy said, "Now we're on our way to New York."

We left Baton Rouge early Friday morning. Jimmy said we shouldn't have any problem getting to Fort Bragg by 4:00 p.m. We hit traffic and Jimmy was getting very uneasy. He said, "We've got to get there. We can't have a layover until Monday." We were so close; they were just closing the gates. Now we're stuck until Monday.

We stayed in the 401 truck stop and that's when I found out why Jimmy didn't want to be stuck in Bragg, North Carolina. There were signs up in the truck stop. Restaurants, "Whites Only," TV room, "Whites Only," beds, "Whites Only." And while I ate in the restaurant, watched TV and slept in a bed, Jimmy ate in the kitchen, slept in the truck with no air conditioning and listened to the radio. Jimmy was five generations American and I was a foreigner.

There's something wrong with this freedom for all in America.

In the moving business, they have everything in cardboard, even wardrobes. When we packed the trailer, Jimmy put in a wardrobe for the both of us. He would hang his suits, shirts, and ties, and put his shoes in the bottom.

"Come on, man!" he said to me. "You've got have a suit and a blazer and some nice pants. When we're stuck in those towns, from Friday evening to Monday morning, we have to make the best of it, baby!"

Stoney and Jimmy Reese

One time we were on our way back from California to Fort Worth, Texas. We stopped off in El Paso. We met an old-time trucker who told us, "If you're going over the border to Juarez, Mexico, don't drive. The cops over there will lock you up on a bogus charge and when you come out, you'll have no truck."

So we parked our truck and walked over. We bought some things. Jimmy bought two small half ounce bottles of something he called "sex juice."

The following Sunday, we were in Fort Worth. Jimmy found out about a roadside gathering and we went. There were a lot of people, food, music, tables. It reminded me of when I was a kid. We used to have crossroad dancing music on a flatbed truck and you danced on the road. The big problem was if you danced a lot, you had no soles on your shoes.

But the people in Fort Worth were smarter; they weren't dancing. Everybody was very friendly. Jimmy saw this beautiful tall girl and moved in. Everything was going great. He was talking to her for an hour. She had her hands around him and she was kissing him. This big, good-looking guy showed up and she introduced him to Jimmy. Then he wanted to talk to her.

She turned to Jimmy and said, "I'll be back." Jimmy comes talking to me. It's me she wants. She's coming back. I'll give her a drop of the "sex juice."

She did come back and Jimmy put a drop in her drink. It took about five minutes. She jumped up ran to the other guy, jumped up on him, with her legs around his waist, telling him, "Let's get out of here." He had a big smile on his face, carrying her away.

I said to Jimmy, "There goes a guy who wants to thank you but he doesn't know who you are."

I was accepted better in most cases by blacks than Jimmy was by whites or I thought I was. We were in Selma, Alabama, for a weekend. George Wallace, the Governor, was getting so much attention with his speeches, "Segregation yesterday, segregation today, segregation tomorrow, segregation forever." The world media was giving him daily attention.

Jimmy was smart. He said people were not traveling. The top shelf motels were not much more expensive than the cheap motels and we had a better chance in the class places than in a cheap white trash motel. Let's give it a shot.

We left the trailer at the moving company dock and drove the tractor right up to the front door. Both of us got out. There was a young black doorman. Jimmy went first. He wouldn't open the door for Jimmy. Jimmy opened it and walked in. I was next and he opened it for me.

Up at the desk, Jimmy said, "We need a room with two beds for three nights." I think she was more shocked than anything else. Jimmy asked if breakfast came with that and she said yes. Back then everything was paid in cash. Jimmy said, "We will pay by the day."

He told me later, "Never set yourself up. If we paid for three days, tomorrow she would tell us we owed. You've got to know how to handle Whitey." Then he went on about the whites. "They're so bad. They go to war with each other," and on and on and on.

"But, Jimmy," I said, "Sure, I'm white."

"No, man," he said, "you ain't white, you're Irish!"

The next day we went for breakfast and the black doorman gave Jimmy a dirty look. Jimmy took no notice and said to me, "He's an Uncle Tom," but I didn't know what that meant. "He doesn't want any change."

We got back to the room. Jimmy was laying on the bed and I was sitting in the chair when a young girl knocked on the open door and asked if we wanted our room cleaned. "Sure," said Jimmy, "come in."

He talked to her about this-n-that and everything else. He had her laughing. He said, "Do you ever make a little extra money with the customers?"

"If the timing is right."

Jimmy Reese and a Lady Friend

Slave Quarters

Jimmy Reese on the left with Stoney at the State line

Jack Becket   Stoney and Lt. Flaherty

"Is the time right now?" asked Jimmy.

"No, I'm behind schedule," she said. "Are you here tomorrow?"

"Yes," said Jimmy.

"Well, I'll get the rooms done fast and I'll see you tomorrow."

That night, Jimmy called a cab and we went to a church dance. I was the only white guy there. I asked this girl to dance. She did and when I got back to the table, Jimmy said, "It's a good thing this is a church social. You're going to get us killed," but everything went off fine. We went back to the motel.

The next day, Jimmy met the maid. I went to the truck outside. A half hour later, Jimmy called me in. The girl was in the bathroom. Jimmy called her out and said, "This Irish boy is shy." He said to me, "Look at this young, beautiful and good pussy."

She said, "Come on, baby! He's right on all three." She wanted to put me at ease.

Jimmy left the room.

The next time we went from New York to Florida. Goldstein told us, "I have a piano going to South Carolina. Here's the deal: I'll give you seventy-five dollars. You put it on the tailgate but that'll make you five feet too long. There's a good possibility that you will get caught in Virginia. If you enter the state in the morning, the fine will be twenty-two fifty. You will still have fifty. So, what do you say?" I said yes.

As luck would have it, we crossed the state line into Virginia at 7:00 a.m. At 7:50 a.m., a state trooper going north makes a U-turn. Jimmy says, "Don't piss him off. Pull over."

"Good morning, gentlemen. I think you're a little over length."

"Yes, officer, I understand."

The cop said, "We must make sure. You hold the end of this tape and I'll go the length of it." Off he went the full length of the tape.

"You, come here."

"Yes, sir."

"You see that says fifty feet? Now, you hold the tape here and we will measure the rest." Then he said, "Come here. Look. You're five feet over length."

"Yes, sir."

"Lock your truck and get in the patrol car. We'll all go to see the justice of the peace."

We drove back north about five miles, made a left turn onto a dirt road, went another two miles onto another lane and went another quarter of a mile and finished up at the side of a house. I was loving this—it was more backwards than Leitrim.

He got out and told us to get out. A woman came out the back door.

"Good morning, Bill."

"Good morning, Mary Lou. Is Mason around?"

"He's down in the field feeding the calves." (That's what I had to do before I went to school back in Ireland!) She said, "You all come on in. I got the coffee on."

The back room we were in looked like an office. It had a coat rack with three coats hanging on it. The office had two large windows. We were all chatting away when, fifteen minutes later, Mason arrived with five empty buckets, which he dropped into each other. He had a farmer's overcoat on. He walked in and said, "Good morning, Bill," as he was taking off his coat.

"Good morning, Mason."

"How was the fishing yesterday, Bill?" he asked as he put on a robe that was hanging on the rack.

"Caught a few nice ones."

"Good. Good. A nice relaxing day. What have you got here, Bill?"

"These gentlemen had the tailgate down which leaves them five feet too long."

"Which of you gentlemen was driving?"

I put up my hand.

"You sit here."

He took a plaque, turned it towards me. It said, "Justice of the Peace," and he started writing. Nobody said a word while he was writing.

"Okay," he said, "twenty-two fifty."

I wanted to see his reaction, so I said, "Is there any way I could beat this ticket?"

"Well," he said, "we can lock you up in our jail. There's a judge coming through here in three weeks."

"And what would it cost me then?" I said.

"Twenty-two fifty."

I paid.

We got back in the car. He drove us to the truck and told us we must be out of the state by midnight or we could get another ticket. We got to South Carolina, got no more tickets and got our fifty dollars. Strange incident and I wouldn't have missed it for the world. It was a real Andy Griffith, Mayberry experience.

We delivered the piano to a poor black family. Their son worked for the post office in New York and had saved his money to buy the piano for his little sister. I wish I had kept her name. I often wondered if she became famous.

When the mother saw us taking the heavy furniture pads off the piano, she said, "My, my! They would make great blankets when we're cold." Their house was just a shack. When we gave them four furniture pads, she hugged us.

As we drove away, Jimmy said, "You're the first white boy that black mama ever hugged."

Our next stop was Tampa. We arrived late Saturday night. Jimmy said, "I know Tampa. I lived here." We checked into a motel in the black section of town.

Jimmy was always ready to party. I said that I was staying in and that I was tired.

"Okay," said Jimmy. "I'll see you later."

I went to bed and I didn't wake up until the next afternoon.

I heard the key in the door. Jimmy walked in with a tall black girl. He said to her, "There he is, baby." He said to me, "Wake up, man! You don't wake up to this every day. This is Bon Qui Qui."

She said, "Hello, honey baby. Jimmy's told me all about you. Jimmy says this is what you should wake up to everyday."

He says to me, "Bon Qui Qui is my friend. Everything is taken care of, Stoney. I'll see you all later," and leaves.

She says, "Jimmy is my friend. Why do you look so nervous?" Then she says, "But I can see why you're nervous, sticking it into a strange little black hole but wait until I'm finished. You'll be happy you met me. I promised Jimmy I'd make you happy, Relax, Baby, I'll teach you how to enjoy."

I did relax and I had a great time. I said to her, "You have an unusual name, does it stand for anything?"

"Yes," she said, "in French, it means your steak is ready."

For a young Irish guy in America, I was getting some education. Like about how black people can keep the bad treatment hidden, work so very hard, and still enjoy life. I didn't trust myself to remember her name, so I called her Frenchie when I said good-bye.

The following morning, we started unloading at a private house. By 3:00 p.m. we were on our way to Miami. When we got to Miami, Jimmy knew a black lady who had worked in the Allstate Van Lines office in New York. She had gone back to her hometown and her friends, and bought a rooming house on Second Avenue, the Harlem of Miami. We got in there late, 11:00 p.m. Everybody was standing around on every corner, watching this big tractor trailer with all the lights.

Jimmy said, "Let me go in and talk to her."

While Jimmy was gone, guys were coming all around the truck, asking me if we were unloading that night. I said, "No, tomorrow morning."

Jimmy finally came back, climbed up into the truck and closed the door. He said, "Let me explain. I'm sure you'll understand. She's got rooms. I'm going to stay because she needs the money. But she wanted me to explain to you that if she rented a room to a white guy, they would burn her house down."

"Jimmy, I understand very well. I will drive into Miami and I'll see you here at 7:00 a.m.

I get there the next morning at 6:45 a.m. and Jimmy is outside waiting with some guys hanging around him.

He told me, "This is the way moving furniture works. There's always guys in every town watching for furniture trucks. Most of the time, they're good movers. We needed two. I picked these two."

Because we had unloaded a family in Tampa, we had room in the back of the trailer. We put them in the back and went to unload. They were so good we kept them for the two days we were there.

When we had the trailer empty, we called New York to find out where we were to go next. They told us to go to the Garrison Army Base in Miami to pick up a family's furniture. He's some kind of general. His furniture has been in storage for months while they were looking for a house off the base in Fort Gordon, Georgia. When we got to Fort Gordon, we were directed to his house. He was there with his wife. He was acting like a general, walking up and down checking everything with his hands clasped behind his back.

We had most of the furniture in and Jimmy and I were putting legs on a table. We were talking to each other and the general heard my accent. Suddenly he stopped, almost on top of me.

"Excuse me," he said, "is that an Irish accent?"

I said, "Yes, sir."

He said, "This is very important to me. Are you from the north or the south of Ireland?"

"I'm from the south, sir."

He took his wife by the hand, "Honey, let's get out of here."

Jimmy asked what that was all about and I said to Jimmy, "I think I know. That man is Protestant. He may be four or five generations removed from Belfast but because I'm from the south, he's thinking I'm Catholic. The poor man has so much hate that he can't stand to look at me."

"First time I've seen that," said Jimmy. "If we were in a dark alley with him, I'd have a better chance at surviving than you."

When we finished, we said we needed to be signed out. He must have really hated me because he sent a soldier to sign us out. If he only knew the way I felt.

We called New York and got bad news, no jobs coming back to New York. The good news was that there was another full load with families going south, one family going to outside Fayetteville, North Carolina.

We spent a few days in New York for loading. We were in Brooklyn getting the last family on, and it got late. I wouldn't be able to get the paperwork into the office until the next day. Jimmy said he knew clubs in Brooklyn. He gave me the address and the number of a room he had rented on 54th Street between Eighth and Ninth Avenues. He told me to pick him up when I got the papers, and we'd go through the Lincoln Tunnel.

The next morning, I got there and double-parked. I saw a cop on the corner. I ran up to the door and rang the bell. Jimmy opened the door.

"Come in," he said, "grab this bag." Then he said, "Look in the bed."

I guess he wanted me to see that there was a twenty-five or thirty-year-old white girl asleep in the bed.

I said, "I'll see you downstairs," and I took his bag.

I was sitting behind the wheel when he opened the door and threw in a bag and then a pearl-handled gun.

"Put that in the glove compartment."

And he walked back to the side door where he had his wardrobe and hung his suits and shirts. He came back, climbed into the truck and said, "Let's go."

"But the gun. See the cop."

"He's directing traffic, man! Let's go!"

"But Jimmy, what if we get stopped?" I'm nervous."

"Don't be. I've always had a gun. You just didn't see it."

I was relieved when we were on the Jersey Turnpike going south.

The next night, we got into Fayetteville. Jimmy says, "You know this is a black family's private house, if we can find it, we can get unloaded."

We were in the country in black dark; there were no streetlights. We came to a crossroads and there was a grocery store. Jimmy said, "Let's go in here. Somebody might know."

He must have had a reason for asking me to go in. I was behind him. He said, "Good evening, ma'am." I stood back with my back to the wall. "We're looking for a Johnson family out here in this part of the country."

As he walked down toward her, she said, "I don't know any Johnsons."

She walked towards me inside the counter.

Jimmy saw a phone and said, "Ma'am, I'll leave the dime. Can I use the phone?"

"No," she said, Jimmy said, "Thank you, ma'am," and he walks towards the door.

I must have had a look on my face because I was having a flashback. When I was a kid and strangers would come into the shop looking for a family, Mother or Father would send me or my sisters with them so they wouldn't get lost.

The woman was looking at me and I was looking at her with my mouth open in disbelief.

Before Jimmy got to the door, she said, "Use the phone. Leave a dime."

"Thank you, ma'am," and he used the phone but nobody answered.

We went outside and sat in the truck.

The truck stood out in the dark country night, fifty feet long, with all those lights. A car pulled up with six guys in it. The driver got out and spoke to Jimmy. He told Jimmy that he knows the family and he told us to follow him.

"You're my man," says Jimmy.

I followed the car for a few miles; he was away ahead of us. We see the lights turn left.

We got up to where they turned when Jimmy said, "Stop."

"Okay," said Jimmy. "Just turn enough for the lights to shine up that road. Those guys might be bringing us up a road where the truck will sink."

Jimmy got out onto the dirt road. It didn't look good. He walked up one side down the other side and then the middle, and decided that we would go.

As we drove along, very slowly, we saw a light away over in a field. Then we saw a second light.

I said to Jimmy, "Do you know what that second light is?"

"No," he said.

I told him that from living in the country, I knew it was a window light. When they opened the door, the second light appeared. When we got there, the six guys were outside the car. We climbed down and they surrounded us, but you couldn't see who is who.

Then I heard a guy saying, "You're from New York. You must have money."

I heard Jimmy saying, "Yeah, man! We have money!" and then there's a shot and then another shot. Everybody started running. I dove under the trailer. There were three or four more shots, then everything went quiet. I came out. Everyone was gone except Jimmy.

I said, "That was you?"

"Yes, sir. When he mentioned money, I wanted him to know that I had a gun to go along with it."

The people from the house were standing in the field. Jimmy yelled to them, telling them he was from the moving company and that it was okay. They came over. Then the guy came back to get his car and apologized for what happened. He said that he didn't know any of those guys.

Jimmy didn't believe him but used this opportunity to send this guy a message. He told the owner of the house, making sure the guy with the car could hear him, "When our trucks leave the dock, the foreman puts a government seal on with a special tool."

He brought them around the whole trailer, showing them the government seal, and telling them that the seal can't be broken until 9:00 a.m. on the next day's date.

"If it's tampered with, you all will be dealing with the FBI and not the local cops."

Then he said to me, "Let's unhook the trailer. We'll take the cab into Fayetteville."

I said to him, "Do you think that line will work?"

He said, "Those people don't like to hear 'FBI.' It'll work."

We drove to Fayetteville. The only place we could stay was the 401 Truck Stop, me in a bed and Jimmy in the truck. The next morning, we drove out to the house and Jimmy was right, nothing had been touched.

We were there most of the day. The house was four hundred yards up the field. It was on stilts and I could see cats through the floorboards. It must have been cold in the winter. We got on the road by late afternoon. I'm thinking that if we're making deliveries at night in the South, maybe I should get a gun. Jimmy said it's easy in Miami.

The next day, the truck broke down outside of Macon, Georgia. Jimmy says if we can get it going, he knows a place in Macon where we can get it fixed. We worked on cleaning out the diesel lines and after an hour, it kicked over. We started driving but it wouldn't go over twenty miles an hour. When we made it into town, it was eighty degrees out.

As we drove in, I was looking at all those black people, young and old, standing on corners outside the stores. There must have been fifteen to twenty on each corner. In the middle of the town, Jimmy said there was a driveway to the left. It was narrow. You had to go out as far as you could to the right and make a very wide turn, otherwise you'd crash into in a building. When we got down the driveway, we came to what looked like a big field with a big truck mechanic's shop.

Five white guys came out. They looked at the truck and saw the New York plates. They stared at the both of us.

"You all from New York? What's wrong?"

Jimmy said, "We couldn't get it to go over twenty miles an hour. We got dirty diesel."

"The lines need to be purged. Back it away down and unhook the trailer."

So I did.

The civil rights marches were going strong. Blacks were doing their job actions, which meant they go to work but work very slowly. On June 22, 1964, three civil rights kids, one black and two white, Chaney, Goodman and Schwerner, were murdered by the sheriff and his deputies in a town called Philadelphia, Mississippi. A song that was very popular at that time was "Eve of Destruction" by Barry McGuire. Have a listen on YouTube.

I was still naive about what was going on around me. It being 80 degrees, I figured it would take at least two hours to fix it.

I said, "Where can we get some beer?"

A guy said, "This is a dry town but if you want some beer, I'll drive you all out the road to the next county."

I said, "Great! I'll get beer for everybody. Come on, Jimmy."

Jimmy made a sign to me and said, "Let me show you something," and he walked all the way down the field to the back of the trailer. He said, "You dumb Irishman! You're dumber than the dumbest nigger.

You go get the beer. I'll stay with the truck and watch them so they don't put a pound of sugar in the tanks or we'll never get out of Georgia."

I was still carefree. I said to the other guy, "Let's go get the beer."

On the way out the road, he was friendly, "You all from New York?"

"Yep," I said.

We arrived at this store out in the countryside and he drove up to the door. We both got out and he held the door so I walked in, him behind me. I heard the door close. When I looked back, his demeanor had completely changed.

He said, "Hello, Jesse.

"Hello, Billy Joe."

"You know what I got here, I got myself a New York boy and he's ridin' with a nigger!"

I'm looking straight ahead at this guy Jesse and I see a double-barreled shotgun hanging over the register. I think of the three civil rights workers in Mississippi.

When I get nervous, I talk a lot and the first words out of my mouth are, "Listen gentlemen, I'm here only a few months from Ireland and I'm only a driver. I know nothing about this country. If the boss puts a nigger with me, I do what I'm told."

"What do you think, Jesse?"

"I think he really doesn't know, Billy Joe."

Jesse said, "You know what you do, boy? When you get back up to New York, you tell your Jew boss how we feel about niggers down here."

I didn't know how he figured, but my boss was Jewish.

"Yes, sir, I sure will let him know how you feel about niggers."

He said, "How much beer do you want?"

"Give me two six-packs."

We got outside and into the car.

"You're new in this country?"

"Yes sir."

"You're getting to know how we feel about niggers down here?"

"Yes, sir."

When we got back, the truck was fixed. Jimmy had paid and he had it hooked back up to the trailer.

Jimmy said, "Let me drive it out of here." I think he wanted them to see that he was the man.

I left the beer for those white bastards.

I said to Jimmy, "No, you can't drive it. I'm a nervous wreck. I've got to drive."

I drove out, made this big wide turn, had to go two blocks around a circle, and onto the main road. When I got on the main road and started to breathe normally, I finally opened my mouth. "Jimmy," I said, "I just gave you up" and I told him everything I had said. "No more niggers with me down south."

Jimmy looked at me, "That's all right. If I was in your predicament, I'd have given me up too."

From that day forward, I was never from New York. I found out that a southern accent was easy and I picked a town to be from, Rocky Mountain, North Carolina.

One day, we drove into the cross-the-border truck stop in Jacksonville, Florida. The whole front was glass. When you sat in the restaurant, you could see your truck outside. While you were waiting for your food, the waitress kept filling your coffee cup.

Jimmy walked around the back to eat in the kitchen. I went in front. Sat down. The waitress came over, poured coffee.

"How you all doing? What you all having?"

"I'll have a tuna fish on rye. Thank you."

Ten minutes go by and no tuna. More coffee.

"Where you all from?"

"Rocky Mountain, North Carolina."

"My, my. There's more truckers from North Carolina than from any other state. You all must get cheap insurance up there."

I looked out the window and saw Jimmy heading back to the truck after eating.

We had been told that Martin Luther King, Jr. had a big march going on somewhere; any blacks that couldn't go were doing their job actions. The waitress came around with more coffee. She said, "Now, don't you worry, your food is coming. You know," she said, "since this King guy started up, they're getting slower and slower back there."

I'd hear a lot of stuff like that, then I'd go back to the truck and Jimmy and I would have some good laughs.

Back then, it was so interesting: some of the southern white truck stop and restaurant owners thought that if they built a restaurant in the back identical to the one up front, blacks would be happy to stay segregated.

Some truck stop owners knocked down the front and the back and put the kitchen in the middle.

Two identical restaurants, one in the back and one in the front. They would say, "What more do they want?"

Handcuffed and Homeless

We were in the office in New York one Saturday morning and loaded for Los Angeles, California, when Jimmy gets a call telling him that his mother is very ill and he has to go down south. He tells me, "You will have to do this run on your own."

I drive on my own for six days. On my way back I break down twenty-five miles outside of El Paso late on a Saturday night; nothing I can do until the next day, so I sleep with the truck running to keep warm. I don't wake until 10:00 a.m. next day. I cross over the highway and get a ride with a trucker. Luck is with me, his company works out of El Paso and he says there is a mechanic who works on their trucks would be glad to drive out to help get me back on the road, even on a Sunday, for a price. How lucky can I get?

By the time we get to El Paso and he drives me to the mechanic's shop, it's raining. I tell the mechanic my story and he says no problem, but with rain we don't want to be run over so he calls the sheriff's office. They send a deputy over and he escorts the mechanic and me out the twenty-five miles. He got me back on the road at 7:00 p.m. that Sunday evening.

The deputy says to me, "That will take a little of your overhead."

I am back on the road and I am so happy, how could I be so lucky to get a mechanic on a Sunday. I drive about ten miles and see a sign for diesel. With the truck running all night, I was low on diesel. As I drive in, I see a cop car. The station was a run-down shack; it had diesel and that was all. The place did not get too many trucks stopping and the guy looked happy to see me, with a big hello. I told him to fill it up, which would be a lot of money for him. Since it was raining, I went into the shack.

The only one there is a cop and he had with him a skinny, dirty old man in handcuffs. I ask the cop what did he do? The cop says he is a vagrant. I ask what is a vagrant? He says when he stops a person, he must have two dollars in his pocket or he gets locked up. The old guy was a sad looking sight, standing there all wet, and not a word coming out of his mouth.

I say to the cop, "Can I take him?" "Sure," says the cop, "as long as he is not in my town," and he takes the cuffs off him.

I felt sorry for the guy. He looked so skinny and wet that he looked like a drowned rat. He seemed very stiff for a man in his forties. The truck cab is very high up and I had to push him up into it. When I paid the guy who pumped the diesel, he had a big smile for me, and he told me in a low voice, that this was a very nice thing I was doing. I think he did not want the cop to hear him.

I drove all night and he slept on the seat. I did not suggest that he sleep in the sleeper, since he was dirty and he did smell a little. By the time daylight had come, we were getting close to Dallas. He pointed to the countryside to my left, and told me that when he is in this part of the country and has no money, he picks cotton on a cotton farm. I asked him how much he gets paid, he says eight dollars for a hundred pounds' weight, and it takes sixteen hours to do that, but, he said, black people could do it in twelve.

I said to him, "You're like a hobo, but they know how to look after themselves. Why do you look so dirty?"

He said, "I don't think I am that smart."

I laughed, because I did not think you needed much brains to be a hobo. I asked if he knew about the big trucks stops and how to wash up. He said no, he did not. I told him he's definitely not a hobo. I couldn't believe I was giving him tricks on how to keep clean.

Just before we came to Dallas we saw a big truck stop. Big truck stops have everything, diesel, food, clothes, and showers for truckers. I told him I was going to buy him a new shirt, pants, socks and a razor blade to shave with.

I said, "I will give you a quarter. Inside the door is a small room. Just watch me. I will put down my twenty-five cents and the girl will give me a small bar of soap and a towel. You do the same and then we go to the showers."

I was showered and shaved, and waiting outside for him, it took him forever to come out; when he did he looked pretty good, and younger. I asked him if he had ever heard of the truck stop showers before.

"No," he said.

"Well," I said, "you don't have to be dirty anymore."

We went back to the counter and I bought us breakfast. When we went outside, he asked if it would be okay if he stayed around here for a while. "Okay," I said, "but you have no money."

So I gave him five bucks and he said, "I have to thank God for all this help."

I said "Fuck God. What about me?" and we parted ways.

I never did ask him his name, and he never asked me mine.

I would go back to cab driving from December to March. Jimmy sometimes would stay in Florida and sometimes stay local, moving. Then he and I would hook up again. We did that for three years. Then Jimmy gave it all up and went back to Florida.

I got tired of furniture and got into freight. I liked it. You backed into a dock and they loaded it onto the trailer. I tied it down and drove away. One of my runs was from upstate New York to Lexington, Kentucky. One was from Rockford, Illinois to Springfield, Massachusetts.

I recall the first time I got to Rockford. I parked away from the dock and got woke up at 3:00 a.m. by a trucker from the same company, Dairy Express. He said to park at the dock so you get away first thing in the morning. The doors opened and sure enough, there were twelve trucks waiting behind us. I was picking up bulldozers and street diggers for Springfield, Massachusetts.

The guy that drove the equipment onto my trailer had an accent. I said, "Where is your accent from?"

"County Cork."

"My, you're a long way from home."

"So are you."

I got into Springfield at 2:00 a.m. on a Sunday and I could not find the address to drop off the load. I'm in the town and I see a cop car. I pull in behind him and I get out and go up to him. He says, "Sit in the car and I'll help you out."

I sit in the front seat with him.

He says, "You're Irish?"

"Yep."

He says, "There used to be a lot of Irish in Springfield. Still are. When I was a kid, my father would take me with him making deliveries to all the bars. I got to know all the Irish bar owners. They became my friends. Every one of them died from cirrhosis of the liver."

Do we ever have a drinking problem.

He said, "Follow me and I'll take you to where you have to go."

He got me there and I said good-bye and thanks. Then I went to sleep. The next morning, a worker banged on the door. He told me where to back in. This guy was talking to his boss and I couldn't believe what I was hearing.

I said, "Where are you from?"

"County Cork."

I said, "You may find this hard to believe, but the guy that drove this equipment on in Rockford, Illinois was from County Cork!"

Winter came again and I went back to driving a cab.

Cab Driving and Pussy Galore's Mink Coat

I had been driving a cab for six winters and I was wondering if I would go back on the road again. I had one woman give birth in the cab outside St. Clare's Hospital on 59th and Ninth Avenue.

There was another pregnant woman I picked up on Columbus Avenue and 102nd Street.

I said, "St. Clare's, straight down to 59th?"

Her friend said, "No, no. Eastside. Mount Sinai."

I said, "The woman is screaming. She won't make it!"

"Yes she will. Mount Sinai. Her doctor is waiting!"

I picked up two people and now I have a screaming baby!

Having babies being delivered in your cab screws up your whole night and you've just got to go to a bar and explain your problem to the bartender. You need a bucket of water and soap to wash out the back seat and floor and to get the smell out, and even then, a customer gets in and says, "Hey, driver! What's the smell in this cab?"

I started driving for a different cab company, called Carrick. It was owned by Terry Tole and his brother-in-law, Frank Earley, from County Tyrone. Terry had eighty medallions and Frank had nine. Terry had come to America in 1928 and was lucky. He worked through the Depression.

When World War II broke out, all the gasoline went to the war effort. Most of the cab owners went broke and junked their cars. The price of a medallion went down to ten dollars each. Terry Tole had foresight; he bought sixty taxi medallions and he threw them in a closet.

When the war was over and gasoline came back, he went to a bank manager and explained that he had sixty medallions and he wanted to buy sixty new cars and put the medallions on them and then he'd be in the cab business. The bank manager thought about it for no more than ten minutes and said it was a sound business deal and gave him two hundred thousand dollars. Terry paid it back in full in five years. His garage was on Northern Boulevard and Queens Plaza.

I drove at night. The day driver started at 6:00 a.m. and I came in at 4:00 p.m. I would be waiting for him. Then I would leave the "Off Duty" sign on and drive over the 59th Street Bridge and go up Third Avenue to 116th Street. Then I would put the "On Duty" sign on. The reason for this was to keep away from the mid-town traffic. For a few hours, most Harlem people went to the Bronx.

One evening, I was on Third Avenue and 122nd Street. This well-dressed man with two shopping bags hailed me.

"Excuse me, driver, but do you mind going to the Bronx?"

"Sure," I said.

He gets in and says, "I'll tell you how to go."

"Thank you."

"Would you like a cigarette?"

"No, thank you."

"Are you Irish?"

"Yes, sir."

"I have a lot of Irish friends. They're all so nice."

We get to his building and he says, "I have to go up and get money from my wife. I'll leave my bags here until I get back."

"Okay."

I wait fifteen minutes, then I get into the back seat and look in the bags. They're full of empty soda cans, bottles, and old papers. My first con and he was so nice. My father's words came back to me, "Never trust a stranger that's too nice."

I said to myself, "This won't happen to me again!"

I was taught to always use common sense but that doesn't happen all the time. The following weekend I find myself on Broadway dropping off two people for a show. When they get out, a big heavyset man with a big cowboy hat gets in. I notice his hat looks different. It looks like silk. With a Texas drawl, he says, "The Waldorf Hotel."

I get there and he says, "Wait here. I'm picking up a friend."

I say, "You can't go. You have to give me what's on the meter."

"Boy, I don't have any small change."

"Well, leave your hat." I say

"My hat cost more than the front end of this cab."

That's when common sense clicked back in. I say, "Sorry, Sir. Go ahead."

A few minutes later, he comes back with a gorgeous young girl about my age on his arm.

She says, "Baby, how is the oil business in Texas?" "Fine, Baby. Driver, 45th Street and Broadway, please."

Years later when I was bartending, I met big company and hotel reps, big guys coming in from out of town. To get their business, they were given the red carpet treatment: free hotel suites, the most expensive call girls and Broadway tickets. Now I know who my Texas oilman's girl was.

I gas up at midnight or whenever I get to Queens. One night back in Manhattan, going up First Avenue at 77th Street, there's a lady in her forties. When you're in your twenties, forty is old. She had leather boots up above her knees and the shortest hot pants I ever saw. I stop and she jumps in the back, says, "Go! Go!" I went through a red light up First Avenue.

I ask her, "Are you in some kind of trouble?"

"Yes," she says, "I'm rich. I live on Fifth Avenue and I can't get a man or boyfriend to go down on me and eat me."

I had heard of this. Now I'm wondering, I've got a rich, forty to fifty-year-old woman who wants something different. She had been drinking; otherwise she wouldn't be talking like this. Maybe I'll try something new for a change.

I knew a guy who owned a bar on Third Avenue and 89th Street, who worked there at night. I took her there for a drink. She went to the bathroom. My friend said, "Where did you pick up this bimbo?"

I thought she looked great. She came back from the bathroom and started on both of us. She goes to class places, not dumps. She knows cab owners, not cab drivers.

She says, "Let's go. Drive me home."

We get to 79th Street and Fifth Avenue and she says, "You're going down on me."

"Right. Yes," I say.

"Okay," she says. "You see that door? That's my building. I'll leave the door unlocked. You go around the block and park this thing. I don't want my neighbors seeing me bringing a cab driver in."

I park the cab and go back. The door's unlocked; I walk in. There must have been someone there earlier as there were two half glasses of wine on the table. She was the type who told you what to do. She's standing in the living room and she tells me to take her clothes off, so I do. She lies down on the couch, puts one leg on the coffee table and the other leg on back of the couch and says, "NOW. Eat me!"

I get down on my knees. It doesn't look very appetizing and I'm thinking it doesn't have a nice smell.

She gets frustrated with me.

I say, "Maybe you go to the bathroom and wash, then I'll be able to go down on you."

She goes to the bathroom but doesn't come out. I open the door and she's sitting on the bowl, legs spread, half asleep, peeing. She sees me, jumps up out into the living room.

"Okay," she says.

I say, "Sorry, I can't. I'll go."

She says, "Okay, fuck me then."

I did.

When it was over, she jumped up and said, "Get dressed and get out!"

She's walking me to the door and I say, "Could I see you again?"

She says, "I need a man to go down on me and eat me. I can meet guys like you every half hour that will fuck me. Out!"

The next day was Sunday. Desmond, Neil Mahon and I go to the Chestnut Bar for an hour before I go to work. I tell them about the rich Fifth Avenue lady I met.

Desmond was the type who always wanted to be in charge, and when I finished telling my story, Desmond was shaking his head.

I said, "What would you do?"

He said, "It's always the wrong guys who get the once in a lifetime break. If I had only met her, I'd be eating my way into a million dollars right now!"

Months later I picked up a girl on Lexington Avenue who was pretty drunk. She was wearing a black, full-length fur coat.

She said, "I want to go to an all-night deli."

Back then there were very few places open all night.

"Yes," I said, heading straight down to Lexington and 66th Street.

We got there and she got out, took off the coat and threw it on the back seat and said, "That's my coat. Don't go away."

I locked the doors, left the meter running and fell asleep. I woke up twenty-five minutes later and went into the store. The poor girl was high. She was so friendly that every guy in the store was around her. She had bought so much food, a half-pound of this, a half-pound of that, that the counter was full of her stuff.

I said, "Do you remember me?"

"No, who are you?"

"I'm your cab driver. You left your black fur coat with me."

"My, my, my! Thank you very much! Okay, let me get all this stuff in the cab."

She comes out. "Can I sit in the front?" she says.

I say, "Sure."

She says, "You know the movie Goldfinger?"

I said that I did.

"Well, I had a small part in the movie and Honor Blackman, the girl who played Pussy Galore, gave me that coat. I'd die if I lost it."

She lived up on 84th Street, on the East side. When we got there, she said, "Would you like to come up to the apartment?"

"Sure," I said.

"You wait here," she said. "Let me bring some of this stuff up. I'll be right back."

She comes back and pays me, gives me a big tip for watching her coat, tells me her boyfriend is asleep, that he was supposed to be out of town.

"Boy," I said to myself, "some of those girls could get you killed."

I picked up another woman on 59th Street and Eighth Avenue.

She said, "I'm going to 89th and York Avenue. It's by Gracie Mansion."

She said she never gets young cab drivers and goes on about how she left her boyfriend. She was going to wake up her friend on 89th Street and stay there, but she was in no hurry getting there. Did I want to stop and have a drink?

We were on First Avenue between 85th and 86th Streets, near a bar called Mothers. We go in there. It has a big barrel of nuts in the middle of the floor and everybody is eating out of it. The floor is covered with shells from the nuts. She plays the jukebox and starts dancing.

The bartender yells, "No dancing!"

She yells back, "Don't be a bore!" and just keeps on.

The bartender says, "You've got to leave!"

I took her outside and she said, "You and I are friends now. I'm riding in the front." I said, "Sure." Then I said, "I'll drive to 89th Street."

When we got there, she said, "This is a dead-end street. It's a great place to make out. Drive in here."

I love it when a woman tells me what to do. It takes all the guesswork out of it. Back then all the women wore nylon stockings called pantyhose. She took off her shoes and pulled up her skirt so as not to sit on it.

Then she put her two feet up in the air and said, "I don't want to put a run in my pantyhose."

One week later, I'm driving on 46th Street, on "Restaurant Row." A lady runs out of Joe Allen's Restaurant with her hand up. I stop, and she jumps in and says, "Wait, my boyfriend will be right out," and it's the same lady. I look at her and she looks at me.

I say, "Do I know you?"

"No," she says.

He comes out and says, "Hello, Driver."

I say hello and he gives me an address in the Village.

We go to the Village and she says, "Good night, Driver," and smiles.

I say, "Good night," and I don't ever expect to see her again.

Fifty-four years later, in August of 2017, I'm the owner of Ryan's Daughter, a bar on East 85th Street. My friend John Healy, who promotes artists through shows and book readings and the like, was sponsoring an exhibition at the upstairs bar. He had put out a few pages of this book before it was published for people to look at, and he asked a lady friend of his to read them and tell him what she thought.

He says to me, "She really wants to meet you."

So I go to meet her, this well dressed little old lady. She shakes my hand and tells me her name is Lara.

"I want to tell you something," she says. "I never forget anything, even when I've been drinking. The story you have in your book, about the girl you made out with at Gracie Mansion in 1963? Well, that was me. I was taken aback when I realized that you were the same taxi driver that my boyfriend and I hailed outside of Allen's Restaurant a week later. That was very nice of you to say, 'Do I know you?'"

We had a hug and a laugh, and talked about our younger days. That something like this can happen to me in a city of nine million people, I find it so hard to believe. Small world.

The Joys of Driving

I was half parked on 45th Street and Eighth Avenue at 3:00 a.m. when two guys got in the back seat, one tall and one short. The tall guy grabbed my head and stuck a gun in my neck with his other hand. "The money, Man!"

I said, "It's in my breast pocket."

The little guy got my money and said, "There's more. Where is the rest?"

I said, "That's it."

The little guy said, "These guys are smart. They hide it in their shoes."

He jumped into the front seat and went for my sock. That was where I did have my money. I was scared now because I had lied. I had my hand on the handle of the door and, as he went for my sock, I came up with my right knee and hit him in chin, then I yanked the door open and dove down to get away from the gun and out onto the street. But because I was parked away from the curb, my left side landed between the curb and the street and I was hurting. I got up to see them run up Eighth Avenue.

I drove to the garage and checked in. They drove me to Elmhurst Hospital. They told me I had three fractured ribs. All they do with fractured ribs is wrap you up from your chest down to your stomach and let them heal. Boy, did it hurt when you coughed or sneezed!

I was back driving in Harlem, and one night, at about 11:00 p.m., I picked up an old black man on 116th St and Fifth Avenue.

He said, "147th Street, off Morningside Avenue." Then, he looked and saw that I was white and he said, "What are you doing up here, white boy?"

I said, "Just trying to make a living, like everybody else."

He said, "It's a poor living when you're dead." He said, "I was going into my house one night and there were five young punks sitting on the stoop. They stuck a gun in my ear and said, 'We need it all, Pop!' One of them said, 'What does an old nigger need money for anyway?' I told them, 'Take everything, just don't pull the trigger.'"

He said to me, "Now look, son, when you get me to my house, I'll pay you while I'm in the cab. Then I'll get out, but you don't leave. My wife and I have two German shepherds. We live on the fifth floor. I have a whistle here and when I blow it, she'll let the dogs out and they'll come down to take me home."

We got up there and there were five young guys sitting on the stoop.

He said, "Look, there they are."

He paid me and got out. I opened the passenger window so that he could talk to me. He blew the whistle and as fast as you could count 1,2,3,4,5, two German shepherds came flying through the door.

He said to me, "You do what I told you. Lock your doors and get out of Harlem!"

He yelled to the dogs and they started barking. He yelled to the guys, "Move or the dogs will move you!"

They jumped up and the old man went home.

I started thinking, in the United States of America there must be sixty percent of the people who live in their own little world, shouting from the hilltop, "Freedom for all!"

The white guys want to kill me because I was with a black man, an old black man needs dogs to get into his own house because of black kids and he ain't doing too well with the whites either. I would love to sit down with that old black man and get his version of the American Dream.

Change My Plans

April came and I was thinking of going back on the road trucking. I was in the Bliss Tavern on 46th Street off of Queens Boulevard in Woodside, Queens, and the bartender said his friend Matty was quitting his bartender job a place called the La Salle. When I asked why, he said there were two reasons: one, there were too many fights and two, he preferred being a waiter. As a waiter you worked lunch, then you took three hours off, went shopping, came back and did supper. With bartending, it was ten hours plus travel time.

I said that I would take that job. He gave me the address of the bar. The next night, I stopped in to see Matty. I introduced myself and told him that I knew his friend, Vinnie. He told me he was going to quit but his boss, Jack Beckett, gave him a raise in salary and he had decided to stay with it for a while.

I asked him where he lived and he told me Sunnyside, Queens. I asked him how he got home and he said by cab. I told him that the cab company that I drove for was located near there.

"Can I make you my last fare?"

He said, "I'd love that, as I'm nervous hailing a cab in this neighborhood at 5:00 a.m."

"Okay," I said, "I'll be here at four thirty or five every morning."

I stopped by the next morning at 4:00 a.m. to see if he had any customers. I was surprised to find the place full. He introduced me to a few local guys, Jackie, Sully, Dennis Cooney and George Kelly, all tough guys, and there were more to come. Over the next three weeks, I got to know quite a few of them. I was happy now that they were familiar with me.

One night, I was in Harlem. I was running late and had no time to pick Matty up. At 5:00 a.m. there was nobody on the streets and no traffic, so I decided to go back to the garage. I was coming across 116th Street, headed towards Lexington Avenue, with green lights all the way to Second Avenue, and I was doing sixty.

A bus had just pulled in and a guy jumped off the bus and ran right across in front of me. I caught him dead center on the hood of my cab and I put my two feet on the brakes. He went flying up the hood and up the windshield, and when the car stopped, he went flying back down the windshield and down the hood to the street. All this happened in seconds. I jumped out and by the time I was out, he was up.

I said, "You need an ambulance?"

He started running towards Park Avenue yelling back at me, "Fuck you! Fuck you, you motherfucking—"

The light had changed red so the bus couldn't leave, so I went over to the bus driver. He opened a small window and bent his head down. I said to him, "Did you see that?" and, with an Irish accent, he said, "I didn't see nothing." The light went green and he drove away.

There was an old Spanish man standing on the sidewalk. As I was getting back into the cab to drive away, he said, "You can't leave. I've got your license plate." I got scared and when I saw a cop car coming down Lexington Avenue, I waved it down and told the cops the whole story. They said to me, "It's okay. You told us. You can go," and they drove away.

After they left, I had second thoughts and I drove to the precinct on 119th Street. I walked in and there was a cop behind the desk and a sergeant standing outside the desk. I told him my story.

The sergeant said to me, "Did you get their shield numbers?"

"No."

"Did you get the car number?"

"No."

"How dumb can you be?"

He turned to the guy behind the desk. "Who do you think would be driving over there?"

He said, "Don't know, Sarge."

The sergeant turned to me and said, "Give me your license and registration," and he typed up a full report. Afterward, he said, "Always take a cop's shield number. When they don't take a written report from you, you could get into big trouble."

I said, "Thank you very much, sir. I'll remember this."

I stopped by the bar the next night and the place was a wreck. "Oh, Stoney!" Matty said, "I can't take this. There's no amount of money that could keep me here. I'll introduce you to Jack tomorrow evening. I told him all about you, how you were in refrigeration, truck driving and cab driving."

I met Jack the following evening. He came out from behind the bar after his day shift and sat down with a beer and I was introduced to him.

He said, "I understand you were in refrigeration, and then a truck driver and a cab driver. So, are you going to use me also?"

I sized him up and I figured that he was the type of man who wasn't into being called sir. I said, "Well, Jack, I did all those jobs plus I did a little bartending on weekends in the Red Mill and in the Ferguson and McLaughlin, and I liked bartending. I think it's time for me to settle into a full-time job and if you give me a chance, I will prove myself."

He said, "I know Ferguson and McLaughlin. There's a big sign over the register. What does it say?"

I said, "It reads, 'If you want your prayers answered, get off your knees and work.'"

Jack liked me and I was hired.

So I call the cab company and tell them that I have a new job. Everything is going great with Jack until he asks me one morning to go into the kitchen and cook bacon, sausage and scrambled eggs. I learned early in life that nobody can cook scrambled eggs and sausage without another person complaining:

"You should have cooked it more."

"You cooked it too much."

"The eggs are too soft."

"The eggs are too hard."

"Jack," I said, "I never cooked in my life. I even order in toast."

"Okay," he said, "I understand some guys do not like to cook, even for themselves."

A Day at the Races

Jack had me work with him for two weeks before he decided he was going to keep me and put me working the night shift. On his day off, he always went to the races. He asked me if I ever went to the races and I told him no.

He said he was going to Aqueduct the next day and that he would meet me and that I would enjoy it. "It's not my favorite racetrack," he said, "but it will do. Monmouth Racetrack is my favorite."

I lived in Richmond Hill, close to the track so I met him there. I didn't know how much money Jack brought with him to the track, but he won quite a few races and bragged to me that they knew him at the hundred-dollar window, and they did. At the eighth race, he put sixty-eight hundred dollars on a horse to win. That year you could buy a cab and medallion for eight thousand dollars.

Jack used to watch the races on the screen with one hand in his pocket and no emotion on his face. Me, on the other hand, my heart was in my mouth and it wasn't even my money.

That race was a photo finish and we had to wait. It seemed like a long time, but it finally came up. He had lost. Keep in mind that five minutes before that race, Jack could have bought a cab. Without even flinching, he turned to me, tucked in his tie and said, "Stoney, give me twenty bucks. I'm taking a cab out of here."

Jack always liked to show off. The next evening when I got behind the bar, he gave me my twenty and, as he did, an envelope fell to the floor. "Pick that up," he said, "see what is in it"—and him knowing what was in it. It was a check for fifty-nine thousand dollars from the Navy.

Later on that night, his good friend, John Flaherty, who lived around the corner, came in. He was a police lieutenant on the short list for captain, but because of his age, the department rushed his papers through and made him retire so they wouldn't have to pay him a captain's pension. I told Flaherty about the fifty-nine thousand dollar check.

"Yes," he said, "Jack got that from the Navy."

Flaherty said, "Let me tell you about Jack," and he told me. Jack's wife had two brothers, one in Ireland and one here. Jack had this dream of going back to Ireland to live on a farm. Every year, he and his wife went back to the Galway Races. One year he met up with his brother-in-law, who knew of a farm for sale. He looked at it, liked it and said that he'd buy it.

He wasn't going to move to Ireland for another ten years. At that time, the taxes were high if you lived outside of Ireland but owned land in it, so the brother-in-law, McHugh, said, "Put it in my name for the ten years."

And so he did. Jack paid for it in cash.

Jack and the wife went over every year for the Galway Races and would go admire his farm. When the ten years were up, Jack and the wife packed up and went back to Ireland to live on their farm.

Bombshel! McHugh said, "It is in my name and I feel that it's mine. So it's mine."

Jack told his wife, "You can stay here, too," and he returned to New York.

He was thirty-five years old. The Second World War was on and the government was looking for men, so he went to the Navy recruiting office and signed up for five years. That's where that check came from.

When he came out of the Navy, he bumped into the other brother-in-law who lived up on 190th Street in Washington Heights. Jack held no grudges; he was looking for an apartment. McHugh knew of one in his apartment building, one floor above him, on the fifth floor and Jack took it.

It was a large building. When you walked into the big lobby, the left side of the building, the side that Jack lived on, was a walk-up; the right side of the building had an elevator. Jack would take the elevator to the roof and walk down one flight.

Jack got a job as a salesman selling glasses to bars and restaurants. Working on commission, he was an expert salesman. McHugh owned a bar and he told Jack that he would make him a twenty-five percent partner for five thousand dollars. Back then, you could buy a bar for five thousand dollars, but Jack went for it. McHugh and Jack both could waste money. The bar went bust and Jack was out of business again.

Jack never did go back to Ireland. He started working as a bartender in high-class places, but he always liked bartending in rough middle-class places. It was interesting because Jack was highly educated, five years of college, and he had no problem cutting you down to size with some fifty-dollar words.

He met a man, Donahue, who had five bars and restaurants, who asked him to become a partner in one of his bars in Harlem, at Amsterdam Avenue and La Salle Street at 125th Street. Jack went for it again. The contract was that Jack had to work five days a week for a forty-nine percent partnership, with an inventory and split of the profit every three months.

Two years after he started working for Donahue, the City decided to put in housing projects on Amsterdam Avenue, from 122nd Street to 125th Street. Donahue found an empty storefront on Amsterdam Avenue at 90th Street. He and Jack remained partners and they brought the La Salle name with them.

Jack settled in and found himself a girlfriend who had a husband. According to gossip, she wasn't the brightest. Jack's brother-in-law, McHugh, still lived in the building on the fourth floor, underneath Jack. He got married and started having kids. When Jack and he met, they tolerated each other.

Flaherty said, "Fourteen years had passed. I went into the bar one night. Jack brought me into the kitchen and handed me a letter and said, 'Read this.' The letter was from Jack's wife telling him she was coming back the next month. Jack asked me what he should do.

"I said, 'The first thing you do is you get rid of that bimbo. The second thing you do is fix up your apartment. She is your wife.'"

He never went to Ireland while his wife lived there. She came back to New York in June; he was at the Galway Races in July and he never missed them ever again, but he never took her. I guess it was his way of getting even.

The brother-in-law and his wife still lived underneath Jack when she died from complications giving birth to her fifth baby. Since Jack and the wife had no kids, she took the place of her brother's wife. The oldest kid was eight years old. Things started to run smoothly after a few months.

One year later, her brother had a heart attack and died. Jack told his wife, "Let's keep all these kids together. It would be like a duplex apartment. You be the mother and I'll pay and we will put all of them through school as far as they want to go."

When I started working for Jack, one of the kids was then seventeen. Jack had him cleaning and mopping and packing out beer, just like he had me do when he hired me.

The kid would say to me, "I hate Uncle Jack."

Because I knew the story, I let the kid know how foolish he sounded and how he and his brothers and sisters could have ended up in foster homes.

He said, "Yes, but I still hate him."

Kids do not appreciate things until they are much older.

Cops and Robbers

Flaherty was pushed into retiring before he became a captain. He would go to the track with Jack and Ernie. Ernie was married to Jack's partner, Donahue's, daughter. He owned and operated a garage one block away on 89th Street.

Flaherty told me that when he had been a lieutenant on patrol in Midtown, he had finished his 4:00 p.m. to midnight shift and walked home. Back then Jack worked nights. It was

2:00 a.m. He stopped in to see Jack and he was down at the end of the bar talking to a customer. Two other customers were arguing and Jack got annoyed. He yelled at them to stop.

A customer asked for a whiskey. As Jack grabbed the bottle, it slipped out of his hand and hit Flaherty smack in his face and forehead. Blood was everywhere. Everybody wanted to call the cops and an ambulance. He was the only one who kept a cool head. He said, "No, nobody call nobody!"

They wrapped his head in towels. He told Jack to call Ernie and when he arrived, he said, "Here's what you do, Ernie. Take your car out of the garage. Bring it to Amsterdam and 89th Street and park it as if you were turning onto the avenue. I want you to know that I'm going to pay for all of this. Then we break the windshield. I'll break it the rest of the way with my head, to get my blood on the glass. Then, I'll lie in the front seat as a passenger and you call an ambulance. I won't talk. You'll do the talking. Tell them a car went through the light and you hit the brakes and I went through the windshield."

They kept it as low-key as possible but when the top brass got a whiff of it, they were all over it.

I asked Flaherty why he would go to so much trouble. He said that the Internal Affairs Division, the IAD, was always looking for something. "They would have it make the front page of the newspaper. The headline would read "Police Lieutenant in Bar Room Brawl at 2:00 a.m. Got Forty Stitches." I could never tell the true story to anybody I worked with."

He said to me, "You know, we had a poem back home about a secret."

I said, "Hold it. I bet I know it:

'If you have a friend, just keep him so.

Never let that friend your secret know.

For if that friend should turn your foe, Then all the world your secrets will know.'"

Now that he was retired, on quiet nights he would tell stories. I liked most of them, but there was one that I didn't like. When he was a cop on the beat, he once pulled a car over. He noticed the guy's glasses on the dashboard. He asked the guy for his license and registration. His license said he wore glasses to drive.

Flaherty gave him a ticket for having no license, which I really didn't like. He went to court on his court date and the guy was present. When the case was called, the guy produced his license.

The judge said, "Dismissed."

Flaherty stood up and said, "Excuse me, Your Honor, I'm the police officer who wrote that ticket."

The judge said, "Okay, officer, explain to me why you think this man didn't have a license."

"This happened back in the late 1930s," Flaherty said. "So I said to the judge, 'Your Honor, there are three states in the United States that do not require a license to drive a car. This gentleman has a license but he must be wearing glasses when he drives. He was not wearing his glasses; therefore, he has no license.'"

The judge agreed. Flaherty was so proud of himself. I was not.

He was extremely smart. He had a photographic memory and he was very well known and liked in the Department. The captains, lieutenants and sergeants from the 20th and 24th Precincts used to stop by at night to talk to him about cases that they had going on.

From listening to them talk, you'd know that there's a big book on law on the desk in every precinct. They would ask Flaherty a question about their cases and he would stand up and say, "You will find it on page 1,020," and then he would recite it as if he was reading it out of the book.

Flaherty came to New York to Ninth Avenue and 17th Street in the winter of 1923, a very cold winter. All the houses were cold-water flats with bare wood floors. You needed a lot of blankets to keep warm. The first morning he got out of bed in his bare feet he stood up and he couldn't move.

He looked down at his feet and they were stuck to the floor. He hadn't known yet that winters in New York were so cold that you went to bed with your socks on so your feet wouldn't stick to the floor when you got out of bed in the morning.

He had wanted to become a cop but he was racing against the clock. You had to be in the country for five years to become a citizen and you had to be a citizen to be a cop. He had to go to night school, and get his high school diploma, and then take the cop test, all before his twenty-ninth birthday. If you passed before your twenty-ninth birthday, you were on the list. He passed, but didn't get called until he was thirty-three and that was old to become a cop.

He was sent to the Bronx where his beat was the Grand Concourse and Fordham Road. He said that back then there were no cops in cars. Sergeants and lieutenants were the only ones with cars.

The sergeant made the rounds every two hours and you'd better be out there when he came around or you would get a complaint. One snowy night at 3:00 a.m., he was standing in a doorway on 188th Street, when the car came around and stopped. The sergeant opened the window. Flaherty gave him his book. The sergeant signed it and drove away. Flaherty said to himself he'd better start studying harder and get that guy's job.

Two years later, he was transferred to Manhattan. He kept studying and the next year the sergeant's test came up. He took it and passed. His new assignment was back in the Bronx where he had been a beat cop.

The winter came and the snow came. One night he was going up the Concourse at 3:00 a.m. and he thought of himself standing in the doorway, freezing while waiting for the sergeant. He said to the driver, "Turn here," and there was a cop standing in that same doorway. He rolled down the window and signed his book. As the cop walked away, Flaherty said, "The same to you."

His driver asked him what that was about. "Oh," he said, "three years ago I was standing in that doorway freezing and when the sergeant signed my book, I said, 'Fuck you,' under my breath. I knew what he was saying to me so I was just answering him, 'the same to you.'"

Flaherty told me, "As a sergeant, I learned the ropes. You pay for nothing while you're in uniform. The local bookies were the best at paying us off. The Mayor brought in a new commissioner, Murphy, to stop the cops who were on the take. I got transferred to Harlem, 28th Precinct. I found it hard to believe there were no racial problems in the 28th Precinct. There wasn't one white person living in it when I was sergeant.

"My first night there, I got in the patrol car and I can tell the cop is nervous as he drives up the street. I say, 'Where is the action?'

"He says, 'What, what?'

"I said, 'Never mind this Murphy guy, where's the action?'

"He said, 'Maybe down this block,' and he pulled down into the middle of the block and stopped.

"This guy runs over saying, 'Hi Man.'

"The man throws a bag over my shoulder into the back seat and we drive away.

"Thank you bookie."

On a Sunday in the 28th Precinct, as a sergeant he'd get three hundred and sixty dollars and give ten dollars to the cop driver. I told him if I was the cop, I would consider ten dollars an insult, that I should get at least a hundred or he could just put me back out on the beat.

Flaherty said, "I did a lot of walking. The old black men shining shoes on 125th Street had a spare shoebox and it wasn't full of polish. It was full of miniature vodka and whiskey bottles like you get on an airplane.

"He gave me two bucks. I went down some steps to a basement. That guy had bars on the windows wide enough to let a bottle through. He didn't see the uniform as he was coming with a bottle in his hand. I told him I'm not here for the whiskey. Then he sees the uniform. He says, 'Okay, Man,' and gives me ten dollars.

"The following year the sergeants and lieutenants called for a meeting. I noticed a lot of Jewish names. The meeting was about changing the structure of how the money was collected. They wanted to pool the money and split it every month. I knew their game immediately; come the Sunday, when they had to make the rounds, they would call in sick, but they would be there at the end of the month to collect. I stood up and said, 'What you walk for, you keep. What I walk for, I keep.'

"Five years later I made lieutenant. Now I'm part of the top brass. They would bring lieutenants from the high crime precincts to One Police Plaza for round-the-table talks to discuss how to handle situations. I explained to them how it worked in Harlem, 'Gentlemen, conversation around this table flows like buttermilk. But uptown, where eighty percent of the people use the word motherfucker, and you get a call to a bar with trouble and the walls are actually moving with an angry crowd at three in the morning, the only way you get their attention is to fire two shots in the ceiling and yell, 'Back up, Motherfucker!' That way, you may get out alive."

Flaherty would never tell young cops how times were because a cop named Frank Serpico completely brought down the corruption in the Police Department; but he liked to talk to old-timers. I recall a retired sergeant from Brooklyn asking him how it was as a lieutenant in the Midtown area known as the Tenderloin. He said being a lieutenant on patrol in Midtown was like being nominated for Vice President of the United States, you went to work tired, hungry and broke and you came home well rested, well fed and, if the dice rolled right, with a pocket full of money.

He said the interesting thing was that all the top brass were cops at one time, so when a cop got a complaint, they would transfer him to Central Park where he could make no money; nothing in Central Park but rabbits.

Central Park had an upside. There were more sergeants and lieutenants made out of the Central Park Precinct than any other precinct in the city. Rabbits don't need policing. The smart cops took their books to work.

Flaherty said, "When I became a lieutenant in Midtown, I worked the desk. There were two thousand arrests a year. You had one hand on the phone full time and the other hand was writing in arrests. If you didn't know the big law book on the desk off by heart, you had problems.

"The interesting thing about Times Square was it had a lot of hustlers. They worked their craft very well. They weren't out to hurt you, just to get everything you had. The smartest thing in a hustler's brain is picking the right person.

"I walked to work every day through Times Square, wearing civilian clothes and nobody approached me.

Now here's a phone call we got often, here's one of the stories.

"A young guy, five feet, two inches tall, just out of college, first day in New York, his parents have given him a thousand dollars. He's walking down Broadway. The hustler approaches him with pictures of girls, White, Asian and Black. 'Ha! Man, you look like a nice guy. You want a girl?' Shows him the pictures. Then says, 'You're not a cop, are you?' Back then you had to be five eight to be a cop.

"Instead of this guy catching on, his ego takes over. 'No, I'm not a cop.'

"The hustler shows the pictures again, 'Which one do you like? The Asian? Okay, she will be ten dollars for you, she is young but old enough to screw, that okay?'

"'Yes,' says the kid.

"'Okay,' the hustler says, 'Come with me a few blocks.' He says, 'Man, I'm so glad I met you. You're going to have the time of your life.' They get to a brownstone, a five-story walk-up. They go inside. The hustler says, 'You wait here until I make sure the girls are ready.' He disappears for five minutes then comes back with another guy. The other guy is angry, yelling at his buddy. 'Why do you pick those guys up? What if he's a cop?' The kid can't wait to tell them, 'No. No. I'm not a cop!' 'Okay, we believe you,' the hustler says, 'Here's the way it is. We have had trouble with our girls. Some of them are not honest.' He pulls out a large brown envelope and says, 'This is for your protection. Put everything you have in here and we'll seal it in front of you.'

"The college kid puts his thousand dollars, his watch, even his change, in the envelope, and they seal it in front of him. The guys tell him, 'Wait ten minutes and ring Apartment 5E.' They go to the roof and go over two buildings and they're gone."

Flaherty said, "I often wondered why they use not just the same building, but the same apartment. The phone call comes in. I answer, 'This is the police department.' 'This is Mrs. Murphy calling. They're banging on my door again.'"

I recall a young cop telling him that he bought a house out on the Island. Flaherty said, "Tell your neighbors you are anything but a cop, because in the suburbs they think cops are lawyers. They don't realize that ninety percent of us were lucky to pass the test for a high school diploma."

The cop says, "What should I tell them?"

Before I give Flaherty's answer, I must explain what a longshoreman is. A longshoreman works on ships and docks. That's all he knows, is ships. So when the young cop said to Flaherty, "What should I tell them?" Flaherty said, "Tell them you're a longshoreman and hope there's not a big flood and a ship sailing up the block at two o'clock in the morning."

On a snowy January night, a guy came into the La Salle at 1:00 a.m., made his way to the end of the bar and started talking to Flaherty. Flaherty had a way of putting people at ease. (Keep in mind it is fifteen degrees outside.) The guy tells Flaherty that he sells Swiss watches, Swiss army knives, etc. Does Flaherty want one?

Flaherty asks to look at one. The guy had on a big heavy overcoat, which he opened. Flaherty shouts to me and I look down the bar. All I could see was watches and Swiss Army Knives on both sides of his coat. There must have been at least hundred and that's all he had on, not a stitch of clothing except underpants. I fell down on the floor with laughter. Flaherty tells him he had better close his coat and he did. He figured Flaherty to be a cop, so he says to Flaherty, "I have a permit for a gun."

Flaherty says, "Do you have it on you?"

"Sure," he said. "Let me show you."

Flaherty takes it into the kitchen where there was good light. He shouts to me, "Stoney, I know you're busy, but you got to see this," so I go into the kitchen and he reads it off. Can't believe it; it is an up-to-date gun permit.

He takes it back out and says to the guy, "You're right. It is an up-to-date permit. "You know," he says to the guy, "I don't mind you having this gun permit, but it's the guy who issued you this permit that I'd like to meet."

After working three years in the La Salle, I bought a car. There were two old guys, Chuck and Hank, who would wait for me to drive them home. Flaherty would go home at one or two in the morning. He liked to go to the track during the daytime. One night, he left early. But he was back in half an hour. He says to me, "Call the cops. I got mugged." He had got off two rounds but as a cop you can't let off rounds and not report it in case one round went through a window and hit somebody. When the police car came, he explained the situation and they took him to the station house.

I remembered him telling me, when you work the desk, you do it by the book. You always cover yourself. When he went to the precinct, the young cop behind the desk asked him for his permit. Flaherty was shocked. His gun permit was out of date. He says, "I'll go down tomorrow and get it renewed."

The young cop says, "I'll have to take your gun."

Flaherty says, "This gun wasn't out of my hand in thirty-four years. Can't you overlook it this time?"

"No, Mr. Flaherty, I cannot. You know the rules better than anybody. Now hand me your gun." He tells me that young prick took his gun.

"Well, Flaherty," I say, "you could have overlooked the poor bastard that had his glasses on the dashboard."

What goes around comes around.

Every night after that, he asks Hank to walk him home. I say, "Look here Flaherty, you got some nerve. Your apartment is only a block and a half away. Poor old Hank, he has to walk back here."

He says, "But he doesn't have to worry about a gun and making out a report."

"No," I said, "But he has to worry about his life. He stays here, him and Chuck, and I drive them home. So they won't get mugged. And you're putting Hank's life at risk, and you have a gun."

After that, he stayed until I closed and I drove them all home. I liked it better that way because he had no problem using the gun when there was a stickup.

Flaherty was in very good shape at age sixty-nine. He was always talking about not drinking. Because he had a drinking problem, once he started, he couldn't stop until he got help. He always dressed in a suit and tie, but the one time I saw him drunk, it was sad.

I had been on vacation. I drove into work on a rainy Monday evening. As I pull into a parking spot, I see Flaherty coming down the street in the rain with no shoes. Because his socks are wet, they're half off his feet and coming off more with every step he takes. The socks flip back and forth.

I say, "Hey Flaherty, what happened to you?"

He lifts his head, gives me the long look trying to figure out who I am. It took him a couple of seconds, "Oh Stoney, I need help."

I say, "Do you have the gun on you?"

"Yes."

"Can I have it?"

"Yeah."

I get the gun and put it in the trunk of the car and he comes with me back into the La Salle where Jack is working. Jack says, "He wouldn't listen to us all week."

I say, "He knows he's got to stop or he's gonna die."

Jack says, "I'll work late tonight for you. See what you can do."

So I call Dan McRory and Paul McMoro; McRory was a cop in emergency service and Matt had just joined the FBI. Flaherty knew them and their fathers and mothers.

When they arrived, McRory says, "John, we'll take you to the hospital."

He says, "No you're not, taking me to no shithole. I'm going to Long Island." He fumbles for his wallet. "I got a card in here. The police department has a place on Long Island where they send cops to dry out."

"Okay," I say, "Let's go to the car."

McRory asks where his gun is and I tell him that Flaherty gave it to me and I'll give it to you. The last thing I need is to be pulled over with a police lieutenant's gun in the car. We drive him to Long Island and bring him into the front desk, and he's in bad shape. There's a young girl there, eighteen or nineteen. You could tell the job was new to her.

She said, "I have to ask you some questions, Mr. Flaherty. Are you allergic to anything?"

"Yesss," he says, "I'm allergic to bullshit!"

He was back out in three weeks and back to his old self— shined shoes, suit and tie—stopping in to see Jack at lunch hour on his way to the track, where he would always put on a bet for Jack.

I go into work one evening and Flaherty has a great story for me. He tells me that, "Because of all the construction going on across the street, I came in here at twelve noon. This place was full with construction guys. I look down the bar and see an undercover cop who's in the gambling squad. I see another guy at the phone and another guy at the door.

I sneak out down to Broadway so I can call Jack and tell him he's been raided. Then I have second thoughts. If I call Jack, he'll probably tell the guy with the hard hat to be careful—who I thought, by the way. I decided to go back and make like I walked in to use the bathroom. You need to do it fast; don't give the guy a chance to say anything. So I walk down the bar fast, spot the undercover, say, "Hey, how you doing? Nice to see you in the neighborhood. Let me introduce you to my friend, Jack."

'Well,' he says, 'that's not what I came up here for.'

"Then he called the guy off from the phone and he called the guy off from the door and he had two more guys outside. They would have taken Jack like Sherman took Richmond. I asked him why he was up here. He said an Irish woman called and said the bartender was running prostitution and gambling and we were sent up to close it down."

There was an old Jewish man, Sam, who took some bets. If Sam had been there and took a bet over the phone, Jack would have been closed down for three weeks.

Jack's partner had a son in the police. They decided to have a gold shield made for Flaherty and when they presented him with it, he was highly insulted. He tells me, "I saved them from being shut down with a mark on their license and they gave me a gold shield? I got a drawer full of that shit."

Flaherty, Hank and Chuck used to wait for me every night. While I was ringing off and packing away the beer, Flaherty used to run from the kitchen to the front door and then back. Then with a closed fist, he would hit his chest and say, "I'm in great shape. But, I have this pain in my chest, it's not bad but it's there."

Then he stopped coming in. We thought it was because of the gold shield. Two weeks went by. One day a detective, Mike Sheehan, come in. He knew everybody, so Jack asked him to check on Flaherty. He comes back in two days, and tells us, "I found him. He's in the St. Claire Hospital morgue. His toe is tagged. I got there just in time. Tomorrow he was going to a potter's field."

Mike Sheehan said what happened was that Flaherty checked himself into the hospital. When they asked him his next of kin, instead of their son who lives out on the Island, he gave his own address. The mail kept coming and the building super kept putting it under his door.

I must say I enjoyed him, and I miss him.

Chuck and Other LaSalle Characters

Now I must tell you about Chuck. Chuck was a small, skinny man. As a young man, he worked the coal mines in Pennsylvania and got black lung. When I met him, he was breathing bad and he drank Schenley whiskey and ginger every day. He would be in the La Salle every day when I got in until I drove him home. He drank very slow; he never got drunk.

One night I went in to use the bathroom. Chuck was in there after taking a leak and he was grunting and moaning because of his lungs and he can't get his penis in his pants because it's so big. I said, "I'll leave you to it. You'll make it."

The next day I said to Jack, "Do you know Chuck is deformed?" He knew right away and laughed. He said that twenty-five years ago, Chuck was the James Bond around here. One girl told the next girl and they all had to have him.

When I drove Flaherty, Hank and Chuck home, I made Chuck the last to drop off. I asked him how old he was when he started having sex. He said he was twelve. I asked, "With all the twelve- and thirteen-year-old girls?"

"Yes," he said, "plus my teacher. She was twenty-one years old and one day she asked me to stay late and she took me into the coal shed. After that, she took me in twice a week."

I said, "In a lot of cases young guys like to brag, but you never told anybody?"

"Never," he said, "In my day you never talked. A good thing was a good thing, and I was smart enough to know she would lose her job and I might go to a reformatory school. Back in Pennsylvania when I was a kid, you were taught to think like a smart old man. Not a young dumb one."

Working in the coal mines as a young man took its toll on his lungs. He had a small oxygen tank in his pocket and he walked very slow. He came from the doctor one day and showed us the papers: he only had eight months to live.

Let me explain that back then, every bar in New York at Christmas time gave the good customers a bottle of whatever it was they drank. Chuck drank Schenley Whiskey but because Jack knew Chuck is dying, he didn't give him a bottle. I thought it was very mean, but Chuck took it in good spirits. He said to Jack, "I know why. Because I may be gone." But poor Chuck didn't die, and next Christmas comes and Jack gives him a bottle.

At 5:00 a.m. Christmas morning, I drive Chuck home to his cheap hotel called Haten Hall. It had a doorman, but he was asleep half the time. I see Chuck to the elevator as usual. The next night I go into work and there is Chuck at the end of the bar. Somebody says he got mugged last night. I asked him how that could happen.

He told me that when he got off the elevator, two black guys were waiting for him. They took him into his room. One sat on him so he couldn't breathe and the other ransacked the room and left. Well, I said to him, at least Jack gave you a bottle this Christmas so you could have a drink, because you needed one, but he said they took that too.

Then there were the Henderson Sisters. Betty was a beauty. I was working there about a month when I met them. Flaherty was there and they came right down the bar to talk to him and stayed a few hours and then left. Flaherty says, "That woman that just left? Betty Henderson. One night you'll have to put her out and when you do, she'll piss on you. She wears no panties, and it will flow out of her."

Four to six weeks later, Betty came in on her own. She sat beside a guy in the middle of the bar. He's buying her drinks and Flaherty brings it to my attention. "Check what's going on with Betty and her new friend." I walk around the bar and Betty has her shawl thrown over his lap. She has his penis out and she's fondling his balls. I ask him and Betty to leave. He does.

Betty says, "I ain't leaving!"

I say, "Yes you are!"

She says, "Don't put your hands on me or I'll piss on you."

I can't believe she's telling me this. I grab her and I only get to the door before she spreads her legs. Holy Mackerel! It came out of her like the young mares back on the farm. I got her out and mopped the floor.

Flaherty said, "You were warned."

Then there was Harriet. She came from Wisconsin. She was in her fifties, but looked older. You could tell she had been good-looking. I was told that she was Jack's girlfriend for a time.

She told me her first husband was a salesman. They lived in a small apartment with a Murphy bed. One night she's in bed with a boyfriend and she hears the door opening. She jumps up, flips the bed into the wall, with the boyfriend in it, throws a nightgown on and meets her husband at the door.

"Oh, Honey, I was going out for cigarettes and milk. Would you be a doll?"

Off he goes. She runs to the Murphy bed and pulls it down. The boyfriend's almost out of breath.

"Come on! Get dressed and get out."

She runs to the fridge, pours the milk down the sink, hides the cigarettes, sits down and waits for hubby. That was too close for comfort!

She met a Jewish guy who took her to Florida. They had an argument, he broke her teeth and she went downhill from there. She would come in to the La Salle and people would always buy her drinks. She liked to play the jukebox. Jack didn't want nobody playing the jukebox when the races were on or when the Kennedys were on, but he never would unplug it.

Once, she plays the jukebox, Jack gets mad, comes out and unplugs it and then plugs it back in. Goes back behind the bar. Harriet plays it again. Jack, her ex-boyfriend, comes out from behind the bar and pushes her out the door; it's very cold outside. He goes back behind the bar and he looks to the door. There's Harriet back in, standing by the radiator with her skirt up above her waist.

Jack says very loud, "WHAT ARE YOU DOING NOW?"

Harriet says, "I'm warming your lunch."

Losing her teeth sent Harriet into a tailspin. What a bastard that did that. And she was a beautiful, fine-looking woman. She went downhill fast after that. She got sick, and started walking slow, like she had nothing to live for.

There was a supermarket at 90th Street on Broadway. I was coming into work one evening, down Broadway, and I see this tractor trailer backing up. I'm watching him because I used to drive a tractor trailer. Harriet is coming across the street behind the trailer. He gets a glimpse of her in the mirror and he gets a shock; he jumps out, comes running screaming at her, "I could have killed you lady!"

Harriet acted like she didn't hear him until she got one foot on the sidewalk, then turned real slow, looked at him straight in the face and said, "You'd have done me a fuckin' favor."

Harriet must have told the family lies back in Wisconsin about New York City being where the money was because when she died, she had nieces and nephews and a sister who came to New York wanting to know who stole her money.

In the end, they did a nice thing and they brought her back to Wisconsin. It made me feel very happy.

Harriet was a funny lady and had a heart of gold. R.I.P.

Bryant's Brothel

Lee Bryant lived upstairs in the same building as the La Salle. She would tell us all that she had no education; she was a very tough lady. She ran a brothel, using young girls, out-of-state students trying to pay their way through college, most times having them work out of their own apartments. She had a young black man, Lloyd, helping her run the business. He was a gentleman. He was a big man who always wore a suit and talked softly.

Lee often took in black runaways and had them do robberies for her. Bruce and Jason were two guys that she had for a while. There was another friend of hers, a guy who had a good job at Madison Square Garden, named Cecil. He was friends with both Lee and Lloyd, and he took Bruce under his wing.

They would hang out in the La Salle together and he would buy soda for Bruce and advise him to try and get away from Lee. Since I was there behind the bar, he would include me in the conversation and ask me my opinion. I became close to both of them.

One night Lee was drinking with some people from the building. She bought a round of drinks for the group with a traveler's check. The round was twenty-five dollars, but the check was stolen and it bounced. A few days later I meet her and tell her she owes the twenty-five dollars she did not pay, and she did not care. I told her I would not serve her until she paid. I kept that bounced check. She was mostly a day customer of Jack's, and he would serve her.

Another night I am behind the bar and the building superintendent is drinking by the door. She comes in and starts to argue with him and gets loud, using bad language.

I say, "Lee, keep it down."

She yells at me and says, "What? Are you eavesdropping on me you white, Irish, blue-eyed motherfucker?"

She finally left.

Two months go by and I come in for my evening shift and there she is with a group of her friends and they are buying the rounds. It's 7:00 p.m., and she must have thought I had forgotten about the check and felt guilty for drinking for free off her friends.

She says to me, "Let's forget the past. I want to buy my friends a drink," and she puts up a fifty-dollar bill. I give her friends a drink, ring it up, add the twenty-five dollars, give her change and wave the bad check at her. She goes ballistic; she storms out yelling, "I'll be back to get my money!" But she didn't come back and her friends left.

At 10:00 p.m., the bar is full and she storms in with Bruce. Bruce is carrying a large laundry bag. Before I can stop her, she is at the cash register. I grab her before she can open it and run her out the open end of the bar. Sitting there was a regular couple, Lucy and Pablo, a Puerto Rican guy who liked to say he was tough.

Lee shouts to Bruce, who takes a sawn-off shotgun from the bag and places the barrels on the bar between Lucy and Pablo. It was close enough to Pablo that he could have grabbed it and pointed it towards the ceiling. He always acted tough; if I was where he was, that is what I would have done. I'm not sure if it was my training in the LDF as a teenager, but that shotgun would be facing the ceiling.

Bruce calls me by my name, "Stoney, give her the money." I said I couldn't. By now, Lee is walking down the bar. My thoughts are to get away from the shotgun and, as I walk down the inside, I keep telling her I can't give her the money.

She yells out, "Shoot the Motherfucker!" and every customer who was sitting on a bar stool dives into booths, including my friend J. from Kerry. When Bruce doesn't pull the trigger, Lee yells, "Let's go!" He puts the shotgun over his shoulder and swaggers out like you would see in a western movie, carrying the laundry bag.

Everybody came back to their seats. My friend J. said to me, "Your face was white. Why didn't you give her the money?"

I said, "If I gave her the money, I would have to quit my job here since she would be running the bar, and I am not quitting yet."

Someone had called the cops and a sergeant and two cops arrived. I knew two of them well, Callaghan the sergeant from the robbery squad, and Bob.

Callaghan said, "You got robbed by two young guys?" I said, "Listen Callaghan, I was not robbed and I am making no complaint."

"Stoney, please. Off the record. I would like to hear your version of the events, because at 9:30 p.m., two young blacks with a laundry bag and a sawn-off shotgun stuck up the liquor store on Broadway and 108th Street."

Now I knew why Lee had not come back right away when she went to get Bruce; he was out with Jason doing a robbery. Being friendly with Bruce may have saved me.

Callaghan tells me that he and two cops will do a stakeout across the street from the La Salle, but their shift ends at 2:00 a.m. So the first night, they park across the street and at 2:00 a.m. Callaghan comes over and says they're leaving. He tells me to close my doors. I say, "Callaghan, you must be kidding. Lee probably knows you guys are parked across the street. She can get me anytime she wants."

They do this for three weeks; same routine; what a waste of manpower. One night it was raining and I see Jason at 1:00 a.m. with his two hands up against the bar window looking in at me. At 2:00 a.m., Callaghan and the two cops come to me to say they are leaving.

"It's amazing the balls of some guys," says Callaghan, "this little black guy was banging on the police car window asking us if we would go get him a pack of cigarettes from the bar since the bartender didn't like him. We told him to fuck off. We were not going to get out in the rain."

I started to laugh. I said, "Callaghan, that was one of your stickup men."

A few nights later, the cop I did not know so well stopped in to say that Callaghan had a plan. If I went to the front entrance of the building and pushed Lee's intercom and called her every bad name to piss her off, she would get her two boys and come down to get me, and then they would move in.

I said no, that Lee will know I got somebody backing me up, and then she will really get me. After that, they said they would be leaving the stakeout for good. I told them they were never any protection for me anyway.

At 3:30 a.m., Bob, the cop I knew, came in and said, "Stoney, I'm glad you didn't go for Callaghan's plan. He's desperate to get an arrest."

And I thought Callaghan was my friend.

Don't Get Flaked by Popeye Doyle

Every year the bar would get new customers, families would have sons, daughters, reaching legal age to drink, or some just come in to use the pay phone. One college guy, Luke Gallagher, used to come in with his girlfriend. He would talk about his brother, Bill, going to college in Arizona. He said that he was coming home for a few weeks and, "You got to meet him."

So one night he comes in with a guy on two metal crutches. He says, "Stoney, this is my brother Bill." I have a big hello for him. They order drinks, Bill has a Seagram's 7 with ginger ale. They stay for an hour before Luke and his girl left.

Bill stayed until closing, left and got a cab. He told me he lives six blocks away, on 96th Street. The next night, he is back and stays until closing; I am thinking it is a sad way to spend your weeks out of college. He did not drink to get drunk. I never asked about his legs, but it looked like polio.

When Bill had been coming in for about two weeks, a young black guy named Leroy started coming in to use the phone only. He would say hello, but never ask for a drink. On quiet nights he would stop and chat for a while. He told me his father was a cop. He looked like he was about seventeen years old and had the looks of a young Muhammad Ali. I asked him what he wanted to be when he got older? He said he wanted to own a stable of girls.

I say to him, "A brothel?"

He says. "Yes. That's where the money is."

He told me something else, also. Maybe he was trying to scare me. He told me that one night he had a problem with a guy, so he stole his father's gun and stuck it in the guy's mouth. "That guy knew where I'm coming from!" he says. Now, he said, he got three guys that hang out with him. Sure enough, the following night he walks in to use the phone, has a big hello for me, he has three Puerto Ricans with him. He uses the phone, smiles to me and says thank you, Stoney. He used to come in three or four times a week on his own or with his buddies.

One night at 2:00 a.m., only two customers are left, Rafferty with the sleeping disease snoring in a booth, and young Bill Gallagher at the bar with his crutches. In walks Leroy with a girl. He goes right to the phone. I could tell she was very new to this, but he had her under his spell.

While the two of them are at the phone, I see him pointing to Bill, telling her to go chat to him. She moves up beside Bill and starts chatting. Bill is thrilled to have a girl beside him and he buys her a drink. Leroy gets off the phone and leaves; Bill is in heaven. She goes to the bathroom and I see my chance.

I tell Bill, "You're being set up. Please make sure you don't leave with her."

"Don't worry Stoney. I am okay. She is so nice."

I walk away; there's nothing I can do with a young guy on crutches and a few drinks in him, who maybe never had a girl. Leroy comes back, says a few words to her and leaves. She helps Bill with his crutches and off they go.

It's 4:00 a.m. now, so I close the door and I put out the lights so I can watch them. They cross the street, then they are talking, and then she hails a taxi. As she gets the back door open, something is said that registers in Bill's brain. He won't get into the taxi. Instead, he starts back across the street and I see Leroy follow him. I know something is going down, so I run to the booth and pull Rafferty out of his stupor. I run him to the door and I yell, "You stand there."

I'm thinking that if something happens, having the extra person is important. I look out the window and I see Bill has reached the door. Leroy hits him and down he goes, and so does Leroy. I fly the door open and push Rafferty out and yell, "What are you doing?" Leroy is trying to get into Bill's pockets.

Leroy spins around with a gun in his hand, saying, "Get to fuck out of here."

I say, "Leroy are you going to kill all three of us?"

He walks away. I pick up Bill and his crutches and bring him inside. I sit both of them at the bar and give them a drink. Rafferty hadn't a clue what had just happened.

The next night my friend J. from Kerry is in and I am telling him about what happened, when in walks Leroy with a big smile and his three buddies. They all walk to the phone. I say to J., "I can't let them leave without saying something. Otherwise they got me, then I may as well quit."

I see Leroy getting off the phone and I walk to the front of the bar by the door. I still don't know what I am going to say. Here he comes with his crew behind him. As he gets to where I am, I say, "Leroy," and before I can say another word, he says, "What is it Stoney?" I say, "I don't want you in here anymore."

Then one of his buddies jumps on the footrest of the bar and says, "We will come in here any time we want and you won't do a fucking thing about it."

I have a genius flash in my head and I stick my face into his and say, "You decide to come in here again, I know enough cops in the twenty-four precincts to flake you guys with enough drugs to put you all away for twenty years!"

It worked. I never saw them again.

At that time, the Knapp Commission was investigating lots of cops. A detective, his nickname was Popeye Doyle, had made eight thousand arrests in his career and his detective partner was put on the stand to testify. He spills the beans and tells how they used to "flake people," but no one knew what this meant.

He explained they would be driving in an unmarked patrol car and Popeye would see someone he did not like the look of. He always kept drugs in a closed fist, so he would tell him to stop the car then he would jump out run over to the guy and slam him against a wall. Then he would put his hand in the guy's pocket and then pull out his open fist and say, "See, what have I got here?" A lot of innocent people were wronged.

At the time it was all over the papers, a famous movie was made about it, The French Connection. It was a big hit, with the actor Gene Hackman as Popeye Doyle. It is nice to know that ninety percent of cops, given the opportunity, want to be decent and do the right thing. But you still have a percentage of Popeye Doyles. I knew cops who carried an extra gun. They explained to me that when they stopped someone who had a gun, they would take it from him and tell him to fuck off and keep the gun. If they shot someone who did not have a gun, they would plant the spare gun and claim he had a gun.

Law Enforcement

The La Salle was a tough bar to work in for the eight years I was there. There were a lot of disputes. I took five guns and fourteen knives off guys and I gave them all to cops. The next night when these guys would ask for them back, I would tell them that I gave them to the cops. I got away with saying that because a lot of cops from the 20th, 24th and 26th Precincts hung out there until the Knapp Commission was set up.

After the Knapp Commission got rolling, cops couldn't drink in the precinct where they worked, but cops from the 20th and 26th Precincts still came in occasionally after work. Flaherty told me how to handle a situation if a sergeant comes in and cops from the local precinct are in the bar. He said to say, "Hi Sarge. I was having trouble with a customer and I saw the police car and ran out to ask the cops for help, and they put him out."

About a month went by and two cops I knew come in, in uniform. I was surprised, but I liked them so I give them a drink. They tell me they have a new sergeant, transferred from the 108th Precinct in Long Island City, Queens. I'm looking towards the door and I see this uniformed cop walking in. I grab the drinks and throw them down the sink so there's nothing on the bar. It was their new sergeant and, to my surprise, he was from my home place in Ireland, Dowra. I pretend not to recognize him, but I see the stripes.

I say, "Sergeant, I had a troublemaker, and I ran out into the street and I was lucky those two cops were driving by. They came in and got him to leave."

He puts his hand up at me, "Okay, I heard you."

They talk and leave. At 1:00 a.m., the same sergeant, Bob McGovern, comes back in civilian clothes. We have a big hello for each other and talk about Dowra, etc. Then he says, "Stoney, don't go out of your way to protect cops."

I stop him right there, "I was not fibbing to you when I told about the patrol car."

He says, "Okay."

The next night, I tell Flaherty about how he came back. "He was checking you out," says Flaherty. "If you told him the truth, he could never trust you. You did a good job."

I was very strong and I had a great technique for putting a guy out. I would come out from behind the bar and start talking to the guy who was giving me the most trouble. After I got him calmed down, he would drop his arms.

I would make like I was walking away, but I'd walk around the back of him. With his hands still down, I'd throw my hands around him from behind, lock my fingers and fly out the door backwards, all the way to the street, and drop him fast. I would run through his pockets, pull out the knife or gun, and run in shouting, "call the cops! call the cops!" After that, I'd lock the door and he would run way.

I had a few scary incidents. But first I'll talk about some of the characters. There were quite a few Irish and Irish-Americans in the neighborhood. There were Jackie Sullivan, McMoro, Frank Lynch, Donny Treller, and McRory. All those guys went to school together.

Jackie Sullivan, known as Sully, worked for the Port Authority, went on drugs, but held on to his job. He lived with his father, who was an alcoholic. They slept in the same bed, but they didn't get along, so they never talked. Sully would get up in the morning and go to work. The father would be on the other side of the bed sleeping. After work, Sully would stay out drinking and more until all hours. The father would be in the bed when he got back.

Sully woke up on a Sunday morning and decided to make coffee. While he was waiting for the water to boil, he realized there's a terrible smell. He checked the bed and the smell is the father. He called the cops and the ambulance. They took the body out. The next day the cops come to talk to him. They told him he had been sleeping with the corpse for three nights. It didn't seem to bother him, though. After his father died, he would come in to the La Salle in the mornings.

Jack, my boss, had known his father very well; he didn't like the idea of Sully sleeping with the corpse. One time, Sully is talking and Jack is answering, sometimes with a question. Finally, Sully leaves. Jack says, "Stoney, in this business you can handle piss. You can handle shit. You can handle corruption, but you can't handle piss, shit and corruption, and that's what just walked out that door."

About a year later, Sully hooked up with an old school buddy, Emmett Conlon, who taught at Columbia University, but was on heavy drugs. He had joined A.A. and he asked Sully to come with him. He did. They both quit drinking and smoking. Emmett went to California to become successful building houses. Sully saved his money, bought a house in Breezy Point, off the Rockaways, and lived there, enjoying the ocean.

Back when Sully was on whatever he was on, they would all go skiing on Hunter Mountain. Wherever they were going, they asked me to go with them and I did. My boss didn't like it.

One night Paul McMoro and I were standing in the middle of the floor. After the music stopped, Sully came running up, looked Paul straight in the eyes and said, "I know everything. Ask me anything. Anything. Come on, anything."

Paul says, "Who's the first president of the United States?"

Sully closes his eyes, shakes his head, opens his eyes, looks straight at Paul and says, "Ask me another one." Those damn drugs.

Paul became a building inspector. He said building owners would give him cigars wrapped in fifty-dollar bills. McRory always called him a genius and I reckon he was. But he was also a bully.

There was a building super, George, and his wife Patricia. They lived on Riverside Drive. Patricia would dance by herself and make jokes. She never bothered anybody. I would leave her in the bar while I was cleaning up. One night there was Nappy, a cop and a very nice man, and Paul, and Patricia dancing in her own little world. Paul and Nappy were sitting in the middle of the bar. Patricia danced over to them and said to Paul, laughing, "Would you like to dance?"

He spun around and, with his knee bent, he caught her in the stomach with his shoe and then flung her with all the power he could exert. She went flying backwards twenty feet and hit the wall. Down she goes and doesn't move. He yells, "Stay away from me, you dirty rotten scumbag." I went and picked her up and put her in a booth. She didn't move for a long time. Then I gave her a drink.

There came a knock on the window. It was Tommy from Kerry. He was bartending in McGlades on Columbus Avenue, one block up. He was double-parked outside with the warning lights on. Paul knew him to see, but didn't know him personally, but didn't like him. I opened the door and let him in.

Paul says, "Why did you open the door for that scumbag?" then continues with, "scumbags like you should stay on Columbus Avenue."

Tommy comes right into his face. "You take them words back."

Paul says, "I'll do better than that. I'll shove them down your fucking throat," and he jumps up.

They went at it, stools falling everywhere. I'm putting all the stools up on the bar to give them room. Nappy and I look at each other and I could tell from the look on Nappy's face that we both wanted the Kerryman to win this one. It went on seven to ten minutes. Finally, the Kerryman got Paul's legs under his arms and lifted him like a baby, and pinned his shoulders and head to the floor.

He says, "If you don't apologize, I'll snap your neck right now."

Paul was barely able to breathe, but he said it. "I apologize. I apologize."

The Kerryman said, "I don't think you mean it," and leaned harder. I thought his neck was going to snap.

Paul says, "I mean it! I mean it!" and he let him up.

Tommy says he's leaving. He goes out and his car won't start. He comes in and asks me if I could give him a boost. His battery is dead. Paul says, "I got cables," and tells Tommy he'd be right back. He goes away, gets his car, comes back, and gets Tommy started. They shake hands and off Tommy goes.

I say, "Paul I can't believe you gave up your parking spot to get him started."

"I respect him. He beat me fair and square."

I said, "Patricia can't beat you. She won't hurt you, and she may have to go to the hospital. She only asked you to dance. Maybe you can apologize to her."

"I don't apologize to no lowlife bitch."

Paul and another school buddy, Tim Bradley, joined the FBI. Bradley had two years of college. He was left in the New York Office. Paul had five years and he was brought down to

Washington, D.C. and when his mother passed away, he gave up his apartment on 90ᵗʰ and Columbus.

The FBI wanted him to infiltrate the Chinese coke and heroin cartels. They sent him to China for two years to learn Chinese. This was where his genius showed. After he came back from China, he met up with his friend Dan McRory in their favorite restaurant, the Red Blazer. McRory knew the owner, Dennis Carey. McRory was in doubt that Paul could speak Chinese. He asked Dennis if he could bring some of the Chinese porters out of the kitchen to talk to Paul. "Sure", says Dennis, "but don't hold them up too long. As you can see, it's busy."

McRory had two Chinese porters come out and talk to Paul. The two Chinese boys were impressed. Later on, he brought out the chef and the assistant. Later, the chef told McRory, not only does your friend speak Chinese but he speaks different dialects. McRory is right; he is a genius. Paul went back to Washington for a year and then came back to New York with an FBI friend who lived in Bayside, Queens.

They came to the La Salle. Paul asked me if I had anybody living with me in my house in Flushing. I told him not right now. Paul says my friend here wants me to stay with him, but he has a wife and kids. I'd prefer to stay with you and get a good night's sleep. I said I always leave the back door open. All you have to do is walk right in, take the bedroom on the right. And off they go.

I close up and get home at 6:00 a.m. Paul is in bed, but awake. He tells me he had just gone to sleep, but he woke up with two big flashlights shining in his face and somebody asking him who is he. He explained he's FBI and shows them ID. They tell him the next-door neighbor called saying there was a prowler next door. We talked for a while, then he goes to bed and I go to my room.

I'm almost asleep when I hear noise. I open my eyes and Paul is in my room, opening the dresser drawers. I say, "What's wrong Paul?"

He says, "I'm missing my three thousand dollars." I jump up. I say, "Where did you have it?"

"In my pocket," he says.

"Paul," I said, "I just came in. How could I have it?"

He said, "The two cops stole it. I'm going to the precinct."

"I'm going with you."

We get to the precinct and he demands and gets into the Captain's office. He was Italian, what a cool guy. The Captain says, "Before we call the IAD and maybe destroy those officers' names, did you look everywhere?"

So Paul explains, "There was nobody in that room, but me and the two officers. They took my money."

"Ok," says the Captain, "let's call IAD before the cops come in off their shift."

We're sitting there in the 109th Precinct and in walk two women in their fifties, rumpled clothes and granny shoes. They looked like they had just milked cows and one of them had an Irish accent. I've heard guys say they could spot a cop fifty yards away; well, those two would fool cops.

Paul and I come out in the hallway; Paul says to me, "You've got to work tonight, go home."

I say, "Paul, you were in my room, going through my drawers. You think I took your money. I ain't leaving your sight until this is solved."

There was a public phone on the wall. Paul says, "I got to call my friend. Let him know the story." He calls his friend and tells him how the cops were in his room last night and stole his three thousand dollars and he's in the 109th lodging a complaint against the cops and IAD is here to interrogate them when they come in off their shift.

Maybe it was good Paul went the whole nine yards telling his friend, because his friend says, "I've got your money."

"How?" says Paul.

His friend says, "I came out of the house and I saw something on the street at the passenger side door and I picked it up. I knew it had to be yours. You were tired, so I thought I'll give it to you tomorrow."

Now Paul has to go back in and tell IAD and the Captain how he found his money. Paul kept saying, "You understand where I'm coming from?"

But the Captain says, "No, I don't. You were prepared to bring down two good men."

Paul was Federal Narcotics. He was a good Federal agent and he was against all dope. He stayed with me for a few nights after the money incident. Two nephews and one niece of mine stopped by on their way to California, wanted to stay over, sleep on the floor and smoke dope. They're in the kitchen talking to Paul, they were not smoking yet, and Paul tells them he's a Federal Narcotics agent.

I'm in the living room when James, the oldest nephew, comes running in and says, "That guy in the kitchen, he's a Federal Narcotics agent."

I say, "Yes."

He says, "Can I smoke a joint in front of him?"

"Why?" I say.

"Oh," he says, "I just want to be able to say I smoked dope in front of a Federal Narcotics Agent."

"You go ahead, I don't think anything will happen."

Paul only made a comment that it shouldn't be done, but he did care. Then again, back in the La Salle, Patricia should not have been kicked either, and I cared.

His friend, Tim Bradley, stayed in the New York FBI office for a year or two. He was told to study and he did, but in the meantime, one of his jobs was going to doctors' offices with an older FBI agent, checking up on how the doctors distributed pills and how they kept their books. They were doing this for a month when they went into a doctor's office on Fifth Avenue and asked to look at his books. The doctor tells them he has an assistant, Mr. Flannery, who does all his books, so they go in the back and explain who they are. They need to see the books. Flannery gets very nervous and tells them he keeps them at home. They say fine, they'll give him two days to get all the books and records. "See you in two days."

After they leave, Bradley's partner says, "I don't like what I see. That guy Flannery is too nervous. We'll call the office, and give them the lowdown. See if we can get a surveillance on his apartment." They were told to watch the apartment for twenty-four hours. That evening Flannery packed up and took a cab to the airport. They approached him as he bought his ticket.

They brought him to the FBI office, interrogated him and he broke. He tells the FBI that he had been a priest for ten years, that he is gay and his roommate and lover was another priest, Father Cooke. Cooke was in love with him and still is; he wrote him very intimate letters, which he kept in a strong box. Cooke went his way, and Flannery went his. He got a new apartment and a new roommate and a new job in the doctor's office. Years went by and Cooke became the Cardinal of New York, the richest Catholic Diocese in the United States.

Flannery said his new roommate was an Italian named Joey; claimed he was tied to the mob. While he was at work, Joey broke into his strong box, found the letters and stole them. Then he came to Flannery and told him to give him all the drugs he wanted and he wouldn't go to the press. And that's how that all started.

They leave Flannery in the room and they go to their bosses. They get scared. Cooke is a faggot, holy shit! We better call Washington. The boys in Washington tell Hoover. Every law enforcement agency in the country was scared of J. Edgar Hoover, but it was a known fact he was a cross-dresser, and back then careers were lost on silly stuff like that.

Hoover gives the order: find Joey, get the letters, kill him if you have to. Flannery lost his job and disappeared. No jail time.

What interested me about all of this was Bradley's reaction. Here is a guy who, with his parents' consent, joined the Air Force very young, flew million-dollar planes in Vietnam, came back wounded to the State of Utah, and, with three more buddies on crutches, got refused a beer because they were not twenty-one years of age. But he was so happy the way the Flannery case turned out. "My poor mother," he says, "if she ever thought there were gays in the Catholic Church, she would have a heart attack."

I don't know how long she lived, but she could have learned a lot about the Catholic Church.

Junkies, Drugs and Money

Donny Treller was one of the group's school buddies. He became a junkie and robbed everybody. His specialty was break-ins. He would get caught and be sent to Rikers Island jail, one time for nine months. I asked him how he could go nine months without heroin, then come out and do it again.

He said, "Once you know you can't get it, then you psych yourself up. It's easy. You do the time, but when you get out, you already know where it is and you just have to have it."

I asked him about break-ins, how did he know where to look in a house? He said, "You check the inside of toilet paper rolls, pull out drawers and look underneath, some people tape money to the bottom, or under the mattress, or under the bed, and, last but not least, you rip up the carpets."

Now I know why homes that are robbed are left a mess.

Like all junkies, he worked by his wits. One day, McRory was there with a young cop and he had to leave, but the young cop stayed. Donny moved in on him, telling him how he had given cops tips in the past. The young cop asks, would he have a tip for me? Donny says he knows a few heroin dens, but if he wants them, he'll give them up for three hundred dollars.

The young cop came back three days later and gave Donny the three hundred. Donny gave him two fake addresses and left. When the young cop realized he had been taken, he went to McRory, and McRory went to Donny, telling him he better give the money back or some guys will come up from downtown and beat it out of him. Donny stood his ground, told McRory the entire precinct can come up. He never gave it back.

He came into the bar one night and says to me, "I hear you're looking for a remote color TV." At that time remotes were very hard to find. I told him, "I went to a few stores, but they're all on back order."

He hung around for a while watching the TV. A customer asked me to put on a sports channel and when I did, Treller turns around and says, "Stoney, that's a remote TV." I said it was. "Can you leave the back door unlocked and I'll have a remote TV for you tomorrow evening."

He got caught shortly afterward and did more time in Rikers. Came out clean of drugs and looking good. He hooked up with a neighborhood girl, Susie, who he knew from school. Her mother was from back home with the bar owner, Jack. Susie never took drugs, never drank. She wasn't too bright and could be conned into doing anything. She thought it was the greatest thing that Donny was off the drugs.

He asked her to marry him and down they went to City Hall. They came back to the bar with some friends and family. Her father, who I had never met because he never drank, came in. He voiced his objection with disgust and left. Three weeks later Donny comes in nodding on heroin. I told myself that it's time to keep an eye on him.

One night I'm chatting with Lieutenant Flaherty. A regular customer comes in and he says, "I'm two blocks away and there's a girl lying on the sidewalk asking for help. When I go to help her up, a guy appears out of nowhere shouting, 'You're robbing my wife. Now I'm going to rob you. Give me all your money.' I broke loose and ran here."

About twenty minutes later, Donny and his new wife, Susie, walk in. The customer says, "Oh my God, oh my God, that's them, that's them." They walk out; nothing was done.

Some time passed and Donny would come and go. One night I'm ready to leave and I see him outside. I decide to stay inside. When he realizes I'm not coming out, he uses sweet-talk first. He only wants a pack of cigarettes. I yell that the machine is broke.

He says it wasn't broke early today. "Let me in, I need to take a leak."

"Go between the cars like you always do."

Then he loses it and starts banging on the door. I say, "Donny, let me give you two cigarettes. I'll push them out to you under the door." Finally, he went across the street where I could see him. If he was having a bad trip, as they call it, I could have been in trouble.

A week or two went by. I went into work and there were Donny and Susie talking to a tall southern truck driver. He left with them. The next day the truck driver was still with them. Donny tells me they're all going south to Memphis, Tennessee for a new start in life. The truck driver was a very shady dude; he never spoke to me, never looked me in the eye. I thought at first that I should wise him up as to who he was with. Then I thought to myself he might rob me.

That night they all headed south. About five weeks later, Donny is back. He needs money from his mother-in-law Winnie. Susie is dead in Tennessee, run over by a truck. Winnie brought the body back to New York and buried it.

They had no money for a lawyer to go to Tennessee and check into foul play. Donny seemed to have money for a while. McRory got talking to him one evening, for all the good it did. McRory said to him, "Donny Baby, you're smart. You took her south and you got that lowlife trucker to run her over and you and him collected the insurance. It's too far away to get lawyers to prove it. But you did it, Donny. Right, you did it."

It was the first time I saw Donny not talking. He just stared McRory in the face for a long time, and says to McRory, "I think you got it wrong."

Nothing ever came of it.

Army or Post Office

McRory, Paul, Donny Treller and Tommy Lynch were all about the same age. Tommy Lynch had a younger brother, Francy, who was twenty-one, five foot three inches tall and weighed two hundred and eighty pounds. When he got called for the Army, everybody was surprised they took him. He did his training in Fort Dix, in New Jersey. He always seemed to be a nice young man. I liked him.

Ten or twelve months went by and one Saturday night he walked into the La Salle with a friend, both in Army uniforms. He was so thin I didn't recognize him. Now he's five foot three inches, one hundred and twenty pounds and looking fantastic. I asked him where the other half of him went.

He tells me that they are being shipped out to Vietnam the next Monday morning. I let them stay late, bought them some drinks and I shook his hand and wished him luck and a safe return.

A year went by. We heard that he went out on a patrol with his buddy, I don't know if it was the guy I met. They came back into the big tent with big wide tables where they ate and played cards. They threw their guns on the table and started playing cards. Then they got into an argument and Francy grabbed his gun and opened fire on his buddy across the table, killing him instantly.

There was a lot of bad stuff going on in Vietnam and some of it got out to the press. It was big news when a Lieutenant Calley killed twenty-five women and children, an entire village. He got court-martialed. The Army didn't want more bad news getting out.

Francy got a disorderly discharge and he walked free. He moved out of the neighborhood and nobody had seen him in a year and a half. One night in he walks, all two hundred and eighty pounds of him back again, wearing a postman's uniform.

At the time postmen were getting bad press for going nuts at work and shooting up post offices and colleagues. When I saw him in the postman uniform, I said to myself, he's got the perfect job. He'll go nuts again.

I figured it was okay, so I gave him a drink. There were about twenty people in the bar. There was a local guy, Buddy, who liked to think he was kind of tough. There was Puerto Rican named George, very nice man, and Jack Santos, a nice guy but always complaining. Santos was drinking at a table with two older guys. Lynch staggers over to them and starts talking.

Santos calls me, "Stoney, come out here." I go out. Santos whispers in my ear, "Lynch has a gun. He's threatening us."

If anybody other than Santos had told me I'd have took them seriously. I said, "Okay, Jack, I'll take care of it."

So I put my hands on Francy's shoulders and I say, "Listen, you haven't been around for a long time. Those guys want to gang up on you. Now you and I know each other, so you know what I'll do? I'll get you out and lock those guys in; then you'll be safe."

He goes for it and says, "Yeah, yeah, okay." I get him out, but I never frisked him, which I usually did, because I thought Jack Santos was doing his complaining act. I lock the door. I'm so proud of myself. I figure I'll have fun and stay inside by the door. When Francy realizes he's locked out, he starts shouting to get back in. There was a small pane of glass in the door and I would put my ear to it and then I'd shout, "I can't hear you!"

I take my ear off the glass and look out. And Jack Santos was right. Lynch has a gun in his hand! I run from the door and duck behind a brick wall under the big window and I yell, "Hit the floor! He's got a gun!"

Well, he empties the gun in through the window. After, I stand up, look out and he's gone. So I open the door. Buddy says, "Are you crazy? Keep the door closed. He'll be back."

I say, "He ain't coming back. It's impossible that a guy puts five or six rounds through a window and then comes back. I'm open for business."

"Well, fuck you," says Buddy. "I'm leaving." And he did.

Puerto Rican George very quietly calls me over and says, "I'm hit."

"Where George?"

"On my neck,"

And sure enough a bullet just nicked him. There was blood. I say, "Come on George. You'd get a worse cut shaving. Have a few drinks, you're ok," and I walk behind the bar. I wasn't going to call cops, but Santos got George's ear, telling him he could sue and George says, "Stoney, I need an ambulance".

"Okay, George. I'll call the cops."

The cops arrive, start taking down all the information, and in walks Paul, the FBI agent, just in from Washington, D.C. He asks me what happened. I tell him Francy shot up the place. Paul says, without moving from where he sat, he says, to the sergeant, "You want Francy? He's handcuffed to a lamp pole down the block."

Paul shows the sergeant his shield and says, "I know the guy and his brother." He says, "As I parked my car and I'm getting out, I see Francy coming across the street towards me with a gun, so I pull out my gun. He comes right up to me, and says, 'Give me your money.' I hit the gun out of his hand and put my gun to his head and say, 'How about your money?' Paul laughs. "You know what he said to me? 'My first victim and he's got a gun.'"

Two weeks later, I get off the subway and I'm walking up Broadway and I see Francy a block away, coming towards me. He's wearing a trench coat down to his ankles. I walk across the street so I won't meet him. I get into work and tell them how I saw Francy and I crossed the street.

A customer says, "Are you scared, Stoney?"

"Well," I say, "If the guy is carrying a handgun when he's wearing a postman uniform, if he's wearing a trench coat down to his ankles, he must be carrying a shotgun." That was the last I saw or heard of him.

The Boys in Blue

McRory like his friend Paul joined law enforcement and he became a New York City cop. He would talk to people as if he wasn't in uniform, always using common sense. You would have to be very bad before he would give you a ticket.

After the Police Academy training, they were all lined up and told what precinct they were going to work in. A lot of the young cops wanted to go to a quiet precinct. When they called out, "Dan McRory, 26th Precinct, Harlem," he jumped in the air with joy. He wanted all the action he could get.

He was put on the night shift with an old Irish guy, Sweeney. First night on patrol in a police car, Sweeney says to him, "Listen here, Kid. You don't have to worry about the blacks up here. There is still a percentage of Irish up here and they're the bastards you've got to watch out for.

"There's a brother and sister team called Scanlon," he says. "My partner and I locked him up one night. We brought him into the precinct, took the cuffs off him before putting him in the cell and he went haywire. He beat us bad before the other cops got to him and we got him in the cell.

"A few months went by and we knew he was out. We knew something else. He wasn't that good a fighter when he was drunk. We had the midnight to 8:00 a.m. shift and we were watching all the bars, and one night at 4:00 a.m., we spotted him stumbling out of a bar on his own.

We throw him in the back seat of the patrol car and drive into Central Park, pull him out and beat him until we were tired. Then we threw him against a tree and as we're walking back to the car, he yells, 'Sweeney!' We turn around; he's using the tree to pull himself up, and he's got his two hands grabbing his balls. He says, 'Ha, Sweeney! I got your mother by the throat.' We were going to go back, but we were too tired. Kid, these are the guys you watch out for, not the blacks."

McRory gets a new, older, black partner named Frank. One night on patrol, they spot a car on a quiet street. It was shaking back and forth and Frank stops a few cars back, gets out and walks up to the car and bangs on the window. The poor guy in the car was nude, with a woman. Frank says, "If you go to a motel you pay, and it so happens you're in my motel." The guy reaches for his pants and takes care of Frank. Frank got transferred and became an instructor at the Police Academy.

After that, McRory was put on foot patrol. He's walking the beat off 125th Street one night when a cab pulls up. A passenger gets out and walks away. The cab driver jumps out and shouts, "Officer! He won't pay me."

McRory follows him into the hallway of a building, takes off his hat and shouts, "Hold up there a minute!" The guy spins around and fires one round, hitting McRory.

Somebody called the cops. They searched the building and got the guy. The bullet had hit McRory's shield dead center and put a big dent in it. When his shift is over, he comes into the La Salle to tell his friend Lieutenant Flaherty. He shows Flaherty the incident report he has written up. Flaherty could be a little too much for the detail. McRory shows him his shield with the dent and tells him how he took his hat off.

Flaherty says, "Listen young man, you got to be careful how you word this. You may get a complaint that you had your hat off. That means you were out of uniform."

McRory says, "I could be dead and you're talking about a complaint?"

After that ordeal, he gets transferred downtown. His new partner is Bobby Gates. Bobby enjoyed McRory so much. He'd laugh at anything he would say.

One day they're on foot patrol on Second Avenue and 11th Street. There's a lot of junkies and prostitutes. They see this junkie coming towards them, bobbing and weaving.

Knowing that Gates might laugh, McRory says, "Listen here Bobby, don't you laugh."

The junkie says, "Hello, Officers, I wwaas going to woork."

McRory says, "You're going nowhere. You're a junkie. You got no job. Get out of here."

The junkie says, "YYooul Caant Taallkk Tooo Mee Llikke Thhatt. I I'm a Huumminee B Beenn".

McRory says, "You're not a human being, you're a shit machine. You should be used for parts." He turns to Gates, but he's walking down the street, laughing.

He's working on Lexington, a hangout for streetwalkers and he notices that ninety percent of the cars picking up the prostitutes have New Jersey plates. He starts pulling them over for kicks and he notices all the drivers with New Jersey plates have Italian names.

He says to one Italian who was rude, "What is it with you ginnys? Are there no whores in New Jersey? Your wives or girl-friends are starving for sex because you guys say, I respect them, and put them up on a pedestal, then come over to New York to get a blow job from some dirty whores."

McRory pulls over a guy who was talking to a prostitute.

He says, "What are you doing?"

The guy says, "Nothing."

"What do you mean nothing?"

The guy makes an excuse; he was looking for directions. McRory asks for his license. When he sees the guy's address is Hicksville, Long Island, he says to the guy, "Do you see any hay coming from under my hat?"

The guy says, "What?"

McRory says, "Do you see any hay coming from under my hat?"

The guy says, "No."

"That's right," says McRory, "You're from Hicksville. Don't try to fool a cop in the Big Apple. Get out of here!"

It was very hard to get into the Emergency Squad, but he got in and he loved it. You would see him in the front page of newspapers a lot. He was perfect for it. He loved heights and the smell of dead bodies didn't bother him. He never wore a mask. He said if you could do it, it was best not to wear one. He said some guys that wear masks get sick in them and then they're worse off.

McRory would always give credit where credit was due. When Emergency got its first female, none of the guys in the squad liked it. Her first partner made it so hard for her that she asked for another one and she got McRory. He told me that on his first day with her, he was so happy.

On 23rd Street and the waterfront, they got a ripe one, which means a body that's been dead for a week and is falling apart. When they got there, they put plywood under the body and lifted it onto the dock. Everything had to be accounted for before it goes in the bag and he told her that he would hold the bag while she pushed it in. When she started, the body started to break into pieces. Her stomach and throat were making attempts to vomit, but she wouldn't give in until she had it all in the bag. "You pass the test baby. You're one of us," he says.

Like he said, every part of the body must be accounted for. A guy broke a window on the ninetieth floor of the Twin Towers and jumped. At ninety stories, the body splattered. They found all of the body, but one of his balls was missing. They were going to fill out the paperwork saying he only had one ball. Instead, they tied up traffic for an extra two hours until they found his ball two-and-a-half blocks away. "Let's get his ball in the bag and open up the street to traffic!"

One time it was rush hour. McRory and his partner were on Third Avenue and 44th Street in Manhattan. A call came in reporting a bad accident in the Bronx. He said to his partner, "Let's put on the siren and go for it!"

They get to 60th Street and he notices a car riding behind him. He stops, goes back, asks the guy for his license and registration, says to the guy, "You like following police trucks? Then follow me." He brought the guy all the way to the Bronx and gave him his license and registration back.

They were once called to the forty-fifth floor of an office building on Wall Street. Two emergency trucks, McRory, his partner, a sergeant and a cop all show up. It turns out it was a false alarm, so they get back into the elevator and the sergeant gets in last as he wants to be out first.

The elevator cable snaps on the thirty-eighth floor and the elevator takes off. It didn't look good, but the elevator stopped on the eleventh floor. They all get out and walk to the street. The sergeant goes to the truck to call in.

When he is gone, McRory's partner asks him what he was thinking when the cable snapped. He said, "I thought it was all over. What were you thinking?"

He said, "I was watching the floors. When it got to the third, I was going to jump on the sergeant's back to cushion the crash. I never liked him anyway."

On a very hot July morning, he had a rookie cop with him. They were dispatched to Bruckner Boulevard near where there were four blocks on 150th Street where trucks carrying long steel girders would park. They arrive at the scene and their job was to keep an eye on the body. What happened was an old Puerto Rican man, on his way home from church, stopped at a bakery and picked up a half dozen bread rolls and put them in the back seat of his car. He was driving down Bruckner Boulevard past the trucks carrying steel and loses control. His car goes under the steel, which comes through the windshield, catches his forehead, and, like a razor blade, slices the top of his head right off. The top of the head landed in the back seat, but the body stayed behind the wheel.

The top brass told McRory and his rookie partner to stay with the body until the ambulance arrived. McRory is there taking no notice of anything, telling stories, when he glances in the back seat, sees the top of the head, grabs the hair and puts it back on the head behind the wheel, and keeps on talking. Then he sees the rolls, reaches in, takes one and starts eating it. That did it for the rookie. He got sick and vomited. Later, I asked McRory why he moved the top of the head.

He said, "It seemed like the normal thing to do. Put it back where it belonged."

He bought five bungalows in Rockaway, very run-down. The electric went out and he asked me to fix it, which I did. Temporarily. I told him the main feed was pulled out of the pole outside. He had to call Con Edison.

"McRory," I said, "my old boss, Harry Odem, was a licensed electrician. Him and I was called to repair a job somebody else installed and Harry was going around in circles for over an hour. Then Harry said, 'I see what he done. When you're wiring a job that has motors working off temperature-control windows with louvres opening to let air in, closing when it gets cold, there are different ways it can be wired.' He said, 'When I was a young electrician, I would always do what I did here, trace the wires and see what the other guy did. Today, they're lazy and they want to look good in front of the customer, so they run down the other guys' work.'

"McRory," I said, "what I did here is perfectly legal. But don't' be surprised when the guy comes, that he may talk bad about me."

He comes into the bar two nights later. "Stoney," he says, "the guy looked and said, 'Ah! I got to get a ladder.' He went up the ladder and without taking a tool out of his pouch, said, 'What fucking idiot did this?'"

Was I glad I told him the story, because otherwise McRory would be doubting me.

McRory had one bad fault; he never wanted to lose an argument. Down in the precinct's locker room, Joe the Italian and McRory is slagging each other. Joe wins the argument. The next morning, McRory goes to his wife's chest of drawers, takes a pair of her panties, puts them in his pocket and goes to work. They're all sitting around having coffee when the Sergeant comes in, "Okay, gentlemen, time to go to work."

McRory pulls the panties out of his pocket and says, "I almost forgot Joe, here's your wife's panties. I took them by mistake."

Horses or Mules

There were quite a few Irish still living on the West Side in the 1970s. I'll talk a little about a few of them. As customers, there was Hughie O'Connor from County Cork. Him and his son owned two horse and carriages. They drove around Central Park. Hughie was also a blacksmith and he put shoes on all the Police Department horses.

Back in the 1960s, when I was driving with Jimmy Reese during the Civil Rights era, they told me Dr. Martin Luther King was doing a march and he was using mules. The southern establishment blocked the march, saying the mules must have shoes when walking on the road surface. The local governments stopped all blacksmiths from putting shoes on mules. The organizers brought twenty-five mules to the New York Police Department. Hughie O'Connor put the shoes on them and they were trucked back south for the march. When I was told this I found it very interesting.

Then there was Brendan O'Mara from County Galway, who worked in an insane asylum in Galway City and refused to leave his mother until she died, so he came to America late in life. He was in his forties, which is old for coming to a new country. He got a doorman's job, lived in a room and spent his day off in the La Salle. Jack the owner, who was also from Galway, said Brendan loved only two women, his mother and the Blessed Virgin. He sat at the bar but talked to nobody. He smoked cigarettes only halfway and lined them up around the ashtray until the circle was complete. Then he would ask me to empty it.

One evening, a young, obviously gay man comes in, orders a drink alongside Brendan and starts talking about politics. Brendan says he don't know and turns his back. The young man walks around, faces Brendan and starts talking. Brendan says he don't know and turns again. The young man really wanted to talk to Brendan and goes around again. Brendan says, "You know what's wrong with you? It's called mental deficiency. You're nuts," and he turns his back again. The young man tried one more time.

I was just about to speak to him when Brendan says, "Listen fellow, if I was born in Switzerland, I'd be a watchmaker. If I was born in Germany, I'd be an engineer. I was born in Ireland and two plus two is five. Don't blame me; blame the guy who taught me."

I said to the young man, "That's it. You leave the gentleman alone or you leave." But I loved Brendan's answer.

Then there was Hughie Molee and Mike Mullins, both from County Mayo. Molee worked very hard in construction, sometimes seven days a week, never married, drank hard every night and never missed a day at work. They both lived together for a time in an elevator building. One night Molee went home early. Mike went home an hour later. Clearly, nobody had come into the building after Molee, because when Mike walked in, there was a big, big hole in front of the open elevator door. Mike wonders if Molee is down there and starts shouting his name. Then Molee starts to answer with groans, so Mike calls the cops and an ambulance takes Molee to the hospital with a broken leg.

He got a plaster of Paris cast from his toes to the cheek of his ass. People started to tell him he should sue and the building insurance man came and talked to him. He tells them he was going to wait until the cast came off, but they give him a few hundred dollars. Molee thought it was great. He would play the jukebox and start dancing with the plaster leg. The insurance guy showed him pictures of himself dancing with the leg and told him he should settle. And he did, for five hundred dollars.

He went to live by himself on 108th Street, off Amsterdam Avenue. He had a bed and that was it. He started working for a church on 99th Street and the priest gave him two chairs and a table. He asked me if I would bring them up to his new apartment and I said I would, but he had to wait until I closed.

At 4:30 a.m., we drove the table and chairs over to his apartment building. I got the two chairs and he got the table. I was going up the stairs ahead of him and I get to the second floor, there's the door open. He says that it's in there, I say but the door is open. He says the only thing of value is the lock and he doesn't want them to break it.

He had a brother in Boston who owned a bar and restaurant, a mini supermarket and a laundromat.

Molee told me about a terrible tragedy his brother and his wife had.

His brother was digging out the basement in the supermarket to make more headroom and he moved all the old stoves and fridges to one side. He would fill the truck full of the clay and bring it to the dump. His eight-year-old son used to go with him. One evening, he was leaving at 7:00 p.m. The mother said that it was too late. He shouldn't take him with him. The son said he wanted to go, but the mother said no.

When he came back from the dump at 10:00 p.m., the mother says where's the kid? He says that he didn't take him. They call the cops. The search is started and there's no sign of him. A week later, he's moving the fridges in the basement and he opens one of the doors, and there is the kid. They think he ran and hid when the mother made him stay home. She was never the same after that.

Back in Ireland, the same week, his sister's seven-year-old son was run over by a car and killed while coming home from school.

Molee was very rough around the edges, but everything he said, he said with a smile. So he got away with everything. The cops in the precinct knew him and liked him. Back then you could drink beer on a construction site. He was working two blocks from the La Salle one lunch hour with a black partner as crazy as himself. He came flying in the door with the black partner in a wheelbarrow, telling Jack he needs a double before he can stand up. There was a woman with a camera and she says, "Stay in the wheelbarrow, I got to get a picture."

One Saturday, his day off, Jack couldn't take him anymore and pushed him out and told him to stay out. Molee knew a guy named Rafferty who worked in Clairmount Stables around the corner on 89th Street. He was always asleep. They say it's a disease you get from horses. Molee ran in and shook the hell out of him and brought him outside.

Rafferty didn't know what was going on but he would always do anything you asked him to for a drink. Hughie gives Rafferty forty dollars, sends him to the liquor store one-and-a-half blocks away, and tells him to get two bottles of different liquors, some plastic cups, and soda and ginger ale.

When he comes back, Molee sets up everything on the window outside and starts shouting, "New bar! New bar drinks cheaper out here!" Some people did come and Rafferty loved his free booze. Jack just kept on working and never looked out.

When Molee didn't show up in the La Salle for a few days, Jack sent somebody to check on him. They found him dead. All anybody knew was that he had a brother in Boston, but nobody knew where in Boston. We knew a detective in the 24th Precinct, named Mike Sheehan, who also knew Molee. He became well known later for arresting the "Preppy Killer," Robert Chambers, in 1986. Jack asked Sheehan if he could try and locate anybody belonging to Molee. Jack knew of a sister in Ireland and got a collection going for the funeral. It was amazing all the money that was collected. We waked him in the local funeral parlor.

Sheehan came in before the wake. He had traced a sister to London and she had given him the brother's full name and phone number. So he called Boston, and the brother was on his way down right now. He gave him the name of the funeral parlor. That night, when his brother walked in, there were twenty-seven people there, including Sheehan and a few cops in uniform. The brother was so impressed he could not believe his eyes. He said, "We always thought Hughie would die without a friend and be buried in a potter's field, and we'd never know a thing." It was great seeing the smile on the brother's face.

Talking about funeral parlors, there was a Jewish funeral parlor one block from the La Salle bar on 91st Street. They hired an Italian immigrant, Sal. What a trickster! He had a very outgoing personality and spoke broken English. They paid him very little but they let him sleep in the basement with the bodies. He told me they were training him how to embalm the bodies and have them looking nice for the family at wakes. One night I was going to call for Chinese food. Sal was in the bar and he said, "Oh, I'll go and get it for you. It will be much faster."

I gave him twenty dollars and he went to a bar on 89th Street and Broadway, Willoughby's. I knew the bartender there,

Fast Eddy. Sal was gone a long time and he came back high and said he got mugged, but it was clear he drank my twenty dollars in another bar.

On another night he came and said it was his birthday and he wanted to get drunk. He asked me what the strongest drink in the bar was and I said 151 Bacardi Rum, ninety-five cents a shot. He counted out four dollars and said give me four of them, and I gave him one on the house, and ginger ale on the side. He drank them straight down and walked out. He came back at 3:00 a.m. with two big buckets and said his boss had sent him for ice, so he loaded up from the bar's ice machine.

The next evening I am working behind the bar and it is very busy. I see this little Jewish-looking man standing by the door and he looks nervous. He just stays close to the door, I guess he was asking himself, should he stay or should he go.

Probably he was never in a bar in his life and now he finds himself in the La Salle with fifty people screaming and shouting, but he had to talk to me. After ten minutes I look at him and shout at him, "Can I help you?"

In a low voice he says, "Can I talk to you?"

I shout again, "I can't leave the bar I'm too busy," and I lean out over the bar as far as I can, with my head between two customers. He squeezes into the bar. Man, is he nervous.

He says, "I own the funeral parlor up the street. I have a man working for me, Sal."

I say, "Yes I know Sal."

He says, "Would you please give him no more ice. We had two bodies in their coffins all ready for today's wakes and last night he thought they smelled so he threw ice all over them."

Well I could not stop laughing; I apologized for laughing and promised him faithfully that I would never, never, never again give Sal even one ice cube.

Mike Mullins, the man Molee shared an apartment with, hurt his neck and back and he couldn't turn his neck; he had to turn his whole body. McRory came in late one night. Mullins knew him well and turned to say hello holding his neck.

McRory says, "You got a pain in your neck?"

Mullins says, "Ya."

McRory says, "I can get rid of that pain for you."

Mullins says, "Can you really? Can you?"

McRory says, "I'll kick you in the balls right now and you'll have no pain in your neck."

Mullins was out of work in the late 1950s. Once, he was driving up Amsterdam Avenue and got stopped by the cops for going through a red light. Two weeks later, he went in front of a judge and the judge says ten dollars or ten days. Mullins says he's out of work; he'll take the ten days. The judge asked him if he really wanted to go to Rikers Island. "Yes, let the city feed me for ten days."

Later, he said it was the toughest ten days he ever had. Mullins was a very stubborn guy; he hated to be told what to do. They let him out at 9:00 p.m. on a Saturday and there was a taxi right outside the gates. He took it to the Blarney Stone on 84th Street and Third Avenue. He knew the owner. As he stepped on the sidewalk, a drunk bumped him and said, "Stay out of my way." It felt so good to be free. He hit the guy and he fell through a plate glass window and then Mullins took off running. He didn't want to go back to Rikers ever again.

Mullins was a carpenter. One summer there was a strike and he had no money. He had been evicted from his room when he met up with another Irish guy named Lally who was also out of work. They decided to walk from 80th Street and Broadway to the Bowery. By the time they got to Columbus Circle, the soles came off their shoes but they kept going and got to the Bowery at 7:00 p.m. They went to the Salvation Army to get something to eat. They stayed in the Bowery for two months, panhandling and eating in a soup kitchen.

When they heard the strike was over, they got cleaned up and went back to the West Side to the Union Hall, and got jobs. Mullins got a job as a carpenter on a building site near Wall Street. There were a lot of Irish and Italian workers there also. On the train from work one evening Mullins noticed an Italian reading the Irish Echo news paper, a weekly Irish paper. After a few weeks Mullins was curious, he sat beside him and asked if his wife was Irish, with a growl the Italian said NO. Mullins asked him why do you buy the Irish Echo every week, the Italian said do you want to know the truth, sure said Mullins. The Italian said I hate all ye Irish, I know if I get into argument there are so many of you Irish I will get hurt. So to get rid of my frustrations I take the paper home and when I go to the bathroom to take a shit I use it to wipe my Ass. With his first paycheck, Mullins got himself an apartment on 88th Street near Central Park West. A prime area today.

He is in McGlades Bar on Columbus avenue and he meets a southern guy, who says he is down on his luck. He also carries his own pool stick in a case. Mullins felt sorry for him, thinking of his own past. He tells him he can stay with him for a few nights.

They get drunk and they go to the apartment and Mullins tells the guy he can sleep on the couch, and Mullins sleeps on the bed. Early the next morning Mullins hears the guy getting up and leaving, Mullins falls back to sleep.

Later that morning Mullins wakes up to six cops in his apartment. They pull him out of the bed and take him to the police station. A news reporter named Gabe Pressman and cameramen are there and he's on the TV news. Gabe's asking him, did he know the guy was going to do it? The cops held him for two days.

The story was that the southern guy had a German girl-friend who left him. He knew she took the subway at 86th Street and Central Park West to go to work, so he got up while Mullins was still asleep. He left with his pool stick. Or was it a pool stick?

It was a double-barrel shotgun. He waited at the subway entrance until she came and shot her dead. Then he shot himself. When the cops searched the body they found a will made out to Mullins saying he was leaving all he owned to his good friend Mullins and giving the address of the apartment. It took Mullins two days to convince the cops that he didn't know the guy. Mullins said, "He willed me everything and he had nothing."

Turn of Events

Mullins moved to the Euclid, a run-down hotel on 86th Street and Broadway. No air conditioner, just open windows. There were pimps and prostitutes on every corner. As he was going home one night, a girl approached him and asked to go home with him. He said okay. She gets to his room and now she knows the room number. She asks him for some money to get a pizza. When he takes out his money she knows he's worth robbing.

So she leaves, but doesn't come back because she can't find her pimp. By the time she finds him, Mullins has fallen asleep. When they come back, they get rung in because she knows the room number. They get up there and start robbing him. Mullins wakes up and the fight is on. He breaks loose and he fires pots and pans at them. He even throws his shoe and it flies out the window. They run, but he was out of puff.

He lays back on the bed and falls asleep to be woke up by two young, scared cops and the pimp and the girl. They're saying that Mullins invited them to his room to rob them; that they got away and he threw his shoe at them and they had it for proof. He had the other one in his room.

The cops arrested him and he had to hire a lawyer. It cost him fifteen hundred dollars. It is amazing how the tide can turn when you got a young cop with no common sense. The old-time cops would have known to lock up the pimp and the girl.

He retired with disability and decided to go to Los Angeles. He went to live with a guy named Fahey, who we all knew. He wrote short stories. Some were published. When Fahey came back to New York for a visit, he came to see me and I asked him how Mullins was doing.

"I don't know at the moment. I had to ask him to leave. When he first arrived in Los Angeles, he moved in with me. The first day, I took him out for a walk. When we came to a red light, I said, 'Mr. Mullins, you must wait for the light to turn green here in Los Angeles.' He said, 'What the hell are you talking about?' and took off across the street. When he got to the other side, there was a cop, and he got a ticket. He said, 'Big deal! Go ahead, give it to me.'

"The next day he does the same thing and gets another ticket. Third day out he does it again. The light had turned green for me, so I was able to get across. Mullins is talking to the cop and he's changing his attitude. I walk close to them to hear what he was saying, and he's telling the cop he's retired and he's on disability.

"'The cop says, 'You're retired?'

"'Yes,' says Mullins.

"'Well,' says the cop, 'sure, you have all the time in the world to wait for the light,' and he hands him a ticket."

The Troubles, Northern Ireland

J. was from Kerry. He was a quiet, private man. He worked for Con Edison downtown. He drank in the La Salle uptown and lived in the Bronx. Kept to himself. Would talk politics. He worked with black guys and what surprised me is that, when they found out where he drank, they would come to the La Salle on a Friday night and buy him drinks, have a laugh and then leave.

In the late 1960s and early 1970s, there was a lot of trouble in the north of Ireland. J. and I would talk about the troubles. He figured out that I was a sympathizer to the Republican cause. One night he tells me that he raises money to free Ireland from England and would I like to subscribe twenty-five dollars or more? I give him a hundred dollars, which was a lot at the time.

Irish people gave little to the cause. They were all suspicious and they would tell you that the guys collecting for the cause were stealing off the top. Bernadette Devlin, a young Irish woman very involved in politics, came to America in 1969 to raise money. She went to Chicago, Philadelphia, Cleveland, Boston, San Francisco and New York, and, in three weeks, she raised one hunred thousand dollars. In 1967, when Israel fought the Six Day War, in New York City alone they raised fourteen Million dollars in seven days.

J. knew I had bought a house and that my mother had gone back to Ireland to babysit my sister's kids. So J. must have figured I was okay. One night he tells me he's in a spot and needs help. I ask what kind of a spot. Tomorrow evening, he says, he's got to pick up a machine gun on the Upper East Side. Could he meet me on 86th Street and Lexington on my way to work and would I keep it for him for a few days in my house? I say okay.

The following evening on my way to work, I stop on 86th Street and Lexington, he hops in the front seat and I drive to the West Side. I park the car across the street from the La Salle and we put the machine gun in the trunk. I go to work. He says he's got to meet somebody else and he'll see me tomorrow night.

I went home that night and put it in the attic. The attic is the full length of the house with a seven-foot ceiling. When I had bought the house a few months before, I had decided to renovate, so I had no tenants.

J. comes into the La Salle most every night for a few drinks and he tells me he'll pick the gun up in a few weeks. He comes in one Saturday night and says, "Can I stay over with you tonight, and would you drive me to Woodside with the gun?"

The next morning, I drove him to Woodside and dropped him off at 48th Street. He thanked me and I drove away. Over the next month, we would talk about the troubles in Ireland and he would tell me how devoted some guys are. He once spent a night and a morning in a guy's basement breaking down machine guns, AK-45s, etc., getting them ready for shipment.

He said, "You don't want to know how we ship them."

I said, "Correct. I don't."

One night he said that since my house had been vacant, would I mind storing some more guns for a while. I said okay and he said he'd stay with me that night. The next morning at 9:00 a.m., we'd pick up a van at a diner on Astoria Boulevard. We went there and saw the van, but I spotted a car with a guy sitting in it.

I said, "J., that car is watching us."

He looks and says, "I think so." He makes a phone call and comes back and says, "He's okay. He's watching the van. But I'm glad you spotted him. It makes it look good for us."

The key is under the seat in the van. We park my car, then drive to my house. There were two drums in the van and it took us an hour and a half to take all the wrapped packages to the attic. Two weeks later, we do it again.

The Irish operated in groups of four or six and they never used phones. They would drive a hundred miles to leave a note in a designated place for a guy they never saw.

He comes in on a Saturday night and says he'll stay over tonight, that we have a lot of work to do. He says he has a big list to go by. The next morning, we go to the attic and he has his list. We spread everything out all over the place. His list is pretty simple. It's set up in letters and numbers say,

| 1 | 2 | 3 | 4 | K5 | Done |

| P1, P2, P3, P4, P5, P6, P7 | | | | | Done |

| S1, S2, S3, S4, S5, S6, S7, S8, S9 | | | | | Done |

I ask him how it works. He says, "As you see, the 'S' has more parts than the 'K.' When the list says done, you know you got it all. It's not good when they're assembling an AK-47 in bogside and they're missing the bullets."

When you're involved in something like this, you don't talk to nobody, not even family, so it was a big surprise, almost a shock, when my cop friend McRory approached me about guns. Here is the way it went.

McRory knew an Irish rebel singing group, called The Wolfe Tones. They played a lot for a multimillionaire who owned a lot of places all over the world and had ties to the IRA. His name was Bill. He knew Derek from The Wolfe Tones, who knew McRory. He approached Derek to ask if McRory had any connections for getting guns. Derek goes to McRory and McRory comes to me. The fact is that I have an attic full of guns. I'm asking myself, "Does this guy know something?" I was so taken aback that I just said that I wouldn't have a clue. I tell J. and he says, "McRory is a cop. He's fishing for something. Just act dumb."

McRory would never get himself jammed up. But when he told a story, true or false, you had to laugh. Two weeks later, he comes in to the La Salle and says, "Derek called me and asked me to meet Bill on Second Avenue at the Bus Stop on 32nd Street at 5:00 p.m." He says, "I'm at the bus stop and it's raining. I feel like I'm in a European espionage movie. A blue Mercedes Benz pulls up. The window goes down; it's Bill. He says, 'Get in, Dan.' He drives down Second Avenue. With this heavy Irish accent, he says, 'Dan, Derek tells me you might be able to help us with some items to free Ireland.'

McRory says, "Yes, I might be able to get handguns, shotguns, AK-47's."

Bill says, "Dan, I would be looking for something a little larger." "Like what?" says McRory. "BAZOOKAS, Dan."

"Holy Shit!" says McRory. "I know I can't help you."

Back in the La Salle, J., who knew I drove a tractor trailer, asked me if I'd drive a tractor trailer load of guns from Baltimore to Woodside, New York. I said I'd think about it. Two nights later, I told him I would do it, but only if he rode with me.

I knew he was a deep thinker. Once he knew he was going, he would do a lot of thinking. A few nights later, he tells me there's too much confrontation going on. He decided no. I'm okay with that. I say to him that if all those guns are coming to Woodside, why not get a driver from San Francisco or Chicago?

In the end, they decided to bring them down in five vans. They got stopped on Skillman Avenue at 47th Street and the whole story came out in the newspaper. They were so dumb. It was all hatched in the Breffini Bar on 46th Street in Woodside because that's where they held meetings.

The FBI had rented an apartment across the street and filmed their movements for two years. They tailed them from the Breffini to Baltimore and back. The five drivers got three years in Fort Worth, Texas. They were called The Fort Worth Five.

My mother wrote me saying her babysitting job was finished and she was coming back. I told J. I'd have to get the guns out before she came back.

He came in a few nights later. Stayed over. The next day, there was a van in the street with the key under the seat. I drove it to the front of the house and we loaded all the barrels into it. I drove it to a diner two blocks away, left the key under the seat and that was it for me.

My view point changed, I was in Ireland some years after. I was in a small town called Muff in County Donegal, close to the border. I met a business man. He told me at one time he had two dance halls one south of the border and one north of the border. He said the IRA approached him, and demanded the money taking from the hall in the north for two dances each month for the 'Cause'. They came a second time and shoved a gun in his moth to scare him, and broke four of his teeth. He had to close the hall in the north. He showed me his missing teeth. Like lots of conflicts, some people get in for personal greed, they are only gangsters and thugs, they are in for the money, not sincere wishes. The Good Friday peace agreement was signed in on April 10th 1998. It took ant of neogations and courage by people on all sides. North, South, British, and the USA. People like John Hume, Gerry Adams, Ian Paisley, Martim McGuiness, Mo Mowland, Albert Reynolds, Bertie Ahern, Tony Blair, Bill Clinton appointed George Mitchell, what great work they did, but to name a few. We have over twenty years of peace, new prosperity for the North. The killings have stopped. The Good Friday agreement does leave an option for a united Ireland in the future by democratic means. In the meantime lets all live in peace and harmony.

Crime, Corruption, Cops

When I started at the La Salle in May of 1968, cops from the local 24th Precinct, plus cops from the 20th and 26th, used to come in. They all paid for their drinks when they were off duty, except for a few. The 24th Precinct cops never paid while on duty. The La Salle was never held up but stickups were common in the neighborhood, and all over the city. It got so bad, the Police Commission set up a robbery squad. Cops were assigned in pairs and they would sit in chairs in back of bars, in super-markets and behind hotel curtains. When the robbers came in, they killed them.

It worked fine until one night in a hotel at Kennedy Airport, three robbers came, two guys and a woman, all with shotguns. From behind the curtain, the cops shot and killed the two guys first, then the woman threw down her shotgun and shouted, "I give up! I give up!"

One cop came out from behind the curtain and said, "Sorry Babe, nobody gives up to the squad," and gave her both barrels. She had been known to the squad. She had killed five people, showing no mercy, but there was a witness to this shooting and the robbery squad was no more.

Stickups increased, but there seemed to be fewer killings. The word was that a lot of these robbers were Vietnam War vets who couldn't get a job.

Frank Serpico was a cop who wouldn't take money. After he spent a few years as a cop, the New York Times decided to publicize his story on police corruption, which left his life in danger. I found that amazing; I remember listening to some cops one night talking about collecting the ten thousand dollars which had accumulated in a kitty for any cop who would kill him. One cop said, "I could pay off my mortgage."

They transferred Serpico to Brooklyn where they got a junkie to do it. The two cops with him left him lying there for fifteen minutes before they called an ambulance, but he survived and the Knapp Commission was set up.

Up to that point, cops had had it made. In and out of uniform, they paid for nothing in their precinct, and a small percentage of cheap cops tried their hand at not paying anywhere. I recall a detective named Crowin coming in and ordering scotch; he had four shots, showed me his shield, said he's new in the precinct, and walked out. The next time he came in, he told me he was transferred from Midtown.

He told me he found an underage kid drinking in the Blarney Stone and demanded a thousand dollars to leave the place open. The manager called the owner, Dan Flannigan, who owned twenty-seven Blarney Stones and was a friend of Lieutenant Flaherty's, both of them being from County Galway. Flaherty was retired by then and lived around the corner. Crowin had the nerve to tell me how he shut down the Blarney Stone, letting me know what could happen to this place.

I told the story to Flaherty, who said, "Isn't it very interesting? This guy Crowin got transferred out of Midtown, where there's a lot of money, to the 24th, where he will make half. The 24th doesn't have a Blarney Stone in it and Dan still has clout."

A few nights later, Crowin came in with another detective at 3:00 a.m. and drank until 5 a.m. A bartender had to stay with those bastards until they wanted to leave. Most cops had a few drinks and left, but those guys took it too far. As they were leaving, he told me to give him a case of Budweiser. I brought him a cold case of Bud. He waited for me at the door. After I put it down on the floor, he put a one-dollar bill in my shirt pocket.

I said, "You don't have to do that."

He said, "Stoney, you don't tell me what I do or do not do."

"Okay," I said.

The shooting of Serpico brought things to a head. After that, they brought in a guy called Knapp and formed what they called the Knapp Commission. Let's just say the shit hit the fan.

No cop could drink in the precinct he worked in. They had undercover cops watching cops on patrol, but like everything that changes, it went too far the other way. An old woman on Broadway and 88th Street saw a young cop on patrol go into a Haagen-Dazs ice cream store and order a scoop of ice cream. The manager gave him two scoops and charged him for one. The old woman called the IAD. They put two plainclothes cops in a car to watch him.

It took three weeks for the cop to get a sweet tooth and go in for a scoop of ice cream. One of the plainclothes stood alongside of him on the line. He didn't ask for two scoops, just one. The manager gave him two anyway and the young cop got a two-day suspension. What a waste of manpower! No common sense. Cops were getting locked up, suspended for taking a free cup of coffee. A bartender could get in trouble if he didn't report a cop asking for a free drink. The tide had turned, but if I knew the cops, I would take a chance and give them a drink.

One night, Crowin came in on his own, I'm sure it was to check me out, and asked for a Chivas Regal scotch whiskey. I poured it and said, "Two dollars and seventy-five cents, please."

He said, "Who the fuck do you think you're talking to?"

I said, "I'm talking to a cop who won't pay for his drink. If you don't give me two seventy-five, you don't drink it."

He said, "I don't pay."

I said, "Mr. Crowin, you're lucky I got a lot of respect for cops. You got transferred from Midtown because of your greed and if I make a phone call you may get thirty days and a transfer to Staten Island. I will do you that honor; no phone call," and I threw the drink down the sink.

He got up and walked out saying, "I'll get you."

I said, "Be careful Mr. Crowin. Don't push it. I may get you."

I never saw him again. Boy, did I feel good.

Up one block on Columbus Avenue, a Puerto Rican man owned a bar. He worked days. Once, when he had finished his shift at 6:00 p.m., as he was walking into the back with the day's receipts, a young Puerto Rican pulled a gun and demanded the money. He was so close to the old man that the old man grabbed the gun. It went off, hitting him in the stomach, but he was able to turn it around and shoot the guy with his own gun. They both died before an ambulance arrived.

There was a young black man who opened up a beauty salon two doors down from the La Salle. He lived in the back of the store and when he closed up at night, he would come in with some younger guys and drink in the La Salle.

I didn't work on Sundays. When I got to work one Monday, Jack, the boss, said to me, "The hairdresser next door got tattooed. They found him in the back of the store. There's a bull in the kitchen wants to talk to you."

The word "bull" was a slang word used in the 1940s and 1950s for a detective. I went into the kitchen and this cop had in his hands at least a hundred photos that he had found in the hairdresser's store, all of men.

He looked me straight in the face and said, "Did you know him?"

I said, "I didn't know him. He just drank here."

"Did you know he was gay?"

"Yes, I did. He didn't hide it."

"Were you ever in his place?"

"No."

"Did you ever get your hair cut there?"

"No."

"Did you know he was very well hung?"

"What?!"

Up to that point, I had never realized I was so naive about what's happening around me in the world. He starts to show me pictures, some with one guy, some with two guys, all with erections. He's watching my face to see my reaction. As he's going through the pictures saying, "Ooh, look at this one." "Here's another." "Ooh, here's another." "Ooh, here, here, now that's a big one."

I could feel my face getting red and so hot I was sweating. I said I had never seen anything like that in my life and I didn't want to see it again. I said, "But it looks to me like it's doing something for you. I'm going to work."

He put the pictures in his pocket and left.

Later on in the week, I heard people say it was a hate and passion crime. Someone had cut his penis and balls off, and pushed everything through his mouth into his stomach with a broom handle.

There was a Puerto Rican man, Louis, who used to come in with his seventeen-year-old son Angel. They were both very nice. Angel would drink a soda and Louis would have one or two drinks and go home. You could see Angel had great respect for his father. This was the 1970s and Angel had a large Afro hairdo, almost as big as O.J. Simpson's in the movie Naked Gun. I said to him that he had the largest Afro I ever seen. He told me some people tell him to cut it.

As usual, I was off on Sunday, and when I got to work on Monday, all the talk was about four young guys put on their knees, heads down into a bathtub, in a vacant brownstone up the block, next to St. Gregory's Church. The old-timers liked to tell you this was a good neighborhood, that Babe Ruth got married in St. Gregory's Church. Only one guy survived.

That night, Louis came to tell me about the killings; his son, Angel, was the survivor. A few nights later, Angel came in on his own. I asked Angel if he could talk about it and he told me that he had three friends who were older than him who dabbled a little in drugs and kept them in the vacant building up the block.

Late that Saturday night, they had decided to go down to Times Square, which back then was very dangerous. The scum of the earth hung out there. At 5:00 a.m., they met two guys who wanted to score some drugs. His friend told them they had some they can sell them. The two guys asked where it was and they told them ten minutes by cab. They took a cab up here and the two buyers told the cab driver not to wait for them.

They ask where the stuff is and Angel and his friends tell them it's on the fourth floor. The guys tell them that, since this is their neighborhood, they were holding all the cards, and they didn't want to go up there with all four guys at once.

They said to Angel and his friends, "We'll go up with one at a time."

They agreed. After a few minutes, one of the guys puts his head out the window and shouts, "Okay, one more come up." Five minutes later, he puts his head out again, "Okay, one more."

Then Angel's down there on his own. "I don't know why I didn't go home. I was getting nothing out of it and the whole deal couldn't be more than a hundred dollars. They call me up, and I run up. Before I knew what was happening, I was on my knees with a bullet in my head. I knew I was alive but was too scared to move. I lay there until I could see daylight. I decided to move. I look around and see nobody. I run to the roof, go across two buildings, and come down on the street. I run to Columbus Avenue, see a cop car, and tell my story."

I asked Angel to come into the kitchen to show me. The bullet had gone in an eighth of an inch. It was amazing; the largest Afro in the neighborhood had done the trick. I said, "Angel, what are you going to say to the next guy who tells you to cut your hair off?"

There was a liquor store on 88th Street and Amsterdam Avenue. The owner opened at 11:00 a.m. and closed at 1:00 a.m. He put in floor to ceiling Plexiglas with an S-hook circle in it to push your money through before you got your bottle. He put out the word that they couldn't get him now, but one night, as he was walking to his car, they got him.

Right next to the La Salle there was a bodega owned by Pedro, who everybody called Pete, and who had a mean German shepherd for protection. He was robbed one night. They cuffed him to a steam pipe. After the cops came and freed him from the pipe, he came in to me for a drink. Pete told me, "You know what they said to me, Stoney? They said to call off the dog or they'll shoot him. 'We ain't cuffing the dog,' and then they cuff me to the steam pipe."

Dumbstruck During the LaSalle Stickup

A few of the cops I was friends with would come in to say hello and tease me. They would say, "What are you going to do now? It's only a matter of time until they figure out there are no cops in here. What are you going to do?"

I decided in my head I would faint face first on the floor. What can you do to somebody that fainted? So, every day as I drove to work, I would repeat, repeat and repeat: "I'll faint, I'll faint, I'll faint. I got it now. I'll faint."

I was at the front of the bar one night watching the TV. There was only five customers. Three guys came in fast. One guy jumped over the bar, it happened in seconds, and put a gun in my ear. Yes, my ear.

He ran me to the register, told me to open it. I did. He took the money and what I didn't realize was that there was a second drawer that had never been used. Whenever the boss got a rubber band, he would string it from the second drawer button and clip it to the release button. There must have been ten years of rubber bands on there to stop the button from being pushed down. The guy told me to open the second drawer. I knew what to do.

As I started taking off the rubber bands, he yells, "I'll give you to the count of three to open it!"

I must have kept my cool because I said, "You can count all you want, but if I don't get those rubber bands off, it ain't opening, and there's nothing in it anyway." I couldn't tell if he counted or he didn't count, but I got them off and I got the drawer open. There was nothing there.

The other guy yelled, "Get the customers!" He did and they ran out.

I realized then and there that a person can talk to himself all he wants, but only when it happens does he know what he's all about. My reaction was, do what I was told; the faint thing went out the window.

The customers told me to call the cops and call the boss. I said, "I'll call the cops, but I ain't calling the boss. What can he do? Nothing." But they kept on insisting. I figured they must know something I don't, so I gave in and called him.

When the cops arrived, we gave them what information we could. The cops handle situations like this: there was a sergeant with them. He said, "I'll take the information and let's all have a drink."

Pat Kenny from Dublin, an off-duty cop from the 26th Precinct, who I knew from years before he was even a cop, came in. He wanted to know what he missed. As I'm telling him my version of the stickup, in walks Lieutenant Flaherty, just retired. They knew each other. It was in his blood; he just became very official about things. Now he's calling me "Bartender." He says, "Bartender, did they rob the customers?"

"Yes, sir," I said.

He turns to Kenny, "Officer Kenny, if you were sitting there, how would you handle that situation?"

Kenny says, "You'll have to give up your gun."

"Give up your gun," says Flaherty.

"What else could you do?" asks Kenny.

"As a cop you must move, live or die," says Flaherty. "Let me tell you," says Flaherty, "Jack Beckett, the boss, is a good friend of mine. If I'm sitting at my favorite place at the end of that bar and they rob the register only, I won't make a move, because Jack has insurance. But if they rob the customers and come to me and take my gun, don't you know that the complaint will be wrote up as cowardism?"

Kenny says, "Times have changed. You're too old."

"All right," says Flaherty, "let's hope you never have to find out."

The next evening when I went to work, Jack my boss said to me, "If you're going to stay working for me, there will be stickups. Please don't call me. There's time enough for me to find out when I come in at 7:00 a.m. Last night you woke me up and I never got back to sleep."

I said, "It's no use telling you now, Jack, but I didn't want to call you. It won't happen again."

I find this interesting; if I was uptown on 125th Street the day after the stickup, and I bumped into the guys who robbed the La Salle, I wouldn't recognize them. But two nights later, with thirty people in the bar at 2:00 a.m. and Flaherty sitting in his favorite chair at the end of the bar talking to a man and his wife.

The bar had two doors. When you opened the second door fast, the wind slammed the first door shut, which caused you to look. They came in fast again, three guys and when I looked, I saw it was the same guys.

I ran to Flaherty and said, "The same guys are back," as he jumped off his seat. By now one guy is at the register and the other guys are yelling, "Stickup!"

Flaherty is on his feet, gun out, standing in the middle of the floor shouting, "Police, police!"

One guy says, "Fuck the cops," and comes at Flaherty, shooting and missing him.

Flaherty fires two rounds. The guy turns and runs, the guy at the register jumps back over the bar. Flaherty waits until he's going out the door and lets off another round.

I find it amazing that I never thought of fainting. I never thought of ducking. I was so dumb, I just stood there watching every move like I'm enjoying it and I think maybe I was.

Flaherty says, "Call the cops. I hit them both."

I say, "I don't think so."

He gets a little frustrated and says, "Listen here. I had a lot of things to think about. I couldn't shoot the guy at the register because if I missed, the bullet would go through the window and hit a passerby. I had to wait until he was going out the door. I hit them both, first guy high up, second guy in the leg."

At that time cabs also got stuck up a lot, so much so that the Police Department set up a "Cab Spot Check," where they would have two cops stationed at a busy intersection to look into cabs when the light was red. They would say hello to the customers and the cab driver, ask if everything was okay, and send you on your way.

When the cops arrived, it was good fortune for Flaherty and bad fortune for the robbers. It turned out that there were four of them and they had hijacked a cab to do some stick-ups. It seemed that they had planned it very well, what to do if they got stopped by a cab spot check. When the cab was stopped on 96th Street on Amsterdam Avenue, ten blocks away, the two guys who were shot jumped out on top of the cops and knocked them to the ground, while the other two jumped out the other door and got away with the guns and the money and the evidence.

The cops in the bar were enjoying their drinks, with the walk-ie-talkie on the bar, and a voice comes over saying, "Two suspects with bullet wounds at the 96th and Amsterdam cab spot check."

"That's it," says Flaherty, taking two customers as witnesses.

At closing time, he came back with his witnesses and walked down to the end of the bar, calling me "Bartender." "You got to go up to the Precinct to identify the guy in the cell. Now when you go up there, the guy in the cell is the guy that was at the register. These two people here said it, I said it and you say it. He only has a flesh wound. The other guy is in the hospital. I got him good."

When I went up there, the detective brought me to the cell where I saw the guy. There was no doubt that he was the guy at the register. Man did he have nerve; when he saw me, he came running from the back of the cell, put his hands through the bars, screaming in a loud voice, "You ID me and you're dead, Motherfucker!"

I just thought it was all a joke. I said to him, "What are you upset about? The game you're in, you win some, you lose some." I pointed at him, "Yes detective, that's him, that's him." Haha.

The next evening when I got to work, Flaherty was waiting for me. He told me the guy in the cell is having a court hearing at 10:00 a.m. the next day. He tells me, "You stay with me tonight. I have a couch you can sleep on. I'll cook breakfast in the morning and we'll take the train down to the Centre Street."

We got there and got called up in front of the judge at 11:30 a.m. Flaherty and I were on one side and the guy, whose name was Hudson, and his Legal Aid lawyer on the other. The judge said that bail was set at ten thousand dollars.

His lawyer said that there was no gun found, but the judge said, "Here is the police lieutenant who fired his gun. And they dug out two bullets from the wall. The use of a gun stays." His lawyer went to bat for him again saying, "Mr. Hudson has been on good behavior for ten months and he belongs to the Rockefeller program." (The Rockefeller program was a Methadone plan to get addicts off heroin.)

That statement seemed to make the judge think of something he had forgotten. He said to the court clerk, "Pull the yellow sheet on Mr. Hudson."

He was a very unlucky thief; he was in the system and his rap sheet said he had been locked up twelve times in eighteen months for committing crimes with a gun—and still he was out. The jails were so full, the system was letting them out on a promise. The judge seemed to have a sense of humor, though. He said, "If Rockefeller wants this guy for ten thousand dollars, he can have him."

Flaherty says to me, "Good judge," and we all leave.

The next court date was two weeks later. I stayed over with Flaherty again. The next day they brought in Mr. Hudson and his pal on a stretcher. The case was postponed. Next time their lawyer didn't show. The next time after that, the guy on the stretcher was back in the hospital, and on it went for three months and twelve trips to court. By then, both guys were walking and standing with their lawyer, and it was Flaherty and me - and there was a different judge.

The judge hears the case and says three months. Their lawyer says, "Your Honor, my clients could not post bail. It's been three months since their incarceration."

"Okay," says the judge, "Time served."

Flaherty was shocked. They started laughing and walked out with us. They had no fear of Flaherty. Hudson came right over to me, put his fist in my face, and said, "I told you, man, not to ID me. I'm coming to get you." I must say I didn't feel good going to work that night.

Three weeks later, another shoot-out. I give Flaherty credit. He ran from nothing, but it was nice having a gun. It did level the playing field.

Another two guys ran in yelling stickup, but before the guy could get to the register, Flaherty was on his feet shouting, "Police, Police!" The guy fired a round; Flaherty got off two rounds and they bolted out the door. They were not caught. Flaherty told me to call the cops.

I said, "Listen, Flaherty, before I call the cops, I want you to understand I ain't going to go through any of this bull again. I didn't see nothing. It was too fast. I ain't going to no precinct, okay?"

He says, "I tell them what I know. You tell them what you know."

So I call. Two detectives come, one an Italian with pinky rings and a flashy shirt with the collar folded back over the jacket, and a chain hung around his neck. He looked and acted more like a mob guy than a detective. Flaherty went with them. He loved the attention.

Pinky Ring demands that I go to the precinct after I close up, to look at mug shots. I say, "No sir, I am not going to the precinct."

He says, "Yes you are."

I say, "Listen, I couldn't identify nobody. I ain't going up."

He says, "What makes you so sure?"

I say, "When I heard 'stickup,' I put my eyes on the floor and I didn't take them off the floor until they were gone."

He said, "You're sure?"

"I'm sure."

Sometimes you think to yourself, "I wish I had said that," but this time I was very good.

He thought he'd catch me out, so he said, "You're so sure, yeah? Were they black or white?"

I said, "I don't know. I never looked up."

Years later, when I bought a bar, I told all my bartenders the Mr. Hudson story and I told them to identify nobody.

Captaining the Shit-House

Mr. Austin was a black man in his fifties who lived in the building the La Salle was located in. It was a doorman building with the entrance on the side street, at 220 West 90th Street. He tended bar at a place on 135th Street and Seventh Avenue in Harlem, from 2:00 p.m. to 9:00 p.m. He would come in to me every night after work for a nightcap.

He got to like me a lot. He introduced me to his wife. She was a lovely woman, but boy could she stand up to him when she knew he was wrong. I told him the story about trucking with Jimmy Reese in the South. Maybe that's why he said I was the only white guy he liked.

He told me he was eight years old when he and his mother left North Carolina during the Depression and came to Harlem. I never asked, but he must have been an only son because he never ever mentioned any brothers or sisters.

Back then there was no work. He said the rich, white people who lived on Fifth Avenue were all Jews. I wonder. They would come over in their horse-drawn carriages with drivers to 96th and Central Park West when they were throwing a party. They would stand up on the carriages and point to the women they wanted saying, "You. You. You. You…" to all the younger and good-looking ones, but his mother was not a pretty woman and she was never picked. Mr. Austin and his mother would go back to Harlem and on their way they would eat the oats that horses had spilled onto the street from their feedbags, and whatever else they could find in the garbage.

It didn't take him long to figure out what was going on. When he got older, he was told that all the black maids and cooks had to put out for the white men if they wanted to get hired next time. He told me that North Carolina had no electric when he was a kid and I told him I had no electric or gas in Ireland. He said, "How old are you? You're talking like an old man."

Mr. Austin and the wife loved to dress up and go to Broadway shows. They came in one night for their nightcap, her in a beautiful green gown, him in bow tie, suit and tails. He told me they had come out of the show and seen an empty cab. They jumped in. The cab driver, who thought his doors were locked, turned and looked at them and said, "Where are you going? To Harlem?"

Whenever Mr. Austin got a driver who asked that question, he would always give him a specific address, so he told him he was going to 220 West 90 Street.

"I'm your next-door neighbor now," he told the driver.

He had said to the driver, "What's the matter with you? Do we look like we are going to mug you?"

Now, if I was driving a cab and saw a bunch of young blacks with sneakers, I'd lock the door.

Mr. Austin used to say to me, "You think being a bartender in this place is tough? You should be uptown with all the blacks. They're bad drunks. The only way you can survive a shift uptown is to have a few before you start and then blend into the bar room bullshit."

One night, he came in for his nightcap. There was a nice crowd, with many of the regulars, including Rafferty. There was an Italian immigrant, named Tony, who had bought a candy store on the corner. He had no credit so he had to pay cash for everything. He also had no safe, so he brought his money home each night. He would open the store at 5:00 a.m. and close at 10:00 p.m. and every night, before getting on the subway, he would treat himself to a Johnnie Walker Black.

Anyway, that night the door flies open. Two guys. One guy over the bar, the other guy standing by the door, wearing a Clint Eastwood poncho, a sawn-off shotgun strapped to his arm. When he stretched his arm out, the two barrels appeared and when he dropped his arm, the barrels disappeared.

He yells at me to give all the money to his buddy, but I didn't have to since he was already helping himself. I'm standing with my hands holding the bottom of the bar. The double-barreled shotgun has me very scared. My mind is working like two minds; one is telling me to run to the kitchen, the other is telling me the shotgun will get me, so I'm holding the bottom of the bar to keep myself from running.

The guy with me behind the bar got the register but missed a change box. He backs out from behind the bar, facing me with his gun. The guy with the shotgun yells, "Hold it!" I'm not thinking straight. I think he knows about the change box and my hands go straight up in the air. The guy yells, "Put your hands down!" and they come straight down. The guy with the shotgun says, "Did you take the bartender's money?"

I'm quite amazed by what a person says when he's scared. I don't know why I said it, but I said, "I don't think I got that much." I'm also amazed by the stickup guy.

He waves the gun in my face and says, "What you got we need. You don't think we're just out here for nothing, man."

The guy with the shotgun has his buddy search everybody as they put us all in the bathroom. I was so scared of that shotgun; I pushed my way to the back where the toilet bowl was. It was hot in there and we were all sweating when Mr. Austin shouts out, "If you're on a ship, the captain is the last man off but we're in a shit-house and Stoney is the first man out."

I got this thing in my head that they might blow a hole in the door and I don't want to let Mr. Austin down, so I go to the door on my knees to give it a slight push when suddenly it flies open and there's Tony. He had got a bigger scare than all of us. He had walked in for his Johnnie Walker scotch before going to the subway and walked right into the shotgun. The poor guy was as white as Casper the Friendly Ghost.

Afterward, everybody is broke so I gave them all a drink and called the cops. The cops arrived and they were taking notes and the Sergeant said, "Did they rob everybody?" I said yes. Just then, Rafferty wakes up, stumbles to the bar, puts up a ten-dollar bill and asks for a Seagram's Seven and Seven. We all laugh.

Mr. Austin says to me, "I leave uptown to get away from this and come down here to have the same thing happen."

I say, "It wasn't bad, Mr. Austin. We're all alive and you were funny in the bathroom."

I ask Mr. Austin to tell me about one of his stickups, one that will give me a laugh, but Mr. Austin says, "I'm too old. None of this is a laugh."

Around that time, a new group called the Black Panthers had started up and they used to go around with a closed fist held high, shouting, "Black Power!"

Mr. Austin told me that one day the Panthers was marching and a lot of people were enjoying themselves. His bar was full and there were two bartenders on. At 7:00 p.m., this crazy guy comes in, bobbing and weaving up and down the bar with a closed fist, shouting, "Black Power!" He told me, "What we didn't know was that he had two guys with him, one at each end of the bar, wearing long coats with AK-47s under them. To make Crazy happy, everybody put up their hand and shouted, 'Black Power!' At that instant, a few rounds went off into the ceiling. Then Crazy shouted, 'Put up the other hand! This is a stickup.' Crazy had a big shopping bag; he cleaned everybody out and never got caught."

Mr. Austin quit and got a bartender's job on Eighth Avenue and 54th Street, in Hell's Kitchen. There was a bus depot on Ninth Avenue with a lot of Irish drivers, who cashed their checks at the bar, plus a lot of Irish in the neighborhood. After six weeks, he quit and went back uptown. He said to me, "I thought blacks was bad drunks. But you Irish, man, now I know why you Irish have such a bad name. It's because you all can't drink. I'm going to run the risk uptown because I couldn't put up with you lot."

Meanwhile, Flaherty was missing all the action and I was happy because that guy with the shotgun wouldn't miss, but with Flaherty's fast reaction there would be at least twenty feet between them. He'd probably survive.

I could not believe it. One week later, the same guys, about the same time of night. They operated the same way. I felt they did it faster this time. They took the money out of the register, lined us up, and robbed each of us as we went into the bathroom. Everybody was very quiet; after a few minutes, I did the same thing I did before. On my knees, I pushed the door open, then we all came out. A few of the customers got hysterical, shouting to call the cops, but I got annoyed and I hit the bar so hard the glasses jumped. I said, "They're not here and they won't be here when the cops come. I'm going to give everybody a drink then I'll call the cops."

I was pouring out drinks when I got up to this black guy, Aaron. He was standing up as I started to pour his Bacardi and Coke, but he said, "Would you mind giving me a straight shot?"

"Here you go."

He says, "Stoney, how can you pour whiskey? Would you look at my hands? You know, I didn't mind that cat taking my bread, but the motherfucker called me brother."

The next day, the headline in the newspaper read "Police Lieutenant Shot with Shotgun in Parkview Bar on 197th Street and Broadway, in Washington Heights." When I was cab driving, I went in there once to use the bathroom and, to my surprise, a guy, Frank Loftus, who I had met on the boat to America, was behind the bar. I figured it was the same guys, robbing bars as they headed uptown.

On my day off, I went up there hoping he was working. He was and he had been working the night of the stickup. He told me, "The lieutenant is in the front of the bar with his back to the door, talking to a bus driver. They come in so fast."

I said, "I know."

He said, "One guy over the bar, the other guy shouting, 'Stickup, give it up!'

"The lieutenant turned and said he was a cop and the guy pulled the trigger and blew his left arm off at the shoulder. I don't know how he did it, but he shot the robber, and the other barrel went off as he was going out the door and the lieutenant, he got the other guy going out the door. They were both picked up at the hospital later, but they weren't able to save the lieutenant's arm."

When Flaherty saw the story in the newspaper he said, "Now you know why I stay at the far end of the bar. If people want to talk to me they have to come to me."

Good Cops, Bad Cops

It must have been four months later and Pat Kenny hit the news. He and a partner had pulled over a car at 136th Street on Broadway. We all know how cops work when they pull a car over. Each of them gets out. One goes to the driver's side, the other to the passenger's side. Kenny had his gun out when he approached the car and the driver took off. Kenny never thought of his partner and shot off three rounds and hit his partner. "Friendly fire," it's called.

Another time, Kenny was driving drunk up Third Avenue. At 96th Street, he hit a car. Instead of taking care of business he gave the black guy that he had hit a hard time. He was good at that. But the black guy had clout and called the cops. There was a precinct house just two blocks away and when the cops got there, the black man said to the sergeant, "I need him to have a sobriety test." Kenny was in shock. The sergeant gave him one and he failed and the Police Department gave him a thirty-day suspension.

He came into the La Salle one night when McRory was there. McRory had been in emergency services and had a hundred medals for bravery. Kenny, with the chip on his shoulder, started running down the guys he worked with. McRory jumped and said, "I heard from Flaherty that you were going to give your gun up to robbers. You've never gotten a commendation. The only thing you've done as a cop was to get drunk and ram a guy's car and shoot your partner."

When Kenny was a kid, he had a serious knee injury playing football. He came to New York and took the entrance exam for the NYPD and got in, but now he knew the department was out to get him. One time he was running down a flight of stairs after a suspect when he slipped and fell. He blew out his knee again and retired on three-quarters pay and went home to Dublin.

Kenny had a brother, Ted, who married an Italian girl and he asked me to be in the wedding and I agreed. There were four of us groomsmen and four bridesmaids. The reception was in Queens, which was where I lived. Afterward, I asked one of the bridesmaids, Diana, to join me for a drink. We found a small place with a one-man show. We walked in, her in her gown, and me in a tuxedo. The guy singing asked what nationality we were and we said half Irish, half Italian. He sang the song "Danny Boy" and sent us over a drink.

We had a lot of fun for about an hour, when I told her my house is only a few blocks away and asked if she would like to come back for the night. She said sure, so we went back and got into bed and start making out. Then she starts crying and when I asked what was the matter, she told me that she was a virgin. When I heard that, I jumped out of the bed and started to get dressed. She lay in the bed and asked me what I was doing.

"Let me explain," I told her. "When I was thirteen years old I was going out with a girl who was also thirteen and even then she wasn't a virgin. I am now twenty-eight years old and I've still never had a virgin, and I sure don't need one now. Get up. I'll help you get into the gown and drive you home." So I drove her home to Baldwin, Long Island and I never saw her again, why did she get into the bed at all.

Ted Kenny came into the bar a year later with his wife and she said, "Oh Stoney, Diana told me you were such a gentleman."

I was in Ireland about five years later, hanging out with Sean Flynn, a friend from my home place, who was now a big contractor in Dublin. Pat Kenny's name came up during the conversation. He asked me if I knew him. I told him I did and then told him how Kenny had hurt his knee as a kid playing football for the GAA, the Gaelic Athletic Association, then went to New York, became a cop, fell down some stairs, and how the knee got him out on three-quarters pay.

Sean told me Kenny had another brother who was a lawyer in Ireland. Kenny fell down some steps at a GAA dance and claimed there was no light in the stairs. He sued and his brother represented him and they collected. The GAA never put it all together. "That knee is still making money for him," Sean said.

Spirits and Spirits

Charlie, the super of the building the La Salle was in, was an American Indian and he drank most of his money away every Saturday and Sunday. He had worked as a handyman at St. Gregory's School. His boss, Samuel, was retiring. Samuel liked Charlie; he knew he was a great worker from Monday to Friday but he was afraid that Charlie might lose his job after he retired. He knew Moe, the owner of the building, and knew that Moe needed a building super. Moe's supers kept quitting after a few months, so Moe always needed a super. Charlie got the job and kept it.

Charlie had a heart of gold but he was rough-spoken and he was loud. Boy could he drink his liquor. When he got drunk he was very loud. He would push through the crowd, constantly talking about nothing. If he felt he knew you, he would push you.

Once, he was coming out of the bathroom when he met One Punch Hogan, a seventy-year-old man who used to be a lightweight fighter. Everybody called him that because he would knock out his opponents with one punch. One Punch was going into the bathroom when Charlie grabbed him and gave him a shove. One Punch didn't like that and said, "Don't you grab me like that!" and then decked him.

Charlie went on his ass into a booth with his legs up in the air, but he didn't knock him out. Charlie got out of the booth as One Punch was going into the bathroom and he shouted, "You still got it!" and walked back to his seat at the bar not fazed one bit at what happened to him. Even when he got knocked down he praised the other guy!

There was a woman named Peggy who started coming into the bar. She also talked loud, as if there was nobody there but her. She came across like a child sometimes because she would say whatever came into her mind. Nobody was surprised when Peggy and Charlie became an item. For Peggy it was perfect timing. She had lost her job and was about to become homeless and Charlie had a free apartment all to himself. They seemed to think alike and they both drank, so she moved in her few items, one of which was an urn containing her parents' ashes. Charlie also had his parents' ashes in an urn.

One night their apartment was broken into and the thieves emptied the ashes into a pile on the floor. They were so upset and they were also superstitious, so they wouldn't touch the ashes. They got pretty drunk and told me all this late one Saturday night. And I came up with a plan to make them happy.

I told them a story about how back in Ireland, in the Pagan days, certain families had powers. Some families had cures, some had curses, and some had rituals. They would create a circle and, by certain prayers and wishes, they could separate good from bad and bad from good, and I told them I was from that clan. It was very spiritual; it was going to take a lot out of me, but for them I would do it. I would separate the ashes and put them back in the urns.

Peggy said she always believed in spiritual stuff and she believed I could do it. Would I do it for them? I said, "Peggy, it takes a lot out of me, but I can see in your face that you believe. Yes, Peggy, I'll do it."

I told them to go home and I would knock on their door. "It says 'Super' on it, right?"

"Yes."

They left. I cleaned up and then I went into the closet and found two of Jack's ties. I knocked on their door and Peggy let me in. I asked, "Where is your kinfolk?" She brought me into the living room and there it was, a pile of ashes and two urns.

I told them both to sit on the floor facing each other, with the ashes in the middle. "Peggy, you hold one end of each tie. Charlie, you do the same. I'll get into the circle and you all got to complete the circle. Close your eyes and pray in whatever language comes out of your mouth and I'll do mine, but mine is different and I'll pray the spirits is directing my hands to do the right thing. The spirits will tell me when the ashes are back in the urns."

Peggy was the best. She thought the spirits got into her. I filled the urns but I couldn't pick up the last few grains, so I swished to each side and blew with my breath until there was a clean spot between them. I said some more gibberish, got out of the circle, and told them to open their eyes.

I said it was a success. Peggy wanted to pay me, but I told her that what I have is a gift; I can't take money. They were convinced I did it. I had made them very happy.

Every Saturday and Sunday they were in the La Salle talking loud as if there was nobody else there, then Peggy was telling Charlie he's old.

Charlie said, "What do you mean old?"

"You know, Charlie. When you're in bed."

Charlie says, "Peggy, when is a man old?"

Peggy says, "I don't know, Charlie. You tell me."

Charlie says, "A MAN IS OLD WHEN HIS TONGUE GETS TIRED."

Half the bar turned to look at them, most of them younger chanting, "Go! Go! Go Charlie!" If you saw Peggy and Charlie you would never expect them to talk sex. I hadn't laughed so much in a long time.

Clans of Kellys

There were three families named Kelly that I knew on the West Side, none of them related. The family of Kellys was Margaret the mother, two daughters, Beverly, twenty-two, and Sue, sixteen, and a son Larry, nineteen. Beverly was a strong-minded straight talker. Whatever she did or said, she had an explanation for it. Made no excuses. After she lost her job as a receptionist at Goldman Sachs, even though there was a recession, she found one as a receptionist in a cathouse-a house of prostitution-on the Lower East Side.

I found it so interesting. People on the West Side talked so openly and matter-of-factly about some situations. Margaret, the mother, and the daughter, Beverly, talked about the sixteen-year-old Sue, who had gotten into drugs and prostitution. Margaret said, "She's underage; I can have her put away for a year or more."

Beverly said, "Don't do that, Mom. Before you know it, she'll be old enough to do what she wants and she'll only hate you more. She's going to do it anyway, so let me get her in where I'm working. This way I can keep an eye on her."

It's called making the best of a bad situation. I was talking to Beverly sometime later about how her job was going. I asked her if she would make more money working like the other girls.

She said of course she would, "I just don't like to fuck." She married an electric contractor that she met when he was a customer at where she worked. They bought a house out on the Island and moved.

Larry got himself a good education, got married and moved to New Jersey. Sue disappeared; nobody knew where she went, and Margaret stayed in the rent-controlled apartment on the West side.

The second family of Kellys was Fred, Tim, Sean, and a sister, Ellen. Fred was the best of them. He worked in the neighborhood for the City and was a member of Union Local 32B. There was a vacant building on 90th Street where a movie company was shooting some scenes for a movie called Midnight Cowboy. Movie companies always put out a big spread of food for the crew on big tables on the sidewalk.

One time, Fred was walking by and took a fruit. A guy stopped him and asked if he was working on the movie. When Fred said no, he was told not to take anything off the tables. Okay said Fred and he walked away, got a sledgehammer, went into a vacant building nearby and started breaking a cast iron bathtub. All you could hear is the director yelling, "Cut, Cut, Cut!"

The big boss found Fred swinging the sledgehammer, "We're making a movie, stop this noise."

But Fred could be very aggressive, "You got your job, I got mine. I get two hundred dollars to break those bathtubs, today, not tomorrow."

The director said, "Can I give you two hundred dollars and please do it tomorrow?"

Fred replied, "I shouldn't' do this, but okay, I'll do it."

When Fred spotted the guy who had stopped him from taking the fruit, he yelled out to the big boss, "Can I have a piece of fruit?"

"You can have anything you want on that table."

The doorman in the building of the La Salle was named Taylor. His eighteen-year-old son got into a disagreement with Tim Kelly. At two o'clock one morning, Tim shot him dead outside the La Salle and got locked up. At that time the jails were overcrowded and he only did eighteen months for self-defense. After that, he would come into the bar and use the bathroom, say nothing, and walk out.

Sean was the oldest, a full-time junkie. He had gone to school with McRory. I was with McRory one day down at the precinct where he worked when he spotted Sean checking the locks on car doors. He shouted, "Sean what are you doing? Don't you know you're outside a precinct?"

Sean saw McRory, "Aha, Dan. I should have known they were cop's cars. The cheap fucks, there is nothing in them."

I went to work one Monday evening and Margaret Kelly was at the end of the bar. She told me that Sean Kelly got it Saturday night on Tenth Avenue and 19th Street. A Puerto Rican with a machete. He had it in a leather pouch down his leg inside his pants. The first stroke took off Sean's right arm at the shoulder. He didn't stop until he had hacked him good.

Fred had to go downtown to ID the body. A little while later, Fred came in wearing a suit. Margaret shouted, "Down here Fred. Give Fred a drink of vodka and orange." She asked Fred, "Was it him? Was it?"

Without flinching, Fred put his hand in his pocket, pulled out a roll of money and nodded to Margaret, "Yeah, it was him. Stoney, give them all a round of drinks here."

I guess if you live in that type of environment you set your mind to the fact that it's going to happen one day.

Later, Fred got caught taking money for favors. He was subpoenaed to go to court but he skipped to Canada instead. He came back a few years later. I guess he missed the West Side.

Ellen, the sister, went out with a guy named Cooney. He came in very little but, for what reason I don't know, he hated me. He hung out with a guy, Mulahuskie, who wasn't a bad guy. He was on a scholarship to Regis High School on the East Side, one of the top schools in the city.

One time, his brother and a friend were uptown in Inwood at 200th Street, where the train is elevated, heading downtown to where it goes underground at 174th Street. They had decided to ride on top of the train, but at the entrance to the tunnel, there was only one foot of clearance. Bits of them were found for miles. Maybe that's what had turned him on to heroin. He was trying to get off the heroin, so he joined a methadone program, which left him kind of dozy at times.

There was a guy, Frank. He was a limousine driver; he liked to be called Frank the ginny. I had understood that was an insult to decent Italians, but he said no, he's a ginny. Okay. Any night he was in, he never failed to say, "Stoney, if anybody gives you any problems, you tell me and I'll take care of them." It just so happened he was never there when something did happen.

Then there was Paul McMoro, McRory's friend, who came in one night and said, "You have a bat behind the bar?"

I said, "No."

He said, "In this area you got to have something."

So he went away and came back with a three-foot-long half-inch pipe with an elbow on the end of it and a big roll of black tape. He tells me to hold the end and he starts rolling the tape around the elbow and on up the pipe. When he was finished, the pipe looked like it had a lump on the end of it.

"Now," he said, "you put that behind the bar. I guarantee you'll find a use for it."

I put it behind the bar and there it stayed for a long time.

There was a Japanese man, his name was Akio, who came in at night for about a month. On his finger he wore an Irish

Claddagh ring, which is a love ring. Some people use it as an engagement ring. He told me he was married to an Irish girl. He was an instructor in karate and also worked downtown. He was a very quiet man. He got to know Flaherty, and he and I became pretty good friends.

The Night It All Went Down

I had seven customers in the bar, including Frank the ginny and Akio the Japanese. The corner by the door was empty. In walks Kelly's sister Ellen with her boyfriend, Cooney, and Mulahuskie. They go to the corner by the door, where Ellen and Cooney sit and Mulahuskie stands. Ellen and Cooney order two gin and tonics and Mulahuskie orders a coke. As I'm serving them, Cooney pulls a switchblade and sticks it into the bar. He says, "I'll pay you by cutting your fucking throat."

Well, the bar emptied like a stampede. Frank the ginny was first out the door, but Akio walks down the bar, says to Cooney, "Take the knife out of the bar."

Cooney yells, "Stay out of it. It's none of your fucking business."

Akio says, "Stoney is my friend. I'm making it my business."

Cooney pulls the knife out of the bar and goes for Akio.

I'm thinking I must put Mulahuskie out for the count. Now's the time for Matt's pipe. So I grab it and jump the bar. He has his back to me and I hit him down the side of the head with the pipe and, to my surprise, he starts turning his head towards me. He's saying, "Wu wu too wu oooo, what the fuck was that?" I said to myself, "You fuck!" And man, did I hit him again.

I was lucky because I could see out of the corner of my eye that Ellen had stayed in the corner. I turned to Cooney, who had cut Akio, but when I went to go for him, I tripped over Mulahuskie and fell on my face and lost the pipe. I spun around on my back to see Cooney coming down with the knife. I moved my head just enough that the knife stuck in the floor. Shit! That was close! I get him off me, but my pipe is gone. My mind is thinking of a broom handle in the kitchen, but when I come out with it seconds later, the three of them are gone.

Akio is behind the bar with his hand in the sink. I never seen so much blood, trailing from the front of the bar and in behind the bar to the sink. I'm scared Akio will pass out from loss of blood. I call the cops and say, "La Salle bar, Amsterdam Avenue, 90th Street, 1013," which is the code for "Cop in Trouble." Man, oh man, did we get cops and an ambulance fast.

Four hours later, I have all the blood cleaned up and the bar is full. Flaherty is sitting at the end of the bar wishing he had been there. I wish it too. There would have been less blood spilled. Akio comes in with his arm in a sling. He had gotten sixty stitches. He asked me where they live. I tell him I don't know. He says I think you do. I had a hard time convincing him that I didn't. But I wish I did because I would love for them to have some Japanese Justice.

After a few more stickups, McRory called me and said, "I spoke to Dennis Carey in the Red Blazer on the East Side. He is opening Red Blazer Too, another Bar and Restaurant and he will be looking for bartenders. You've got to get out of the La Salle before something bad happens to you. You've had a gun stuck in your face more often than me and I'm a cop for eighteen years."

I didn't leave right away, though. There was a bar on Broadway and 89th Street, one block down, called Willoughbys. The bartender was called Fast Eddie. He stayed open late and I would stop by once in a while. One night he let me in and there was a tall, well-dressed man in the corner by himself and a six foot five inch guy with long blond hair in the middle of the bar. Eddie introduced me as the Irish bartender up the block. It was my style to buy a drink for everybody.

The big blond said he was an actor. He worked with Richard Harris and Peter O'Toole. (As I tell this story, keep in mind 42nd Street at Times Square was very sleazy at the time. There was nothing on it but sex shows and peep shows and male and female prostitutes.)

The blond was okay in the beginning, but then he got nasty to me and started running down the Irish. The man in the corner was a local West Side Irish, listening to all this. He shouted at me, "You call yourself an Irishman and you take this shit from that blond fag? Hey Eddie let me out of here."

As Eddie opened the door, the Irish guy looked back at Blondie and said, "You know where I'm going now? Down to 42nd Street to see one of your movies. I think it's the one where you get fucked in the ass."

Blondie couldn't help himself, he had to laugh and so did the whole bar.

It was my thirtieth birthday; I left Fast Eddie and drove home. Back then if you smelled of alcohol but were not drunk, the cops would let you go. I got stopped on Queens Plaza by two black cops because the left rear light wasn't working.

Now, I had a habit of putting my wallet under my front seat. The night before, McRory had given me a book that had been written about him in the Emergency Police, which did not do him justice. When he gave me the book, I put it under the front seat and it pushed my wallet so far back I could not find it.

When the two cops pulled me over and asked for my license and registration, I could not find either. All I could find was the book. I tell the cops about the book but it does not work. The cop in charge was very nasty and his partner was very quiet, said nothing.

They cuffed me and called for another patrol car and when it came, they put me in the back seat with an old-timer. Then one of the black cops drives my car to the 108th Precinct. When I hear the old-time cop talking to the driver, I hear his Irish accent and say to him, "The cuffs are very tight. Can you release them a little?"

He says, "You got yourself into this mess, just put up with it."

When we get to the precinct, he takes me out of the back seat, walks me to a room, and sits me on a chair with the cuffs behind my back. Fifteen minutes go by, but it seems like ages. The cuffs are hurting. Then, in they walk, the nasty cop still in control. He holds up my wallet and says, "You couldn't find your wallet." Then he sits down and starts writing a ticket.

The quiet cop just stands there; he has said nothing since I was pulled over. I ask Nasty if he would take the cuffs off. "No!" he says. As he is writing, I lean over and ask if I can beat this ticket. He tells me that I can't beat this one.

"Well," I say, "if you don't show up for court two times, then I will beat it."

"Oh," he says, "you know the system?"

"I sure do. With all the cop friends I have, why not?"

He stops writing and puts the pen down. He's still nasty; he says to me, "This is all one big joke to you."

"Well," I say, "I was thirty years old today, and if the next thirty goes as fast as the last thirty, I am FUCKED!"

His quiet partner, with the best black humor, jumps up and down and yells, "Goddamn! That is good!" He slaps his hands and laughs his head off. Now I feel I can talk.

I say, "Look, guys, at the bar I work in, three precincts hang out there, the 20th, 24th and the 26th. As you already know,

I have very little on me, but I do have a case of beer in the back of the car and I come over the bridge every night, except on Sunday. I'll take care of business."

With that, he takes the cuffs off and walks me to the car. I went to court twice but he never showed up and I beat the ticket. After that, I put a hundred dollar bill in the glove compartment of the car and every night for two months I drove slow through Queens Plaza, hoping to meet them but I never did. Maybe they got transferred.

I called McRory a week or two after, asked him whether Dennis had opened up Red Blazer Too. It was ready to go, and I left the West Side for good.

Dennis Carey owned the Red Blazer on 82nd Street and Second Avenue. It was always full of people from 3:00 p.m. to 7:00 p.m. for the Early Bird Special. Then people kept on coming in until 2:00 a.m. It closed at 4:00 or 5:00 a.m. I often wonder about New Yorkers, why they would stand outside a bar and restaurant in the winter or summer, just to be rushed out after they finish eating if they weren't ordering drinks. Waiters and waitresses were told to move them to the bar, if there was room there, or out. "We need the table."

And across the street there's a bar restaurant. Same food, same drinks, looks even better, and, because they're not busy, nobody will rush you. They want you to stay. It makes the place look good to have extra people. But no, they want to be seen standing outside the Red Blazer.

Dennis opened a second place on 88th Street on Third Avenue, seven blocks away. He called it the Red Blazer Too. It was big. He put in a fifteen piece jazz band and a big kitchen. He hired cabs to take people off the line at The Red Blazer and bring them for free to the Red Blazer Too. To no avail. They preferred to stay on the line.

The Red Blazer Too did very good business, but there were no lines outside. I got a laugh one Saturday night. A young guy was parking his car outside and he gave a good bump to the car behind him. The guy who was sitting in the car jumped out and wanted money for the bump. The young guy ignored him, walked away and into The Red Blazer Too, sat at a table for two, got a menu and sat reading it. The older man followed him in, saw him at the table with the menu and figuring the young guy was going to have dinner, ran out to get the cops. Then the young guy got up, walked out, got into his car and drove away.

Ten minutes later, the old man came back in with two cops. The old man kept saying, "He was sitting here at this table." He came over to me, "You see a guy sitting at this table?"

I said, "Sir, I'm the bartender, I don't see what goes on at the tables."

He showed the bump to the cops and they told him that since his car didn't have any damage, they couldn't make out an accident report.

I felt good. I always have a dislike for people who make a mountain out of a molehill.

There were two other bartenders, Nathan and McHugh. They were telling me how many times Dennis had fired them. I asked them why they were still there. They told me that Dennis goes haywire when he's drinking and he fires everybody, but then he realizes he has nobody and hires them all back. But I had made a big mistake: I had said, "He'll only fire me once," and now I had to stick to my guns. I told myself that I'd never drink with him, so he'd never get the chance to fire me.

McRory was a good friend of Dennis and he got me the job. When the Irish folk singers called the Wolfe Tones were in the country, McRory and all his cop friends went wherever they went. After the Wolfe Tones played Carnegie Hall, they all came into The Red Blazer Too. There must have been forty of them.

Some cops are cheap. About twenty of them had formed a pool of five dollars each. The problem was that about half of them had reneged, but they were getting drinks anyway. Sixty dollars on the bar, two or three rounds and it's gone. There's four cops in the corner, two girls, two guys. One cop, Tommy Crowley, put up five dollars and ordered four scotches, a buck and a quarter each.

Dennis was drinking. Watch out! He squeezed into the corner and had me stop service to tell me that the cops were complaining that I was taking their money. He said he knew that was wrong, but make them happy, give them all a drink. I whispered to Dennis, "See this guy Tommy with the five dollars? I got his round poured already, let me collect, then I'll give them all a drink."

Dennis stayed in the corner watching Tommy put the five dollars back in his pocket. I said, "Okay, Tommy, thank you very much. Five dollars please."

Tommy never saw Dennis. He shouted at me, "I had five dollars on the bar. It was right there, you stole it Stoney." My, my, my, Dennis went ballistic. He attacked Tommy for what he saw him do. He ran to the guys who accused me, told them what he saw Tommy do, ran back to me yelling, "Stoney, don't give those fucks nothing!" then yelled more at them, "Coming into my place running down my staff, you cheap bastards. I don't need you assholes as customers!"

The next night a police lieutenant from the local precinct, Burkoski, came in. He knew Dennis and talked to him about the previous night's incident. I heard him say none of those guys were his men. Dennis agreed, and he had a drink and left.

Burkoski came in a few times after that with a friend, Joe. Joe always did the buying. A month went by. One night late,

Dennis, Joe and Burkoski come in drunk. Dennis told me he was saying good-bye to a good friend. Lieutenant Burkoski had retired. Burkoski said, "Dennis and myself were the best of friends for eight years."

One Saturday night, it had been very busy and Dennis had stayed all night. When I finished, he said, "You worked very hard, have a drink with me." He had already been drinking. We drank for two hours and he started abusing me.

I said, "You can do this to Nathan and McHugh. Not me."

He said, "Fuck you, you're fired."

"Okay, Dennis," I said, "Good Night."

I now had to stick to my word, so I went to Ireland with McRory for six weeks.

The All Ireland Football Final

Who's Playing in the All-Ireland?

First, let me tell you, I don't know anything about sports. I don't follow them at all. For example, football (or as the Americans call it, Irish football) is the national game of Ireland. It's run by the Gaelic Athletic Association, also known as the GAA. Each county has a team and the championship game, the All Ireland, is sort of like the Super Bowl in America and is played at Croke Park in Dublin, Ireland's capital. The players do not get paid, they play for the love of the game and the pride of their county.

My father would not let me play football. He would say that when the GAA paid for my broken leg, then, and only then, would I play football. Until then, he needed me in the field. There must have been a lot of fathers like mine in Leitrim, because I have been told that Leitrim has never won the All Ireland Cup. So I grew up knowing nothing about sports.

Years later I was in Ireland at the time of the All Ireland final and my friend Derek Warfield, a member of the Wolfe Tones, managed to get two tickets for us. He didn't know that I knew nothing about football and I didn't know that tickets to the final match were so hard to get that they're virtually priceless.

So there we were and everything was going great. Derek was jumping and hollering. Then halftime came. I can't recall what he said to me, but it was then that I asked him who was playing! He jumped out of his seat shouting, "What have I done? I got a priceless ticket for a guy who does not know which teams are playing!"

He ran away with his hands in the air. To make matters worse, it was his home team playing against some other county team. Derek came back for the second half and now I was hoping for his team to win. And they did and we all celebrated!

After Dennis fired me, McRory and I met up in Ireland with the Wolfe Tones, who knew a Polish guy, Poleiskey, who had come to Ireland as a teenager and came to own five restaurants and two travel agencies. A real success story. Some months before we arrived, the Russian soccer team had played in Dublin and lost to Ireland. Now Russia wanted a rematch, but they wanted it in Kiev. Poleiskey, being a sharp businessman with his two travel agencies, chartered a couple of planes to go to Kiev, with stops in other countries. Derek, from the Wolfe Tones, got tickets for McRory and me.

Our first stop was Warsaw, Poland for one day and one night, and then on to Kiev for three days. When we got to the hotel, they had set up a bank desk for us to change our currency into rubles. Everybody lined up to get rubles.

McRory asks me, "You getting on that line?"

I tell him, "I walk before I stand in line for a bus. If they don't take dollars, I'm not drinking."

When we got to a bar, we asked one of the bartenders if they took dollars. "Only dollars," one of them said. McRory and I had a great laugh when all those Irish guys finally came in with their rubles and the bartenders gave them a hard time, saying, "No rubles! Just dollars!"

McRory, Derek and I were standing outside the hotel on the second night, when a Russian with broken English approaches us and asks if we'd like to go to an after hours bar. "Absolutely," says McRory.

So he takes us two blocks and turns down a dark alley. McRory says, "This don't look good. I think we're walking into an ambush." The Russian is walking ahead of us. We stop and he waves to us. We don't move. He waves again and points to a door.

We decide to take a chance and move up to where we can see the door. The Russian knocks on the door, some kind of signal, and a very small hole in the door opens. We can see one eye looking out, then he opens the door and waves us all in. The place is packed. We can hardly see each other for all the smoke.

McRory loves having a good time. "These Russians don't speak English," he says. "Let's give them all names." He calls to the bartender and says, "Hey you, you Russian bastard, we want four beers. Now. You Russian son of a bitch."

Derek is laughing nervously, saying McRory is going to get us all killed, but the Russian who brought us all in thinks it's funny. He orders the drinks, but we pay. And we keep paying. Plus, we give him twenty dollars for bringing us there.

We're there for about half an hour when McRory says, "Do you all see that big monster of a man in the middle of the bar? He keeps staring at me."

Suddenly, the man jumps off his stool, pushes his way to us with his big fists, and says to McRory, "AMERICAN!"

"That's right, American," McRory says.

The big Russian says, "Second World War. Everybody freezing. American takes off his coat and give it to me. I want to buy you a drink."

McRory says, "Am I glad that American didn't take your coat."

The Irish lost the game.

We went to Bern, Switzerland next, where the Irish lost the soccer game to an amateur Swiss team. A couple of things fascinate me about Switzerland. It's an inland country with no access to open oceans; and they have large, half-acre swimming pools where everybody is naked.

I wasn't even allowed into the pool area with my clothes on. When I went in, I stood in the back by the fence to watch. I see young boys and girls with their parents. I see teenage girls lying on their backs and teenage boys jumping over them as if they weren't there. Grand mothers and grandfathers are sitting in chairs.

Then I realized that it must be our religious upbringing that has our minds screwed up. We could learn a lot from the Swiss. After observing it all, I feel us old-timers should leave being nude to the young folks.

The next day, a guy named Eamon and I met two girls at the pool and they asked us if we would like to go skiing. We said we would. They tell us they'll meet us at our hotel at 6:00 a.m. tomorrow. The next morning, we're in the lobby and they drive up, Sofia and Lina, in a convertible. When we got in the car it was seventy degrees; in one hour, they had us on a mountaintop where it was below freezing and there was real snow. What a thrill!

From there, we went to Milan, Italy for two days and then to Holland. There was a European folk festival going on in The Hague, but we stayed at a hotel in Amsterdam. Folk musicians from all over Europe were there. The Wolfe Tones and the Dubliners were staying at the same hotel as us. The Dubliners were a popular folk group, founded by Luke Kelly and Ronnie Drew. Luke had a big Afro-type hairdo and a flat face that looked like it had lost lots of fights. Sometimes, when he drank, it would break out in pimples. McRory knew him very well.

One morning, McRory and I are standing in the hotel lobby when we see Luke. McRory says, "Look at the sight of Luke. He looks really down. Let's go talk to him." McRory throws his arm around him and says, "Hey Luke. What's the matter? How bad can things be?"

Luke says, "Ah Jesus, Dan. Don't tell anyone. I was down on the canal last night where all the legal prostitutes are and the whore wouldn't fuck me. Said I was too ugly. Don't tell anyone."

McRory starts laughing, gives Luke another big hug, and says, "What, are you kidding? I'm going to tell everybody."

We flew back to Dublin and then to America. It was a great trip. I was glad Dennis had fired me.

When I came back, I thought I'd get a job right away, but I was out of work for months. A bar owner I knew, Pat Looney, hired me for his new place on 37th Street and Third Avenue, which he called The Rambling Rose after a song Nat King Cole made famous. I worked days. Lunch was okay. There was a young couple in their early thirties that came in three or four times a week and sat in the corner. I noticed that she would go to the bathroom and on her way back, she would talk to any young guy. A stranger. After ten or fifteen minutes, the boyfriend would leave. After another ten or fifteen minutes, she would leave with her new man. I saw this happen about four times. I'm thinking she's selling herself. I got to know them by name, Kim and Jim.

Next door, there was a very good restaurant and bar. It was located on the north side of the street and to give it a catchy name they called it Charlie's South. It was known as a gay bar, but everybody went there because of the food. They opened a second place on the south corner of 39th Street on Third Avenue and called it Charlie's North. The entrance was on Third Avenue, with an exit door out to 39th Street. It was strictly a gay bar, no food.

Kim came in on her own one afternoon and used the bathroom, then had a drink. She told me, "I always go to Charlie's South with friends for dinner. So I thought Charlie's North was the same. I walked in; it was all men and dark. I was met at the door by a man. 'Yes, madam. What can I do for you?' I told him I just want to use the bathroom. 'Right this way, madam.' He walked me to the back where there's a door with big red letters: Ladies Room. Before I knew what was happening he had the door open and I'm standing on the sidewalk on 39th Street."

We had a good laugh. I bought her a drink and asked if her boyfriend was working. She said he's not her boyfriend, he's her husband. I said he's a pretty cool dude if he doesn't mind you with other men.

She said, "It's like this. He likes to watch me having sex with other men. Our closet door has a two-way mirror. He stays in the closet and watches." She said that at first she wasn't crazy about it but then she got into it herself.

She said, "What is your day off?" I told her Monday.

She said, "Can I meet you here? You and I will have a good time. Let Jim enjoy himself in the closet."

"Kim, I must be a real clod. I got to pass on this one. It wouldn't be comfortable at all with someone watching in a two-way mirror."

"Kim," I said, "if you like it that much why not charge money?"

Two months later, Pat sold The Rambling Rose to a gay woman and I was looking for another job. I was hoping to buy a bar someday. Some people would tell me that the big money was in gay bars and I thought about it. Gays don't bother me. Why not?

One night I'm driving up Third Avenue. I'm passing the old Rambling Rose. It's 2:00 a.m. I decide to go in and it was full. There was music and a lot of men dancing, hugging and kissing. One of the bartenders was telling a customer his hair was ravishing.

I went to work for a contractor I had met, Aidan Ross, who had opened a new bar at 27th Street on Seventh Avenue, in the Garment District. At the time it was ninety percent Jewish owned, with minimum wage workers. Not a good neighborhood for an upscale restaurant and bar. Across the street was FIT, the Fashion Institute of Technology. There was eighteen hundred girls and four hundred men. Some of the girls would come in, but none of them had any money. I guess everything was paid for by daddy and mommy. They would go to the East Side where they could meet young guys to buy them drinks.

I got to know a girl named Karen, from Chicago. She was very outgoing. She'd stay late until I closed and ask me to walk her to the dormitory. She would say, "I'd take you up but we can't have boys in." She asked me where I lived and I told her Flushing.

"Alone?" she asked.

"Yes," I said.

I would see her from time to time with her girlfriends. They would stop in for a drink before they headed east to meet the boys with the money.

She comes back from the East Side one Saturday night, tells me her girlfriends all met guys, but she came back to me. (What a line of b.s.) She tells me that she told the school she wouldn't be in that night. She says she's going home with me tonight.

We have a few drinks and it's 6:30 a.m. when we get to Flushing. We go in the living room and Karen takes off her clothes. No bedroom for Karen, so we start making out on the couch. Nothing has happened yet, but out of the blue yonder, she jumps up and runs out the door into the street, naked. I grab a blanket from the couch and run after her, telling myself I'll be locked up for attempted rape if a cop car drives down, me with a nude girl in the middle of the street.

I don't know what I said, but I talked her back into the house with the blanket wrapped around her. I start helping her to get dressed and when she is almost dressed, she starts making out again. I tell her it's very late and I've got to work tonight. I got to get her home. She seems to have her wits about her at that point and says that she told them that she wouldn't be home. I say, "You weren't home. Today is Sunday." I drop her off and she's kissing and hugging me, saying she'll be in to see me.

The following weekend she comes in with her girlfriends, jumps on the bar step giving me a hug and a kiss. From there on, I'd buy her a drink, but I was scared of her.

The bar owner, Ross, didn't pay his creditors and everything was auctioned off. I met Mick Carty who was very successful in the business he owned, Rosie O'Grady's. I said it's very sad about Ross losing everything. Not everything says Mike. He has a big house in New Jersey, and it's the cat's meow.

Now I'm looking for another bar job. I decided to take the subway to Wall Street and started walking uptown going into every bar. I had no luck until I got to 43rd Street and Eighth Avenue, a bar called the Blarney Stone. There were twenty-seven Blarney Stone bars in the city. Dan Flanagan, the owner, had working partners in each one of them.

When I went in, it was 3:00 p.m. and lunch was over. I asked the bartender if the boss was around. He pointed to a guy wearing an apron sitting in the middle of the bar. I introduced myself. I knew the right thing to do, so I put a twenty on the bar, ordered a club soda, and bought him and his friend drinks. I asked if he had any jobs and he asked where I had worked. I told him for Jack Becket for eight years. He said that he knew Jack very well and introduced himself, Tommy Stinson.

He said, "I own this bar. I'll give you a few shifts. If you work out, I know another Blarney Stone. Come in tomorrow night."

"Thank you very much," I said.

As we were talking, a young Irish guy, a student out for the summer, walked in casually and asked him for any shifts. Tommy turned and looked at him, and very abruptly told him no. Then the kid asked where there was another Blarney Stone and Tommy told him to just keep walking, he'd find them. This did not faze the student. He walked away. Now, I remember when I first came to the city I didn't know north from south, east from west, so I said, "Excuse me, when you walk out the door make a right. You'll find a Blarney Stone on 56th and Eighth Avenue." He thanked me and kept going.

I said, "Tommy, were you not a little rough on the kid?"

He says, "Let me tell you, we were raised to be hard working. Did you not hear what those students are doing the past five years?"

"Well Tommy," I said, "I did hear something."

"Yes," says Tommy, "they have screwed themselves. They won't pay anybody, skip out on rents, run up hundreds of dollars on people's phones and when you confront them, they're gone. Ireland will have some time in the future with those bastards."

I worked for Tommy for one week. Then he got me a job in a Blarney Stone on Sixth Avenue, 47th Street. There were two across the street from each other, on 46th and 47th Sts. I worked Saturday and Sunday night on 46th Street. Next door was a rundown dump, with X-rated movies and peep shows on the ground floor, and a whorehouse upstairs. They all came in for food at the steam table and took it with them.

A guy came in one night from the dump of a peep show and said he was the manager. I tried to show no surprise but I'm sure it showed. It was now-retired Lieutenant Burkoski.

I said, "It's hard to live on a pension nowadays; you've got to make ends meet."

I'm saying to myself, what a change of pace.

The place on the second floor was called Pillow Talk. It was run by a young black guy named Keith. He was big, six foot five inches, in his thirties and good-looking. He would tell me he was going to college for a degree in business.

I said, "Keith, you're getting on the job experience upstairs."

He had fifteen girls, mostly white. Sometimes two or three of them would come down, get a sandwich, and take it upstairs.

One Sunday night, it was January, it was zero degrees and there was three inches of snow. It's 1:00 a.m.

Keith walks in.

"Stoney, ten pastrami and five corned beef sandwiches on rye with mustard."

As I'm slicing the meat, I'm making conversation. I ask, "How's business?"

"Not good," he says.

"Well," I say, "it's very cold outside and with snow on the ground."

He says, "That shouldn't stop dicks from getting hard."

"Well," I say, "Every business has its drawbacks."

I worked with another barman, Frank Dillon, from County Clare. We had lots of fun, and fun with the customers. There was one black man named Rufus who used to talk a lot, and when he got a few drinks in him, he would talk about different countries and governments. Frank would joke with him and say, "You know everything."

He'd say," Frank, I don't know everything, but I know a little bit about everything. I know that there is over one billion Chinese in the world and there is a pig for every one of them. Man, do these people love pork!"

Frank and I laughed in disbelief, it would amuse you what would come out of his mind.

Making A Deal

Mike Carty, my friend from way back, was now the owner of Rosie O'Grady's bar in Midtown. He called me to tell me one of his chefs, Otis, a German guy from Yorkville, knew of a small building with a bar up in his neighborhood, 85th Street, near First Avenue that may be for rent or sale.

McRory was still a cop and he knew nothing about the bar business, but he always talked about us getting a bar together and being partners. I called the owner, a retired New York City detective from County Cork, named Dennis Forde. He was buying and selling buildings all over the five boroughs, from hundreds of thousands to millions of dollars. He was doing better with his retirement than Lieutenant Burkoski in the X-rated peep show, working for sleazebags.

McRory and I met Forde at the place on Sunday. It looked like it needed a lot of work, but it had a nice crowd of older people. The first thing I noticed was the sewer pipe coming through the ceiling, through the middle of the floor and into the basement; the wood was rotten all around the pipe. They had put clay into the hole, and it had gotten hard. So it was leak proof. There were two cats drinking milk out of it. This is something you'd see in the mountains in Leitrim—cats drinking milk out of a hole in the middle of the floor.

Forde says, "I will rent the bar for key money, fifty thousand dollars, or I'll sell the building to ye."

I'm thinking I can't pay fifty thousand dollars and then gut the place. Anyway, what I wanted was a corner building, so that was the end of that.

Or was it?

I always remember my father saying, "Eyes, ears and feet are worth a million each. Try and hang on to them. Money is secondary, but, if you do make money, buy a building." I had loaned some money months back to an Irish guy in Queens, who had to go back home to Ireland because of the death of a family member.

A couple of weeks after the meeting, I called him up and asked if he could repay me. I was surprised when he told me to meet him on 61st and Roosevelt Avenue, Woodside at 5:00 p.m. today. I took the train to the 61st Street stop. The Irish guy wasn't there, so I decided to walk across the street for coffee. Coming around the corner, a car had to stop for me. I didn't look at the driver, but he shouts at me, "It's Forde!" What a chance encounter.

He says, "Get in." So I do. He parks the car and we go for coffee together.

He tells me, "I'll deal with one guy and that's you. Then you can do what you want. I'll sell you the building. No more haggling, two hundred thousand dollars."

He asked how much cash I could give him; I told him sixty thousand. He said, "That'll do me. Here's what you do. Go to the bank or banks. If they don't lend to you, then I'll take on the mortgage and here's a tip—don't bring a cop into the bar business. I don't know one that was successful yet."

"Thanks," I say.

McRory, as a cop, can't buy, or work in, a premises that's licensed to sell liquor. It's New York State law. He said that he'd put in for early retirement. I got an Italian lawyer named Verini. When we met him he tells us that he's been dealing with Irishmen for forty years and a handshake is as good as a written contract. He must have really believed that because he never held back any escrow money. He did not check to see that there's no taxes owed on the business or the building.

We went to the closing, Verini, Forde and his lawyer. When all the papers were signed but one, Forde tells his lawyer to call the bank and find out the interest rate. Twelve percent. Okay, says Forde, sign that. I charge the same as the bank, twelve percent. We sign the last paper, then go back to the bar. Forde didn't tell me that he had counted every bottle, and every half and every quarter bottle. I had to pay another four thousand, five hundred dollars in cash for the stock.

I was still working in the Blarney Stone, so I tell Colm Brogan, the night manager, that I bought a place.

He asked me do I want to stay on here for a while? I said yes.

"Well," he said, "Dan Flanagan keeps in touch with the Liquor Dealers Association and your name will pop up, and you will be history the next day. Go to the boss tomorrow morning. Tell him your brother-in-law is a cop. He bought a bar but he can't show his name. He's using your name on the license."

I did that the very next day and it worked.

I was working there when Bobby Sands in the North of Ireland made worldwide headlines. He was on a hunger strike in Long Kesh jail in Belfast. He was protesting the harsh treatment of prisoners by the Maggie Thatcher administration. He had been elected to the British Parliament and to the Irish Government while he was in jail. He was about to die when the Northern Aid and the IRA organized demonstrations outside all English embassies in many countries. They went one step further and contacted every bar in the whole city and asked them to close from 4:00 p.m. to 7:00 p.m. on a certain day, in support of the hunger strike. It was amazing. All of the Italian and Greek restaurants closed in respect and they hadn't even been asked.

A few of Flanagan's partners were IRA sympathizers, like Tommy Stinson, the first guy that hired me. Most of the partners wanted to close, but Dan Flanagan was so cheap, he never sat in a cab; buses and subways were his ways of transport. He said he's not closing twenty-seven places for some guy who wants to starve himself for a cause. His places will stay open.

Four days before the bars were to close, I was working on 47th Street with Frank Dillon. His brother had come out from Ireland to visit and because his brother, Frank, is working in a Blarney Stone, he brings with him a clipping from the Irish Times newspaper saying that a partner of Dan Flanagan had sold his share of a Blarney Stone on 59th and Madison Avenue, New York City for one million dollars. Back in Ireland in 1981 you could buy five bars for that.

I took the clipping home. The next morning, Flanagan was waiting for me. He was a quiet man. He said, "Do you have that clipping Stoney?"

"I left it home, Mr. Flanagan."

"Would you bring it in tomorrow?"

"Yes sir."

When he saw his name in the newspaper, he wanted no screwups. He went around personally to all his partners. No misunderstanding. Close all Blarney Stones. I was told later that what scared him the most was the thought of being kidnapped for ransom. Frank Dillon's brother made history. Thanks for coming over!

I left the Blarney Stone. We decided to gut the place we had bought on East 85th Street, which we had named Ryan's Daughter, after the famous movie starring Robert Mitchum and Sarah Miles. We hired Joe Carty and Frankie Dwyer as contractors. We started on the second floor first. When that was finished, we opened it and closed the first floor. We stayed open through all the renovation. The first floor got new everything— new bar and kitchen.

Back in the 1980s it was a trend for all bars to have a canopy inside over the bar. Joe asked Frankie to build the canopy but he built it according to his own height. He's five foot one inch. Our first Saint Paddy's Day I hired two six-foot tall bartenders. They hit their heads when they walked behind the bar.

Frankie Dwyer was one of the smartest guys I met. My father was right. He used to say you measure a man's height from his neck up.

I got a call from my brother Jim in Dublin. A friend of his was coming to New York, could I hire him. I said, tell him to come see me when he gets here. Two days later, a little guy came in, asked for me, told me his name is Henry and that he's a friend of Jim's. I told him I have three or four weeks of work. I had him helping me most of the time. I said to him, "You're from Dublin, but do I detect a slight Northern Ireland accent?" He told me yes.

"How did you meet my brother Jim?"

He said, "When I got out of Long Kesh after twelve years for killing two British soldiers, I came to Dublin, knew nobody. Met Jim and he's the only friend I know."

"Well," I said, "I don't' think Jim is into the cause."

Henry said that Jim never knew until a few months ago, when he applied for a Donnelly visa to go to the States. They had mailed him the form. So he had to ask somebody for advice and Jim was the only one he knew and he told Henry not to lie on the form. So he hadn't and it had worked, he got the visa. I said, "It worked out for you."

I told him I knew a guy who did time in Long Kesh, lied on the form, and came to live in Woodside. He was here one week, a knock on the door at 2:00 a.m. FBI saying, you want to stay in the United States? You join the Northern Aid and IRA and report to us. He said no, no and no. The FBI gave him a free trip home.

I said, "Henry, do you mind telling me how you got caught?"

"We were hiding out up in the mountains. The Special Branch called. The Black Watch got us. They beat us very badly. We were in the hospital for a long time, but we survived. It was their buddies we killed."

I used to cook lunch and sit everybody at a big round table in the back. Joe Carty had bought a new walk-in van and he wanted steel shelves welded into the sides. He knew this welder who worked out of his truck, so he called him and told him he wanted the shelves put in and where he was working, and he gave the guy the address.

The next day, Henry and I were working on the wall up front, when Joe's welder pulls up outside, gets out of the truck. Henry looks out and says to me, "The guy outside by the truck is the Black Watch Special Force sergeant who beat us half to death."

What a coincidence. Three thousand miles away, on a side street in New York City and you guys meet. Holy Mackerel!

Joe Carty was always up for devilment. When I told him who his welder friend was, he said, "Well, we'll have to have them sit together at lunch."

When I told McRory, he was not pleased.

Henry said, "I did my time. No grudges. I have to get on with my life."

When I got them lunch, I made sure they didn't sit together.

McRory's parents were from the north, so he was a sympathizer. When everybody was sitting, he came to the table and said to Black Watch Special Force guy, "You wouldn't put a pimple on a cop's ass. All you are is an invader. I wouldn't sit at this table with a fuck like you. Henry, you do what you want."

He walked away; nobody said a word. By the way, Henry and the welder never did speak.

Henry decided to go back to Ireland. The English Black Watch guy became a religious freak, always carrying the Bible. The last I heard, they put him in an insane asylum in the Bronx.

We needed an accountant, so I called Dennis Carey of the Red Blazer. We had made up and had become good friends. He told me he liked his accountant, Sal Roungen.

"He asks me nothing. Comes in, does the books and leaves."

"Dennis, I don't know about that, but we're so busy if you think he's okay, I'll chance him."

Our business was not good, but there was some money coming in. I ask Sal, "Are we paying our taxes?"

"Yes," he said, "everything is fine."

McRory wanted to take some money out, but I said we've got to pay the contractors and get this work done and get the kitchen open.

We got the kitchen open with a chef, a prep guy, a waitress, and porters. When the meat supplier came in looking for his money, McRory was there and told him there was no money. When I came back later, McRory said, "This white elephant is too much for me, so much work and time and nothing to show for it." He says, "When it comes to paying those guys, I want you to do it. I don't like paying out money. I like to take in money."

Then came the big shock. A lady walked in saying she was from the IRS. "This place hasn't paid taxes in three years. I will be putting a chain on this door in two weeks."

I called a friend, Johnny Mahon. He also had had hard times starting off, but now had five bars and restaurants. He told me his accountant, Jeff Bernstein, was the best. He wasn't taking on new clients, but he gave me his number anyway. I called Jeff and told him our big problem. He said because I was a friend of Mahon's, he'd come and look at our books. When he saw the books, he said first he'd call the IRS, get a stop on the chain on the door. "My fee is ten thousand dollars."

While we're discussing how to go about dealing with this tax problem, in walks a man saying he's from the IRS. Fifteen thousand dollars back taxes on the building. He says it was twelve thousand, but with penalties, it's now fifteen.

After Jeff got everything postponed, he started in on Sal, our first accountant. He looked normal, but he had had a nervous breakdown. With all his clients, for three years, he had come in, taken his check and thrown all the tax papers in the garbage. Jeff was able to talk him into giving us back his salary.

We tried to get Forde to pay the fifteen thousand dollars, but to no avail. Two more years pass; with penalties, it's now up to sixty thousand dollars. Our old lawyer, Verini, had had an assistant, Joe Porcelli who, with a partner named Maloney, had opened his own office. Jeff told me Joe Porcelli was very well liked by the IRS boys. And man, could he negotiate a deal.

So I hired Joe. First, he went to the IRS and got the penalties cut in half, to thirty thousand dollars. Then he went to Forde, explained how it was his twelve thousand dollars originally that had risen to sixty. He told him the IRS would drop it to thirty if it got paid by the end of the month. "Stoney feels he owes none of it, but to get it over with he'll split it with you and pay fifteen thousand."

"It's a deal," says Forde.

Joe was worth his ten thousand dollars.

McRory said, "We got to get out of this white elephant. We'll sell and you go on your own and buy another place. It's not a problem to you to build another place."

I said, "I can't. I know where every nut, bolt, hand valve and shutoff valve is. I can't do it again."

"Here's my problem," he said. "If you stay and make it I can't take it. My friends will be ribbing me. How you made it and I didn't."

"I'll buy you out," I say.

"I'll make you pay," says McRory.

He got a good Jewish lawyer who told him to never make eye contact with me again. I got a fool of an Irish American lawyer. McRory wanted three hundred thousand dollars. I offered him two hundred and fifty thousand dollars, but property values were going up.

We ended up in court and, at a hearing, we went up in front of a woman judge. She went into a long talk about how if we could come to an agreement today it would be better for all the parties involved. Not for the lawyers, though.

If we didn't come to an agreement, then she would start the proceedings, which could last for months. She said, "I want you all to go out into the hall for twenty minutes and try and solve your differences."

We all went out into the hall. I took it upon myself to talk, not looking at McRory, because he wouldn't look at me. I said, "I have offered you two hundred and fifty thousand dollars. You want three hundred. To eliminate months and months of lawyer's fees, I'll give you two eighty. If you're going to fight over twenty thousand, then let's go to court."

He told his lawyer he wanted to call his wife. He came back; she had said to do it. We go back in and tell the judge. She's so happy, "This is always best for everybody."

Now I have no money to pay McRory. I go to my friend Mike Carty, owner of Rosie O'Grady's, tell him my story. (It was him who got me the place through his chef.) I say, I need three hundred thousand dollars. He said he would introduce me to Bill Burke. He's the king in the Bank of Ireland on Fifth Avenue and 51st Street. He says, if he doesn't give it to you, then I will. Ever since, when he and I meet, we never talk about it, but I never forgot him for saying that.

I went to Bill Burke's office and explained to him how we had signed the papers, but our names were still on the deed.

He said, "That's all bullshit. Where is the building?"

"Eighty-fifth and First Avenue."

He said, "I'm going to look at it and you call me in the morning."

"Okay, Bill."

When I call him the next morning, Bill says, "You got the three hundred thousand dollars. Who's your lawyer?"

"Joe Porcelli."

Bill says, "I hate lawyers. I'll call him and make all the arrangements to have everybody come to my office. Those guys can't run things when they're in my office."

A few days go by. We all meet in Burke's office. McRory must have decided to do what his lawyer told him: no eye contact. He didn't come. Porcelli arrives with a trainee lawyer. He keeps telling the kid, "Ignore everything you see here today. Stoney legally doesn't own the building."

Burke says, "The papers were signed in front of lawyers. He'll legally own it in twenty minutes."

Then he gives me a look and says, what did I tell you about fucking lawyers?

Burke told me to meet him in his office the next morning for my money. Back then interest rates were eighteen percent and the news on TV and the papers was that they were going to go to twenty-four percent. Everybody was scared. Including me. I ask Burke to lock in the interest.

He says, "Stoney, is there a bank in New York that would lend you money?"

I say, "No."

"There you have it. I ain't locking it in because it's going to twenty-four percent."

"I understand," I said.

McRory got his check. I got rid of the kitchen, put in a basketball machine and made a few more changes. I don't know why myself, but the place took off. I had five bartenders on Thursday, Friday and Saturday nights. The interest rate on the bank loan fell to fourteen percent, then twelve, then ten, then seven, then five and a half. My last year, I was paying two and a half percent. Was I lucky Burke refused to lock it in.

The Germans Have Arrived

We had no day business. A young neighbor, Neal, came to me.

He said, "I know a German woman, her name is Ruth. She's looking for a job."

I said, "You tell her there's no day business and she will make no money."

Muriel and Stoney

Oil painting of Ryans Daughter by Gerard Carry well
known Irish artist. See his bio carryartist.com

Oil Painting of Stoney

Front Row; Stoney, Nuala, Jim.
Back Row; Bernadette, Josephine, Una, Mother, Mary, Ann, Vera

He says, "Hire her. She'll bring her own business."

I ask him, "If she's that good, why did she lose her job?"

He tells me that the owner of the Heidelberg Restaurant is a woman who doesn't like the way her daughter is running the place. She has a son living in Germany who she asked to come to New York and run the place. He was very old-fashioned and strict and the first thing he did was to fire Ruth and it had upset a lot of the regulars.

He said, "She needs the job."

I said, "Have her talk to me."

I never met a German without self-confidence, but this little older lady came in very nervous, introduced herself as Ruth.

I asked her, "You think you can make it worth your while?"

"Oh yes," she said. "Can I work for you?"

"It's all yours," I said. "When do you want to start?"

"Monday," she said, "I need to tell all my friends. I'll come in Thursday and get familiar with the place."

She arrives at 10:00 a.m. Monday, typical German, very efficient. She got the bar set up the way she wanted it. Germans started coming in by 2:00 p.m. and by 6:00 p.m., there were sixty Germans in the place. I could not believe it. They had come from Ridgewood, Maspeth, Long Island and New Jersey to show support for her. Come 11:00 p.m., the ones who had to travel started leaving to go home. They started shaking hands, saying good-bye as if they hadn't had a drink, and there were many empty bottles of Jaegermeister and Asbach German brandy, and Beck's beer.

It was then I realized that the Irish have the name for drinking, but that's just it, the name. In Ryan's Daughter we have glass doors up front that open up. If we had sixty Irish guys drinking from 2:00 p.m. to 11:00 p.m. there would have been a fight and when they were leaving it would be through the glass windows not the door. Yesiree, the Germans can drink. We Irish can't drink. Well, some of us can.

In the next few years I got to know a lot of Germans' names, like Adolf, Fritz, Jurgan, Vladimir, Claus, Carl, Peter, Louie. I want to talk about them. Big Joe was from Bavaria. He had a great sense of humor. They had an Italian friend, Alfio. He used to kid them and they used to kid him.

One night, Alfio was talking about the Second World War and something the Italians did.

Big Joe says, "Alfio, do you want me to show you an Italian in the Second World War?"

"Yes, Joe, show me," Says Alfio.

So Joe jumps off the chair, turns his back to us, puts his hands up on the wall as high as he can and says, "This is an Italian in the Second World War."

There was a big German who everybody called Berliner Carl. He was born in West Virginia, but his father and mother went back to Germany when he was three years old. When the war started, he fought for the Germans. Meanwhile, Big Joe, Jurgan and Fritz had come to America in their teens and were drafted into the American army. They fought against their own Germans. One evening Berliner Carl was talking about the war and how he saw it. Big Joe said, "But Carl, you must understand we were on the winning side." I found that quite interesting; to hear a German-born tell an American-born that he was on the winning side.

I also found it interesting that back then, if you arrived in the United States and you were under twenty-five years old, you had to sign up for the draft. Orloff, Fritz and Vladimir were all drafted. Vladimir was in the German army at fifteen. He came home to his village once in a German uniform.

The war ended, he came to America and got drafted. Now he was in the American army. And what do you know? He got stationed in Germany. When he got leave, he went to his village in his American army uniform and some of his neighbors said, "You left here wearing the German uniform and now you are back wearing the American uniform? You turncoat bastard."

Berliner Carl lived a few blocks away from Ryan's Daughter. He worked four blocks away in a Gristedes' supermarket. He was the dairy manager there for twenty-five years. He told me they brought in all young guys, in their thirties, with foul mouths and fired everybody they could find who had only three or four years left before collecting Social Security and a pension.

Carl never used a curse word and because of their foul mouths he called them the Ugly Americans. He called his union explaining that they wanted to beat him out of his pension. He had only three years left. To make it hard for him, they transferred him to a store in Brooklyn. It was rough on a sixty-two-year-old, who was overweight and hadn't ridden a bus or subway in twenty-five years, but he beat them and got his full Social Security and pension.

He told me he had no problem coming to the United States. He was born here, but because he was raised in Germany, he had to learn English. He said he was lucky that he was captured by the Americans and not the Russians. He was also lucky that the job he got was to cook for all the Allies. His job was an assistant chef. The head chef was an Irish guy who wouldn't teach him English, so he tried to teach himself.

The Allies came in three separate shifts. First, the French would drive up in jeeps; the Irish chef would say, "Here comes the Frogs," and Carl would write down, "Here comes the Frogs."

Then the Russians would drive up; he would say, "Here comes the Bears." Carl would write that down, "Here comes the Bears."

Then the British would drive up; he would say, "Here comes the Cocksuckers." Carl would write that down, "Here comes the Cocksuckers."

After a few months, when it was all over, everybody went their own way. He got the go ahead to come to America. He wrote to his uncle in the Bronx, telling him when he's arriving at JFK Airport.

"He picked me up. He's telling me he has two German couples over to meet me, to have dinner and celebrate me surviving the war. We get to the Bronx. They were all sitting around the table having dinner, speaking German. A woman asked me what I was doing as a prisoner and did I learn any English. I tell them I was cooking for the Frogs, the Bears and the Cocksuckers. That's when my uncle grabbed me and took me into the kitchen and tells me if I talk like that again in his house, I'll be looking for a new place to live. After everybody calmed down, they all could see in my eyes and face that I was innocent about what I said."

The other staff that worked in the bar while Ruth worked days were Wendy, from Dublin, in her early twenties back then, with the punk hair style, and John Healy from County Mayo, who had curly black hair. Wendy and John got on great and both were great with customers; they became the best of friends.

After a number of years, John went back to Ireland to open a bar with his sister, with help from his brother and mother. He went on to open other successful restaurants and bars, including a well-known one called Mother Hubbard's in County Kildare, which he designed and built himself.

He was the first one in Ireland to provide wheelchair access and toilets for the disabled, before it was a planning requirement, and he went on to campaign for all new buildings to do the same. The campaign was successful, and today it is a building requirement in Ireland.

Wendy went to California, had two beautiful children, and lived and worked there for a number of years.

Some thirty-five years after Wendy and John bartended in Ryan's Daughter, John returns, and lo and behold, so does Wendy. John helped her get an apartment and a job and they rekindled their friendship.

Funny where life takes people, and sometimes takes them back.

John was in New York when he was six years old, with lots of travel in between; his wish was always to return later in life.

Life Is Like a Roller Coaster

When I was twenty-three years, old I met a girl named Brigid, in Rockaway Beach. She was also twenty-three years old and we hit it off well. We had lots of laughs and fun for a week, but I was truck driving then and soon was off to California and gone on the road for three months. When I got back, I called her and to my surprise, she was pleased to hear from me. For the next three weeks, we saw each other every night. Then I was away again.

Every time I was back in town, I would call and Brigid would see me. This went on for two years. Then she met a guy who was nuts about her. On one occasion, I was back in town and we were in bed when her phone rings. She answers it. "Okay," she says, and hangs up. She then jumps out of the bed, grabs my clothes and shouts, "Out! Out! Out!" Her boyfriend's on the corner. She opens the door and shoves my clothes into my arms. Outside, naked, I jump a fence and get dressed in someone's backyard. Phew!

Next time I was in town, I called her again and she said to come over. I asked her if she had the same boyfriend. "Yes, and he wants to marry me." She had been a one-man woman, but now she had two.

We were sitting on her couch chatting about the future and our plans. I tell her that I'm young and I want to travel and see all of America. Maybe I'll settle down in ten years.

She says, "I love him, but I love you more." I tell her that I'm in the same boat as her, as I was seeing a girl in the Bronx, Jenny Mulligan, and I am crazy about her and she is crazy about me.

I told her Jenny is twenty-six and she wants to marry me and I told her the same thing, that I am too young and I want to travel. Just then the doorbell rings. Here we go again! She grabs me and puts me in the closet. Is it him?

Now, I'm in the closet and I can hear talking, but I can't hear what they are saying. My God, what if he stays over. In the closet, it felt like an hour had gone by. My feet are getting tired. With my back against the wall, I lower myself down on my honkers and the wall at the back of me gives way and I tumble down what seems like three steps. I lay there waiting and waiting. Nobody comes. Now I feel safe; it's dark and I fall asleep.

I wake up with Brigid's voice saying, "Where are you?" She did not know there was a space behind the closet wall, which was a door to a boiler room.

I asked, "What's the story?" She said it wasn't the boyfriend but a friend of her brother's selling insurance and she had to do the whole Irish thing and make him tea and cookies, and then chat. Then he got the insurance business.

I said to her, "We got to stop meeting like this."

We kissed and she said it was hard to say good-bye. "Give me a call sometime for old times' sake."

A year later, I met her sister, who knew about us. She told me that Brigid was married and she missed me, that I should give her a call. It was a bad move. I was still in town waiting for a full load to go to Dallas, Texas, so I called her. She was all excited; her husband was away hunting for four days. She invited me out for dinner and I went. She had a beautiful setup for dinner, with wine and candles, etc.

It was getting late and, as we were talking away, I was getting this feeling her husband may come back. I told her I was leaving, but she said, "No, he won't be back." I kissed her good night and went to my car and looked back at her sad face. I threw her phone number away and that was that.

Or was it?

I had also kept in contact with some of Jenny's friends. They told me she had met an Italian guy when they both were going for the same parking spot. It was love at first sight and they were married within a month.

When I was in my twenties, I thought I do not want to bring kids into this world. Some women can be selfish and want to have a baby with no means to provide for it. A baby needs to fed, and loved, and educated. At that time a girl told me she was pregnant, it turned out to be a false alarm. A month later I make an appointment with a clinic on first avenue, 26 street

Manhattan to have a vasectomy, "snip, snip". The procedure was a couple of hours and not all that expensive. My plan was if I ever get married, the woman better already have kids, and that was a slim chance at the time.

Thoughts on Life

Ruth got old and quit the bar job. Then I got Rosie, a Hungarian who had worked in the neighborhood since she came to the country. She had worked in bakery shops and meat shops, etc., but never in a bar, but she knew everybody in the area. She was so efficient. You would think she had been bartending all her life. Her husband had worked here when it was The Old Stream years back. She always said he would turn over in his grave if he could see her behind the bar.

My life is very good and, as my father used to say, I still got the three million I was born with: eyes, ears and feet. You lose one of them and you're down a million. It doesn't matter what business you go into, you're going to have your ups and downs.

When I gave up trucking and became a bartender, I met a lot of Irish-American police who were members of the police Emerald Society Pipe Band. One group of them had a trip to Ireland to play at big conventions for the Irish government. I joined them for a trip and they played in the Dail Eireann at Dublin City Hall. It was there I met a woman named Muriel, who was thirty-six years old. I went out with her a few times while I was there.

The following year, Muriel and three friends came to New York for a trip. We met again, but in the meantime she had met a guy from Baltimore. I told her, "You're on vacation for two weeks. Enjoy yourself and have fun. Go out with anybody that gives you a laugh, but try to squeeze me in for a night or two."

And she did. When the two weeks were up, I drove them to the airport.

The next year, the Pipe Band went to Ireland again and I went with them. They had to play at a wedding for a member of the Wolfe Tones. The press gave it big coverage. I called Muriel and she told me that she had seen pictures of us in the newspapers and on the TV. I met and took her to dinner. She told me she had separated from her husband five years ago and had five kids, the oldest eighteen, and the two youngest still in boarding school.

Later, I met them all. She told me her husband lived in Howth, County Dublin. He would not give her a divorce, but he did take care of the kids. She asked him for nothing; she had a job in a hair salon, rented a small room, and visited the kids four times a week.

Stoney and Muriel

I never seen a room so empty in my life. It had a two-foot fridge, with a small carton of milk in it and some cheese. Years later I asked why the fridge was so empty. She said, "I like to keep slim." She would never say she had no money.

The next year, the guys in the band invited three of her friends to New York and she joined them for two weeks. This time she stayed with me. When I would come to work to bartend, she would stop in later to pass the time. One evening I told her she should go see a movie in the area. I sent Rafferty with her so she would not be on her own. I had to wake him up first (recall he had the sleeping problem). While they were in the theater, he fell asleep and started to snore. People were yelling at him to shut up, so she moved a few seats away from him and when the movie was over, she left him and came back to the bar.

She went back to Ireland and shortly after she wrote to me to say that three of the kids were now working and living on their own and the other two were in private school. They were all raised now.

I was in my sister's house one evening after getting that letter and I told Vera my feelings for Muriel. She said, "Call her now and tell her your true feelings for her."

Is it Love?

I called her and asked her to come to New York. She was worried that she wouldn't get a job, but I convinced her that would all be okay. A few days went by; she called me and said, "Yes, why not?"

Was it Love?

When she arrived in New York, it was a good time as the bar and restaurant had just opened. Vera was working three nights and there were also some part-time waitresses. Muriel was new to all of this and Vera showed her the ropes. She was a fast learner and eager to make the place a success.

On quiet nights, Muriel would work on her own, and on Friday and Saturday nights, she worked with Vera. One customer, Ted Poster, was a regular who was helpful and familiar to all of us as he was in the supply business to bars and restaurants. Sometimes he would leave his tab and tip to be paid the following night. One Thursday night, Muriel was working on her own, Ted came in for dinner, and left his tab to be paid the next night.

He came back in on Friday night and paid Muriel for his previous tab, plus tip, and as Muriel was putting the tip in her pocket, she saw Vera glaring at her. She told me the next day, "I think Vera thought I should have put it in the tip jar, from the look she gave me. I'm sorry now I didn't put it in."

Muriel was so honest and innocent that she did not know she should have explained it to Vera.

The restaurant part was not working out, so I changed the dining room, putting in a pool table and some other game machines. After that it got so busy I had to have Vera, her husband, Gabe, and her two sons work three nights a week. At the time, Gabe was retired from the Long Island Railroad where he was a supervisor at Penn Station. He liked to tell everybody he was a professional at his job. At Ryan's Daughter his job was to check customers' IDs at the door. At the end of the night, after the customers had left, it was usual for the staff to sit at the bar and have a few drinks and chat.

Muriel would say they are my "Great Friends." Gabe was a very conservative Catholic, with strong beliefs. One Halloween night we had a fancy dress party and Muriel dressed up as a little girl, in a pink dress, pigtails, pink bows and pink socks. I said to Gabe, "What do you think of the little girl?" It seemed he did not approve: "Not for my wife," he said. That may have changed his thinking of Muriel but she didn't notice.

Business was still good. Another nephew, Colm, came from Ireland and asked to work just weekends. Now, the busy time was from 10:00 p.m. to 3:00 a.m., but on the really busy nights, five bartenders would be inside the bar at 9:00 p.m. One night at 9:00 p.m., Colm decided to go outside to have a smoke and say hello to Gabe. Colm lights up, says, "Quiet night so far."

Gabe, who had a very loud voice, yells, "Get back behind your post."

Colm was a quiet guy; he just finished his cigarette and went back behind the bar.

On another night, Gabe had some incident with a group of customers coming in. He called the day after the incident and he was yelling so loud, I could almost hear him without the phone.

He said, "I had a problem on the door last night, but I solved it and I don't want to hear another word about it." Then he hung up.

That evening, the bar staff had their view on the incident and said Gabe was wrong in how he dealt with it. (As a good friend of mine often says, there are three sides to every story.)

When Gabe arrived in at 9:00 p.m., I said, "Gabe, I could not hear clearly on the phone today."

He said, "I told you I did not want to hear another word about it! That's it, I'm out of here," and off he went down the street.

He had quit. At the time, the pay to work the door for one night was a hundred dollars. He had left me with no one to work the door that night.

The sons also quit. I could not believe it. St Patrick's Day was coming up and door staff were needed. I called Vera and asked if her sons could do the door for St. Patrick's Day. She told me she'd have them call me.

Anthony called me, "Uncle Stoney, I am very busy but I will work it for four hundred."

I said, "Thank you very much Anthony. I'll get someone else."

If he had said three hundred, I would have gladly paid it.

Sometimes you win, sometimes you lose.

A few weeks later, I came home one evening to find Muriel looking very sad. I asked her what was up. She said, "I called Vera and Gabe answered the phone. He was very cold to me and hung up on me. I never did anything wrong to them. It was you they had the difference of opinion with." As time went on she would bring it up and I would tell her not to let it worry her.

A few years went by and Muriel and I took a trip to Dublin. We planned a night at a nice restaurant and invited friends and family of Muriel's, a group of over forty. It was a great night. Her husband, who would not give her a divorce, had met a woman in the Philippines and wanted to get married, so he wrote a letter to Muriel requesting a divorce and she told him just to send on the papers and she would sign them. Muriel made no fuss and he got his new wife with an extended family.

Soon after, when Muriel's daughters wanted to move to New York, we decided to get married so their immigration process would be easier for them. Two of them, Helen and Sara, went to New Jersey. Helen married there. Sara didn't want to get married, but she did want to have a baby! On one of her visits to us, Muriel asked her who was going to take care of it if she had a baby.

Without hesitation Sara stood in the middle of the floor, placed her hands on her hips, looked Muriel straight in the eye and said loud and clear, "You are! That's what grandmothers do."

Muriel told her, "You are making a choice to have a baby without a father and I am not going to be an American grandmother. You can come and visit on weekends when the kid gets older and I can take the kid to the park, or a movie, or a restaurant, but you better make other plans, because I am not raising your kid."

A year later, Sara had a baby girl. She would come and visit and then go home. Two years after that, she lost her job and would come looking for money. This I did not know until we found out that Sara was sending out emails to everybody and anybody, saying she could be sitting outside Ryan's Daughter, homeless, barefoot and hungry, and we would just let her die there. So Muriel set up a meeting of all her daughters and explained that, "Stoney pays me a salary and I will give ye girls all I can, but I'm not asking him to support ye." She really impressed me.

In the end, Sara moved to North Carolina where she met a guy whose wife had died and left him with a baby girl the same age as Sara's. When they got married, she did not invite her sisters to the wedding.

In 2004, Muriel was diagnosed with breast cancer. The doctor told her she had five years and she should have accepted that, but another doctor told her to go for chemo treatment. She lost all her hair and got a wig, and then two years later she got stomach problems, heart problems, liver problems. As much as she hated it, she needed a cane to walk.

Five years later and she's in Lenox Hill Hospital. Helen and myself stay with her because she can't move as she lays on her back. One evening I step out to get coffee and use the men's room. When I return, she had vomited on herself. There was a lady with a hospital uniform shouting at her to "Use the basin if you are going to vomit."

"Why is she yelling at me? Does she not know I can't move and the basin was three feet away?" Muriel says in a whisper, as her voice is gone.

I say to the lady, "Give me fresh linens; I'll clean her up."

To my surprise, she walked me to the hallway, opened a closet full of linen and said, "There."

After I had cleaned Muriel up, the nurse walked back in. When I asked where to put the dirty linen, she pointed to a garbage bin. No wonder the prices are high in hospitals.

The next day, I called Helen and we took Muriel home for good. It was difficult, but we knew the care was much better. Even in pain she would whisper something funny, but I found it difficult to laugh knowing she was in pain. I installed a large shower unit with a seat, so when we got in she could sit while I washed her. One night I got her all soaped up, I was holding her hands up as I washed under her arms and she said, "Stoney?"

I answered, "Yes Mu, what is it?"

She looked me in my eyes and said, "Are you getting turned on?"

She was still trying to make some fun of a bad situation.

The last few months she kept wanting to walk. She used to tire Helen and myself out helping her walk back and forth the length of the room. One night she had me worn out.

I said, "Please sit on the couch," and she did.

I said, "Let me make tea," and as I was making the tea, she said "Stoney, why did Gabe and Vera stop talking to me?" I ignored what she said.

I said, "Let me help you to the table." I got her to the table and sat down on the other side. A minute later, her head fell forward and hit the table. I jumped up. I realized it was a stroke. I dragged the back of the chair to the couch and lifted her on to it. Then I called the bartender, who was downstairs, to come help me lift her to the bed. I stayed in the bed with her all night.

The next day Helen, was with me to help. After four hours, she noticed Muriel was able to communicate with her eyes. She would blink once or twice in response to different things she asked her. That went on for four days. We took turns staying by the bed.

Then Helen said, "Come, I think she's leaving us." I knew what to do. I recalled Pat Guicken dying when I was a kid and what Willie Oatie did. I got a book, put it under her chin to keep her mouth closed, then I got two one-dollar coins, old ones from 1890. I closed her eyes and put one on each eye. One hour later it was okay to take them away. She got her wish: do not revive me, cremate me, and scatter my ashes on Park Avenue. Keep half in an urn if you wish, and I did.

It's several years since she passed and I think of her every day.

Some would tell me I should find a partner. I tell them I would look silly going out with a younger woman. Lo and behold, a call came to the bar one day; the barman told me it was a woman looking for me. He had the number. He said he could not hear the name clearly, maybe Brigid, says she knew you from years ago.

I wonder who this Brigid could be. I thought of my father saying he took a chance on Dr. Chance. So here goes. I dial the number. A woman's voice.

I say, "This is Stoney, how can I help you?"

I hear a loud laughing voice, "This is Brigid."

Oh man! After fifty years.

Yes, yes. I ask her how her husband is doing? He died five years ago. Wow, my wife died several years ago, coincidence. I am still excited and surprised, why the call?

"My brother is organizing a big dance, he asked me to make lots of calls to get a big crowd to attend. I recall you liked to dance. It will be at the Waldorf Hotel. A lot of hotshots will be there. Will you come?"

I said yes. "After fifty years I have to see what you look like."

I went that night to the Waldorf, lots of familiar faces from way back, and Brigid and I spotted each other right away, which was nice. The night was enjoyable. Brigid was with a bunch of friends. We said good night and that we would keep in touch.

The next day, she phoned and we chatted about the dance, the people there, and how they looked, and how they had progressed in life over the many years that had passed.

She said, "Will we meet again?"

"Sure," I said, "how about next Saturday? I will go to your house."

She said, "I got a lot of cats."

I said, "Surprise, I am allergic to cats and dogs."

"Don't worry," she said, "we can go somewhere."

I drive out on Saturday; she had everything arranged. We went to a hotel for dinner and after dinner she had a room booked, all paid for. I felt strange about her paying. Funny, we laughed, I always like to pay my way. I felt like a gigolo.

Since then, we have gone on short trips, gone for drives, dinners, museums, had lots of laughs and enjoy each other's company. Just like in the old song, "When you and I were young, Maggie."

You never know where life takes you.

"And That's How It All Started!"

ENDORSEMENTS

"Very informative as far as history of Irish people making it in New York City. Great to learn of how civil rights has made us better people. His traveling south, taught me to appreciate what I have today."
Ann Hernandez, New York, USA

"A great read, the author captures glimpses of life of bygone eras, all the while never short of good characters and incredible situations. I really enjoyed the book."
Kieran Moran, The Bronx, New York, USA

"A roller coaster read. Should be on the curriculum in high schools. This book would be banned in Ireland in the 1960s. The author would be in the good company of Oscar Wilde, Salman Rushdie and Brendan Behan."
Michael D. McAndrew, Journalist
Midwest Radio, Mayo, Ireland

"My wife and I read it in bed. We laughed, we cried; insights into sex, drugs, crime, hard work, history and politics. We did not sleep the night we read it. We waited a long time for a book like this, well done to Stoney and John for this production."
Pat and Phil Burke, Co. Tipperary, Ireland

"Entertaining, educational, enlightening, ecstatic, erotic and enjoyable!"

Lizzy Tabor, Massachusetts, USA

'I've known Stoney for over 40 years - and over that time he has regaled me with his stories and memories many times. It's great to see them documented on the printed page - captured in time. Stories that take us from Dowra, Co Leitrim across to the United States - stories of innocence and ignorance, of hurt and healing, of grit, determination and success - told in Stoney's inimitable voice."

Carl Corcoran, Veteran Broadcaster,
Dublin, Ireland

"I always knew we never had any great footballers in Leitrim, But I did not know we had a talented writer. A great read well done Stoney and John"

JJ McHugh, Strasburg Pennsylvania

"Lots of laughs, some tears, history and thoughts on life, I really enjoyed it"

Bridget Scanlon, Atlantic City

"The Prose reads like a motion picture, regaling the reader with tales of an Irishman,s journey and his enduring influence on American culture. Intersting and true."

Brendan Foy, Saratoga NY

ABOUT THE AUTHOR

Stoney was born on a small farm three miles outside of Dowra. Dowra is a small village that the river Shannon flows through, thus leaving it in both County Leitrim and County Cavan. Besides the farm, his family had a country shop. Times were hard, yet the country people were happy.

His early life starts there, school, helping on the farm, in the shop, listening to stories from his parents and neighbors. Stoney is an unusual name, and indeed Stoney is a unique character.

Being close to the border to the North of Ireland made him aware of the struggles on both sides.

Then as a teenager growing up in America, in New York City, he experienced the struggles of the different sides there. Things like racism and the struggle for civil rights in the 1960s, the tensions in America and the south. This is his first book and the stories span many decades and the rollercoaster of his life from the 1940s to present times, Stoney is an excellent storyteller in how he brings to life the essence of the story. Stoney brings you into the story like an old friend.

As the singer Jackson Browne says "caught between the longing for love and the struggle for the legal tender".

I hope you enjoy this book half as much as I did with the production of it.

John Healy

jh4news@yahoo.com

CPSIA information can be obtained
at www.ICGtesting.com
Printed in the USA
JSHW011154020120
3322JS00001B/5